A Unique Destiny

The Memoir of the Last Tsar of Bulgaria,
Prime Minister of a Republic

Simeon II of Bulgaria

With Sébastien de Courtois

STACKPOLE BOOKS

Guilford, Connecticut

STACKPOLE BOOKS

An imprint of Globe Pequot, the trade division of
The Rowman & Littlefield Publishing Group, Inc.
4501 Forbes Blvd., Ste. 200
Lanham, MD 20706
www.rowman.com

Distributed by NATIONAL BOOK NETWORK

Published as *Un Destin Singulier* © 2014 by Flammarion, Paris
Translated from French by Jane Coyner and Konstantin Saxe-Coburg
Translation copyright © 2021 by Simeon of Bulgaria, Sofia

British Library Cataloguing in Publication Information available

Library of Congress Cataloging-in-Publication Data

Names: Saxe-Coburg-Gotha, Simeon, 1937– author. | Courtois, Sébastien de, author.
Title: A unique destiny : the memoir of the last tsar of Bulgaria, prime minister of a republic / Simeon II of Bulgaria, with Sébastien de Courtois.
Other titles: Destin singulier. English | Memoir of the last tsar of Bulgaria, prime minister of a republic
Description: Guilford, Connecticut : Stackpole Books, [2021] | Published as "Un Destin Singulier" © Flammarion, Paris, 2014.—Title page verso. | Includes bibliographical references. | Summary: "The colorful memoir of Simeon II—the world's last tsar—recounts with honesty and humor an eventful life from his homeland, Bulgaria, to exile in Spain and the United States, and then back to Bulgaria as an elected prime minister"— Provided by publisher.
Identifiers: LCCN 2021015919 (print) | LCCN 2021015920 (ebook) | ISBN 9780811739757 (cloth : alk. paper) | ISBN 9780811769730 (electronic)
Subjects: LCSH: Saxe-Coburg-Gotha, Simeon, 1937– | Saxe-Coburg-Gotha, Simeon, 1937—Family. | Prime ministers—Bulgaria—Biography. | Bulgaria—Kings and rulers—Biography. | Bulgaria—Politics and government—1944– | Sofia (Bulgaria)—Biography. | Exiles—Bulgaria—Biography. | Exiles—Spain—Biography. | Madrid (Spain)—Biography.
Classification: LCC DR93.S54 A3 2021 (print) | LCC DR93.S54 (ebook) | DDC 949.903/2092—dc23
LC record available at https://lccn.loc.gov/2021015919
LC ebook record available at https://lccn.loc.gov/2021015920

♾™ The paper used in this publication meets the minimum requirements of American National Standard for Information Sciences—Permanence of Paper for Printed Library Materials, ANSI/ NISO Z39.48-1992.

*I dedicate these memoirs to my five children,
and especially to my grandchildren, so
that they may better understand their origins
and continue to grow with them.*

Contents

Preface

Along the Road of Memory

AFTER A FINAL LOOP IN THE CLEAR SKIES OVER SOFIA, OUR PLANE SETS down gently on the runway of the airport. Spring can be marvelous in this part of the world, when nature all around is dazzling—especially in Bulgaria, where large swaths of land are covered by forest.

Although the flight was short, it seemed to me to have lasted an eternity. I still did not know what awaited me. History has shown us that exiled kings rarely return home. Examples of banished monarchs abound in the years we have lived through since the fall of the Berlin Wall: I have met several. Not one of them ever left his country willingly. And now I was witnessing the opposite: my own return. I knew that I was traveling not just through space but also through time—the time of my childhood, of my parents, of our house with its long hallways and vast grounds, of a certain insouciance.

On this day in May 1996, the circumstances of life had offered me the opportunity of returning to places where I was happy. It is for this that I continue to be grateful to those who facilitated the trip, who encouraged me to go back to my roots. I am thinking especially of my mother, Queen Giovanna—the name she was given in Italian—who is no longer with us. She refused to give up hope, which finally materialized with my return.

I felt the first jolt of the landing gear hitting the runway, immediately giving me shivers. In a few seconds, decades rushed in front of me as if nothing had happened since I had left. Despite living an extraordinary life, I must admit my limitations—almost a sense of meaninglessness. What is left after all we go through, I still cannot say. Seated by my side, my wife instinctively reaches for my hand. Her eyes tell me that she understands. Since our wedding in 1962, she has shared every single step in my political life, making them her own. She knows that I have always been waiting for this moment without ever daring to hope for it, without even admitting it to myself. A chimera. It seemed simply impossible to me, so difficult were the circumstances. The Soviet world seemed an unassailable fortress.

I was finally coming back to my dearly beloved country, my last memory of it going back to the day of our exile in the autumn of 1946, when I had been forced to leave Bulgaria. Half a century had gone by, and yet I kept on speaking the language and being strongly attracted to any reference to the country. Although Italian by birth, my mother always made my sister Maria Luisa and I speak Bulgarian, especially in the years that followed our departure. This was not always easy, believe me, for this was a time when very few people spoke the language outside of Bulgaria. Wherever I go, whether it is for business, family reunions, holidays or visiting exiled Bulgarians, I never stop thinking of my country of origin—a country that reaches me profoundly and to which I am so attached that I am now firmly resolved to live there, no matter what, despite being the victim of petty maliciousness and spite. I am saddened by the basely political nature of this revenge, especially after the bleak years of Communism. All of us must bear a load of personal suffering, I believe; for those who, like me, have seen themselves forced to leave their native land, there is also nostalgia. All exiles will understand.

"As far as I am concerned," wrote my compatriot, the philosopher Tzvetan Todorov, "I would prefer that, in this gloomy century, we keep in mind the shining figures of those few individuals with a dramatic destiny, those with unravelled lucidity who, despite everything, continued to believe that man deserves to remain the goal of man."[1] I can only subscribe to these wise and optimistic words.

As I reach the sunset in my life, the time has come to take a look back. This is something I had ruled out until now, so as not to give the impression of wanting to close a chapter of my existence. Writing about oneself is already a form of dying, but I can neither step back nor discard.

---

1. In *Mémoire du mal, tentation du bien* (Paris: Robert Laffont, 2000).

I sometimes have the feeling that I belong to another era, not because of my age, but rather because I had to grow up more quickly than other children. Early on, I was deprived of the protective veil of carelessness that cuddles childhood. I was forced to be serious, to adopt a "look," to accept what was an almost theatrical performance that did not allow me to express my true personality. That was the way things were, and I am not complaining. There are worse things, one could argue. I often think of my father, King Boris III, who literally sacrificed himself for his country. I have seen so much, loved so much as well, whether in my professional life or in the time with my family—the latter, alas, all too fleeting, for children grow up without your realizing it.

Talking about oneself is always difficult. This is even more true when your education and social circles do not encourage it, and that is the case in royal families. Few of my ancestors wrote memoirs: it was just not done. Sharing confidences, especially in public, was not looked on with favor. "Never complain, never explain," Queen Victoria is supposed to have said. In many regards, I remain unconsciously faithful to this motto. My father didn't have time to even consider it: he was less than fifty when he died in the middle of the throes of World War II. My mother gave herself over to the task, but all these years later, my sister and I are amused by the pages she wrote in 1964, all "milk and sugar"![2] She was incapable of writing—or even speaking—the slightest spiteful word. My mother instilled me that there was no such thing as a bad Bulgarian, nor were any of them lazy or dishonest. Hers was an idealized country, set forever in happiness and the tremendous love she felt for my father. Bulgaria was a divine myth for her, a sort of Promised Land where she had been able to exercise her talents as a sovereign. No one can change my mind about how important her role was, and she proved to be entirely up to the task. She had no desire to judge anyone, and this is what she instilled in us. Another era. Another way of being brought up above all, one that is in contrast with the voyeurism of today, when one is encouraged to wallow in the suffering of others without, however, being able to help them or ease their pain.

---

2. Giovanna di Bulgaria, *Memorie* (Milan: Rizzoli, 1964).

As for the founder of our dynasty in Bulgaria, my grandfather, King Ferdinand I, it was out of the question that he set his memories down on paper. His memoirs, however, would have been fabulously interesting! This extraordinary person left no one indifferent: either you adored him or you hated him. He lived through the last quarter of the nineteenth century and the first half of the twentieth, dying in 1948 in a Germany devastated by war. Grandson of King Louis Philippe of France on the one side, heir to vast estates in the Austro-Hungarian Empire on the other. Adulated by his mother, Princess Clémentine of Orléans, he was one of the last grand aristocrats of old Europe. "Adieu Old Europe," sang French Foreign Legion recruits. But there are no memoirs or recorded memories from him; his life and his personality remain a mystery to us in many regards.

This is proved by a charming incident between him and the Infanta Eulalia of Spain. As a young woman, she had been very close to Ferdinand, perhaps even in love with him, until she published her memoirs around 1930.[3] My grandfather found her confessions scandalous and had no trouble whatsoever in saying so in a telegram that has remained famous in our family: "Dear Eulalia, I convey to you our most utter disdain. Ferdinand." To which the Infanta replied in the same tone: "It's reciprocal. Eulalia." They never saw one another again. She shared this delightful anecdote with me. At over ninety and having just broken her femur, she told me that "a sad old age awaited [her]." This is when we were visiting her in her house in Irun, in the Basque Country in Spain, where she lived until her death in 1958. She crossed over to France every day; the customs agents knew her well. The sister of Alphonse XII, she enjoyed reminding her visitors that she was the daughter of Isabella II of Spain . . . a really extravagant character whose memoirs must have shocked everyone by their indiscretion.

The writing of memoirs, then, was not well regarded. There were, however, some rare exceptions: for example, the correspondence of Queen Victoria with her ministers and with her oldest daughter, Victoria. Or the memoirs of my ancestor King Louis Philippe as a young

---

3. Daughter of Isabella II and married to the duke of Montpensier, she became known for her literary talents: Eulalia d'Espagne, *Mémoires de S.A.R. l'infante Eulalie, 1868–1931* (Paris: Plon, 1935).

general in the French Revolution; closer in time to us is Prince Christopher of Greece and Denmark, who also wrote his memoirs.[4] And let us add Marie of Romania's remembrances, which have become a classic in the field. She was an English princess born to Grand Duchess Maria Alexandrovna of Russia, herself sister of Alexander II and said to be a flamboyant, theatrical character. At the end of the 1920s, Marie had a little jewel of the Romantic period, Balchik Palace—*The Quiet Nest Palace*, as it was originally called—built on the Black Sea. As a result of a change in borders, it is now in Bulgaria; I went back to visit it not long ago in the company of my cousins from Romania. It is still reputed for its impressive botanical gardens.

The kings of Italy, alas, left nothing of the sort to us, surely due to an excess of propriety and personal reservations. Alas—and I say it again—for I think that their testimony would have been priceless in better understand the recent history of Italy. Indeed, memoirs also serve to shed light on a past that we don't know well and that is almost never described from the point of view of royal families inside the story. Uncle Paul of Yugoslavia and King Umberto of Italy, for example, were key witnesses to the events of their times and have often been caricatured for their actions and roles. Why? Because we know only their opponents' versions of what happened. Memoirs would have allowed them to explain themselves, but, again, I think that an excess of propriety and the fear of compromising people still active prevented them from speaking up. In fact, History with a capital "H" is also made with a small "h," and by comparing the two you know more, though perhaps not the truth. But can we speak of truth in history?

Having become, in spite of myself, a sort of link with the pre-Communist past of Bulgaria, I have a duty to relay sixty years of political life. I have noticed that people often write in a biased fashion. The easy way out is always to go for the sensational. If history reflects what is told by the winners only, it is no good. In my life, I have seen a great deal of

---

4. Let us note that his son, my cousin the writer Michael of Greece, pursued this tradition, but in a more private way, with his *Mémoires insolites* (Paris: Pocket, 2006), in which he relates in particular part of his childhood in Morocco, in Larache, with his grandmother, the duchess of Guise, mother of the future Count of Paris.

propaganda—Nazi, Soviet, and, of course, Western—and I have been appalled by it. I have no interest in making things up. Moreover, I must admit that I am reserved by nature and this doesn't lead me to confide in people. Nothing is more difficult for me than to call attention to this inner "me" where I must delve for my emotions, for I think that we are nothing on our own, life being made up of encounters and coincidences. People don't realize that "good luck" often offers them answers that they look for elsewhere. And of course, we must know how to be open to others, to adopt a "listening" mode that respects those around us. I see in "pragmatic realist" a formula that describes me quite well. I have tried to adapt myself as well as possible to the circumstances of life, in order not to remain confined within the universe of my origins only. I have been postponing this appointment with writing for years now.

The last two decades have brought political and technological changes that were unthinkable in my youth, beginning with the collapse of the totalitarian system and with it the possibility of a new life in Bulgaria. It is understandable to be troubled by the speed of these changes. Since the end of the Second World War, humanity has carried out incredible revolutions that we must come to terms with as best we can. New—even larger—challenges are awaiting the new generations.

Although I am writing about the past, the present interests me just as much, and the idea of nostalgia is not much to my taste. I remain convinced that life must remain at the main priority of our scientists and politicians. And as I am a Christian, I believe in loving my neighbor. The paths that lighten our lives remain an unfathomable mystery. This should never be forgotten.

My children, my wife, and my friends encouraged me to write this book. My destiny is unusual: to go from being the legitimate king of a country to its elected prime minister when it returned to democracy. I have met many people, and choosing among them, as I must, is not obvious. The reader must forgive me for struggling to sum up a life that has been long and full of stories. I have never known a day of boredom, not as a child at Vrana[5]—I can even recall the World War II bombings

---

5. *Vrana* means "crow" in Bulgarian: this is the name of the property near Sofia where I now live and is not to be confused with Varna, which is a large port city on the Black Sea.

in the park!—nor during my school years, or later, during a fruitful professional life. This is why I enjoy so much the rare moments of solitude that I can now allow myself. I've always had something to do, not least fellow countrymen to meet, raising a family and making a living. I often felt that I was not in control of my life. As a History enthusiast, my readings have made me realize many times the extent to which someone's life could be manipulated after his or her death. In writing this book, I may be able to help thwart that regrettable habit, where people are judged based on false rumors and ignoring facts or their own recollections. This is also an opportunity to make information available to the reader that may help him or her better understand the transformational times to which I was a participant. It is not easy to be a king in exile, believe me. I am not a politician, or a noble deposed king, or a Russian exile from the days of the Revolution, or even a prince who manages his estate from afar. Nor am I only a businessman who worked for large corporations: I may be a bit of all of these at the same time. The king who remained sovereign despite everything, and who tried to be useful to his country and to his countrymen.

On this note, I hope that my fellow Bulgarians will forgive me, for this book contains numerous details—mostly geographical—which are obvious to them but not to the international public.

As I reflect on exile—which in my case is also to reflect on life—I suddenly remember the philosophy class at the French *lycée* in Madrid, where we studied the letters by Descartes to Christina of Sweden. If, in general, one remembers his "I think, therefore I am" (*cogito ergo sum*), I have always identified myself rather with his *dubito ergo sum*: "I doubt, therefore I am." Yet never did the idea of forgetting Bulgaria or of resigning myself cross my mind. I had a duty to my country, both as an individual and as a king. Bulgaria is the country of my father, my grandfather, my Uncle Kyril—shot in 1945—the country of my early childhood, when certain memories stay in you for the rest of your life.

I am not alone. This is even more true when I remember the happy day of my return to Sofia, where hundreds of thousands of my fellow citizens filled the streets to greet me.

One Day in May 1996

ON THE DAY OF MY RETURN TO BULGARIA, MY EMOTIONS WERE RUN-
ning high. It was May 25, 1996, and my wife immediately realized how
deeply moved I was. I held back my tears, a habit I had forced myself to
learn in 1943 at the age of six for the funeral of my father. Destiny was
bringing me back to Sofia. Through the window of the plane, I saw people gathering on the runway at the front of the plane. We were seated in
business class, not for the comfort, but to be first at getting off the Balkan
Airlines plane, as our national carrier was then known. My wife Margarita and I wanted to face this very important day together, the day when
I was setting foot again in Bulgaria. After the fall of the Communist
regime in 1989, I waited patiently and watched events closely. Finally,
the prospect of living once again in Bulgaria might actually become true.
Only those who have known the constraints of living far from home
understand the feelings of attachment for a place they are forbidden to
go to. It is a beautiful spring day, one of the most daunting moments in
my life for sure, where memories and sorrow mix with the awe of the
present. I did not know then what awaited me, or even if people would
show up at all.

None of my five children had come with us. Although this was a
painful decision, it was one we had reached as a family, for we had no
idea what was going to happen, given the extraordinary circumstances. I
also wanted to avoid being accused of having any intention of restoring
the monarchy. The political environment was not in my favor. Bulgaria
was in turmoil, going through a political identity crisis like many other

ex-Soviet republics struggling to find a new model to follow. Little had changed since the proclamation of the new constitution in 1991. I would realize later, with the experience in government, that the ties with the dark side of Communism were greater than I thought and still outstanding. More than twenty-five years after the fall of the Berlin Wall, Bulgaria is still paying a price for its bad habits.

How would my return be interpreted? It had been only a few years since the end of a regime that had a deep impact on everyone. The population had suffered, and I had no desire to add to the confusion or to give the impression that I was taking advantage of the chaotic situation to attempt to impose myself. But the news—even if it had been rumored for years—that that I was coming back had preceded me, and the preparations for the trip had been made in the greatest secrecy. Discretion was for me the condition *sine qua non*. I was returning to my country, and I did not want to appear surrounded by a mob of foreign media or turn my trip into a show. I was "the man in the grey suit," as my children sometimes called me affectionately. I was wearing a light-colored tie that seemed appropriate to me and wore a Bulgarian flag on my lapel. I didn't want to look too elegant or too unlike myself. My wife, Queen Margarita, wore no jewelry, but she usually doesn't. Indeed, what kind of meeting was this? A people meeting their king? I thought that was a little old-fashioned for our modern societies. Besides, hadn't years of Communism erased memory? Who would remember me, the child who left Bulgaria on a September afternoon in 1946, at the beginning of a long period of ostracism? I had ascended the throne after the premature death of my father three years earlier. "The king is dead, long live the king," as the old saying goes in European monarchies! An entirely different time it was, that of the Second World War and its millions of dead, its limitless destruction. I had left Bulgaria with one of my father's two sisters (my Aunt Eudoxia), my mother, my sister Maria Luisa, and several others from our entourage, for an unknown—in time and in space—destination.

Three months from this day would mark fifty years since then—in other words, a lifetime absence.

During the flight, each of the pilots had come in turn to greet us, as had the hostesses and those passengers who had wished to do so. Despite my anxiety, I listened to them with pleasure. I pretended to be relaxed, but I must admit that my heart was in my shoes. All were very friendly to us, and this touched me. Everyone around me understood my language! The newspapers were in Bulgarian too. I already felt I was home in a certain way. This is not a minor thing, as exiles will share this feeling of vulnerability. Passengers came to have photographs taken with me, and I was pleasantly surprised to see that young people in particular. What did they know of my history, they who could know nothing of a period so long ago? Even our name had been removed from textbooks and our coat of arms from public monuments. As if the reigns of my father and my grandfather had never existed, even though King Ferdinand was the one who proclaimed independence for the country in 1908. In Communist Bulgaria, it was not possible even to refer to my existence without putting one's family in danger and exposing oneself to reprisals. The risks were too great. The media had even reported that we were dead. The regime was merciless toward those who did not think along the same lines as the party and its underlings.

That very morning, we had boarded the plane at Zurich airport. It was eleven thirty. I remember the hour exactly. The details of the trip had been carefully planned. King Juan Carlos had lent us an official plane so that our departure from Spain could take place without being seen. It was for this reason that we took off from the military base at Torrejón, rather than from the Madrid airport where journalists constantly camped out.

First stop: Switzerland.

Before I gave the green light, every detail had been gone over with a fine-tooth comb by my friends in Spain, my office in Madrid and my supporters in Bulgaria. I did not want to risk being turned back at the border, as happened to King Michael of Romania despite the precautions he took. I was afraid the same thing would happen to me, jeopardizing my return. The government would have been able to hold us for a bit and then throw us out, just for the sake of humiliation.

At the beginning of the 1990s, while I was in London, I had lunch at Buckingham Palace with Queen Elizabeth. While we were discussing the events in Eastern Europe, she said to me, "Simeon, I hope you are not in that much of a hurry." This was said in a low voice as she pretended to

3

stare at her plate. As I look back, I am extremely grateful for this valuable advice, for it seems to me that I waited for the right moment, while
everyone around me was urging me to return to Bulgaria as quickly as
possible after the fall of the regime. I was even accused of having "missed
the boat" of History. Sometimes in life, patience is your best guide. My
father thought that a good statesman was one who knew how to bide
his time. I also did not want either the foreign or the Bulgarian media
to know when I was going to arrive, or to pull the rather sickly sweet
stunt of being photographed in the plane, looking out the porthole with
a sad, nostalgic air. I wanted no staged setting, either; I simply let King
Juan Carlos know what my intentions were—I was, after all, a guest in
his country. That was the very least I could do, so that he would not find
himself in an embarrassing position on a question of foreign policy, especially in this so very delicate period when Eastern Bloc countries were
just opening up to Europe. I consider my cousin a great statesman but
also a very dear lifetime friend.

We managed to get there by means of a very low-key approach.
Our plane reservations were made under other names, mine with the
name used by my father (Count Rylski) and my Spanish wife's using her
maiden name (Margarita Gómez-Acebo Cejuela). In Zurich, a city I like
very much (as did my father, apparently), we decided to take a regular
flight the next day for Sofia. At the boarding gates, some of my compatriots recognized me. Some immediately got out their cell phones to let
those close to them know of our arrival. Others shyly came forward to ask
whether they could have a photo taken with us. They hesitated regarding
how to address me, and I put them at ease.

We finally landed at 2:30 in the afternoon, local Sofia time. The
engines shut off, and the plane rolled to a stop at its parking spot. As I
got off, I had a view of the crowd waiting for me on the runway and was
overwhelmed, moved, shaken. After such a long time, I couldn't believe
that we had finally arrived. I had tears in my eyes. There came back to
me the memory of a trip we had made ten or so years before: on our
way to Istanbul on a pleasure trip, we were flying over Bulgaria, and I
recognized the dam in the mountain valley I love so much—the one that
leads to our home in Borovets, Tsarska Bistritsa, an hour south by road

from Sofia, where I spent so much precious family time with my parents. At that altitude, I could spot other details, forests, clearings, valleys and ridges. The weather was clear, the sky cloudless. We were over six miles up in the sky, but almost a half-century in time separated us from the ground. Baron Heinrich von Thyssen was seated next to me, the friend with whom we were traveling to Turkey, and he pointed out to me that if we had engine trouble, we would have to land in Bulgaria. What a joke that would be! His teasing came back to me; I don't know why. In the meantime, a Spanish journalist friend sent by the newspaper *ABC*, Ramón Pérez-Maura, had telephoned his headquarters in Madrid to announce, "I'm afraid it's a flop; the streets are deserted, there's no one. Nothing's happening." As soon as the plane landed, I later learned, the bells of our Saint Alexander Nevsky Cathedral, in the center of town, began ringing long peals as a sign of welcome.

Since 1989, my intention had been to come back. Still, like everyone, I feared that the fall of the regime, run with an iron hand for more than thirty years by the first secretary of the Bulgarian Communist Party, Todor Zhivkov, would be followed by confrontation and settling of scores. Hatred had become exacerbated over years of oppression and it was hard not to imagine the worst. But the behavior of the population was exemplary, and by the grace of God, no blood was spilled. During the two large demonstrations in 1989, only a few people were hurt. The Zhivkov government collapsed at the same time as the Berlin Wall, like a house of cards. I thus took my time to mull things over. I felt it wasn't right to jump on the first plane and put everyone in front of a fait accompli. I would be allowed no mistakes.

In 1991, in this context, my sister and I decided that she would be the first member of the royal family to make a visit to our native country. We had talked about this possibility during our vacation in the summer of 1990, at Estoril in Portugal, where our mother had been living since 1963. As soon as I felt the conditions were favorable, I telephoned Maria Luisa in the United States, where she has lived for many years: "Sit down," I said to her. "Would you like to go to Bulgaria for me in May?" I could feel her emotion at the other end of the line; then she yelped with joy. I wanted someone from the family to go, someone who spoke Bulgarian. My sister's personality would do the rest, and I was certain that she would represent us in the best possible way. As it turned out, to make things difficult for her, the Bulgarian consulate in New York would give her a visa for only ten days. They must have referred the request to Sofia and were busy asking themselves lots of questions. Despite the change in power, I could see that the same old reaction of distrust toward us still prevailed.

Her trip was a great success, even surprisingly so, and encouraging for what was to follow, despite the rumors spread that the trip had been canceled so as to dissuade Sofia residents from turning out. She told me how considerate people were to her, to the point of wanting to greet her on Eagles' Bridge, at the entrance of the city, as a sign of honor. It is there that one waited for guests in the old days before awarding them the keys to the city and offering the customary salt and bread. Night had fallen. There had been a blackout, and rumor had it that the mayor at the time had done it on purpose. The atmosphere was apparently extraordinary. Afterward, Maria Luisa, accompanied by her husband Bronislaw Chrobok, traveled throughout the country, by car, by plane—sometimes an old Antonov—and by train as well: Plovdiv, Ruse, Vidin. Everywhere people came out to welcome her. On her return, she stopped to share her impressions in Madrid, where I was impatiently waiting to hear what she had to say. Above all, she wanted to give our mother an array of small gifts from the people she had met. My mother was very moved by this, for it was the first time she had received anything directly from Bulgaria. She had never forgotten her country of adoption, the country of the husband she adored. At her home in Portugal, she had re-created the atmosphere of a "little Bulgaria," which always impressed her visitors.

During my sister's trip, people were often surprised that she "spoke Bulgarian well," even though she was born in Bulgaria like me! These remarks had bothered her since they put her nationality into question. "You speak it rather well, too," she liked to reply, especially to journalists.

The people she spoke to were receptive, warm, considerate. From what she said, and what I experienced later, I understood that they were also expressing great gratitude to the memory of our parents, my father above all, since he had been very popular during the twenty-five years of his reign. This was reassuring. Yet while my mother approved of these initiatives, she maintained some mistrust. She could forget neither the way in which she had been treated after the coup d'état nor the violent deaths of some of those close to her.

Later, she would be the one returning, at the end of the month of August in 1993, at the age of eighty-six. The excuse we found was for her to attend a religious celebration, at the invitation of Patriarch Maxim, primate of the Bulgarian Orthodox Church, in the very ancient mon-astery of Rila to commemorate the fiftieth anniversary of my father's death. This time the authorities were prepared and had decided that my mother would not have the right to give interviews. It is true that the large crowds that had turned out for my sister's visit had put some people in a cold sweat.

In Plovdiv, Mother went to the Catholic Church of Saint Louis to visit the tomb of my grandmother, Princess Maria Luisa of Bourbon-Parma, buried under a superb white marble statue. I had provided her with a minibus so that she could travel comfortably and better see the landscapes. She was so very happy. We had even arranged for a medical vehicle able to follow her everywhere, but it was fortunately never used.

My mother was very forceful, stoic, and tough, like many women of her generation were, in view of all the suffering they had seen. She endeavored to control her emotions. It was the first time she had been back to Bulgaria since 1946. The "old queen" whom Bulgarians now met was only thirty-six at the time of the death of her husband. Let us not for-get it. She was a young woman who had put all of her heart and soul into her role as queen, had learned Bulgarian—which is not easy—and had shown several times a heroic behavior during the war. In the plane that took her back to Portugal, I know she was thinking, "This is the last time that I will see Bulgaria." She was right. She would never go back again.

During those few days, she was only an elderly lady who wanted to put flowers on her husband's tomb. That's all. People understood the motivation, for every family can sympathize with it. Don't we all have a grave to put flowers on somewhere? I think the dead are never far from the living, and so we should make a gesture in their direction.

*

From 1989 to 1996, I led seven years of discussions in Madrid, several hundreds of tête-à-tête meetings with diplomats informing me about the state of the country, especially those who had been posted to Bulgaria. Journalists and political analysts saw to it that I got audiotapes with their own analyses of the situation. I had suggested this means of communication for reasons of economy and time, as well as for confidentiality. I didn't want Sofia to know about my thoughts, for I knew that in the past I had been subject to close surveillance. My office in Madrid had been "visited" several times, and later in Sofia I found out that large amounts of information had been collected and stored in my political file. The Bulgarian secret services were among the most efficient of the period. I was followed for decades, and the smallest details of my life and my family, even the most trivial ones, had been reported back.

I wanted to feel the temperature myself; I'm not someone who hurries decisions too quickly, a hothead. You have to state your opinion at the right moment. The country was going through pronounced political instability: six governments had succeeded one another up to 1996, and the one that was in place, headed by Jean Videnov—"Jean" for Jean Jaurès and not "Ivan," which would have been the usual transcription of his name—a former Communist elected democratically, was not pleased with the idea of seeing me land in Bulgaria. Long afterward, during my own term in office, I saw him in a meeting aimed at bringing all the ex-prime ministers together. There was even the one from the last Communist government. History plays some unexpected tricks on us: How could I possibly have imagined such a scene only ten years earlier?

To support my return, a group of Bulgarians—"101 Intellectuals"—had signed an appeal in my favor. Even if I had not been formally forbidden to visit Bulgaria, they wanted to express their desire to see me come back by means of an invitation. They were by far not all monarchists but wanted Bulgaria to open itself to the outside world and to reconcile itself with its own past, with me as the catalyst.

In the meantime, I had obtained a Bulgarian passport. The question of passports could be a chapter in itself, so important is the question for us royal families in exile, just like for any other exile who must constantly justify his identity. It is a rather unpleasant feeling to know that you depend on a simple piece of paper: if you lose it, you may not be able to get another one. This makes you vulnerable; it gives you a real feeling of personal insecurity: as a European citizen today, it is unthinkable to find yourself without an identity. I smile when I remember the thick passport of King Leka of Albania, one that he was the only person in the world to recognize.

After the events of 1989, the first thing that I asked the new Bulgarian authorities was for this precious administrative document. I absolutely had to have it: it was a question of principle. In 1946, we had been given a document good for only three months. Then, in Egypt, we obtained a laissez-passer that was accepted at some borders. It was only in Spain that we benefited from temporary identity papers, until my mother, as daughter of King Victor Emmanuel III, was finally granted an Italian diplomatic passport. This type of passport was also kindly issued to my sister and me and bore the name of Count Rylski, the alias that my father had used to travel incognito, since our patronymic Saxe-Coburg Gotha was too well known. As for Grandpapa, King Ferdinand, he was called Count Murany when he traveled, a title that is Hungarian in origin. (I passed it onto my daughter Kalina, who has great admiration for "The Monarch," as he is known in our family.) For the Bulgarian authorities, I therefore became *Simeon Borissov Sakskoburggotski*, in a single word, which is the transcription of my patronymic in Bulgarian. Of course, there was no question of inscribing my title of "king" anywhere, since I was sure it would never make it through the wheels of governmental bureaucracy. I regret to see that people in Bulgaria are afraid of using my title properly and call me "Mister Saxe-Coburg." I am very proud of my family name and thus see nothing personal in this, but rather a subdued attack on the symbol that I incarnate and, in consequence, on the history of my country.[1]

My children, too, were enrolled at the *Lycée Français* in Madrid under the name of Rylski, until one fine day when the king of Spain proposed

---

1. To underline this fact, and fight against the negation of history, I merely wish to remind people that banknotes and postal stamps with my portrait were printed beginning in 1943.

Spanish nationality for them to me. I wanted them to belong to a place, to pay taxes in a country, and avoid being "little international princes" without roots. My fourth son, Konstantin, did his military service in Spain, in the Air Force. They thus became *Sajonia-Coburgo Gotha*, and people couldn't understand why they had changed names. The youngest among them had to explain this "change of identity" at school to their schoolmates. Children are sensitive about this kind of detail, but they didn't explain how they went about it to me.

Throughout my exile, as public enemy number one for all those years of absence for some, I thought I had been deprived of my nationality, but not at all. For the Communist authorities of Sofia, I remained Bulgarian. This legal trick was a way for the political police to exercise authority over any Bulgarian national on foreign soil, even if the latter had acquired another nationality in the meantime. I was as proud as a peacock of my new Bulgarian passport. Royalists wanted my title "Simeon II," or even "King Simeon," to be printed on the document, but this seemed unrealistic and ill adapted to me.

All the years of uncertainty and waiting come back to me. They were not easy. I don't know how else to summarize them other than to say that I neglected my family life in favor of my obligations. My five children needed me at the time, especially the youngest ones, and I know they suffered from it. For them, Bulgaria was an abstraction, a country that stole their father's precious time, time he spent always in meetings, always seeing one visitor or another until late evening, as I can see in the pile of appointment books I kept from the period. I can hardly believe it. All that energy spent . . .

But now it was my turn to go home, and one event swiftly followed another. My wife and I had been invited to visit Bulgaria until June 16, 1996, the date of my birthday. The three weeks were long and exhausting, but so comforting. With the help of our contacts, I had designed the pace of the trip, and especially the places we would go to and the visits we would schedule. After all those years of absence, I thought I could afford to take my time.

As we got off the plane, the mayor of Sofia introduced himself, with a bouquet of flowers for Margarita. I took this gesture from the local authorities as encouraging, and even as a good omen. The airport employees cheered us. I was not only touched by these outbursts, which were spontaneous, but also pleasantly surprised, as I would be many times throughout the trip. You must never say die, never give up hope.

In the reception area, where people were waiting, the scene was one of euphoria. As I came in, cheers rained down on me, and we stayed at least an hour with those who had turned out to greet us. The group of intellectuals who had advocated in favor of my return were also waiting, as well as several priests who burst into a brilliant *Te Deum*: "Long life" was what this ancient song from the Orthodox liturgy sang to me, and to which I was very attached. I guess the Sofia airport had never seen such a numerous, exuberant crowd. I am not head of the Church, but because I was anointed, I enjoy a special status. In fact, I am "King of the Bulgarians" and not "King of Bulgaria," the formula having been borrowed from the kingdom of Belgium and from Louis Philippe, "King of the French," one of my favorite ancestors; the queen is "of Bulgaria" because she was chosen by the king. I was not only moved but also overwhelmed. I remembered my father and wondered what he would have made of such an event. I could have fainted, but I stayed firmly on my feet, buoyed up by the joy of the crowd that had come to support me, to encourage me, simply to say "welcome home!" to me. The first moments are always tricky. I waved. What could I say? How should I react? I was the center of attention. Thereafter, the clergy came with me all along this memorable visit. We made a rather colorful crew, I must confess!

A few days later, His Holiness Patriarch Maxim received me with great warmth in the presence of the members of the Holy Synod. The evening before we had come back from the monastery at Rila, where I had gone to pray by the tomb of my father King Boris, as my sister and my mother had done before me. After dinner, we spent the night at the monastery. But before then, I had asked the father-abbot to take me to the church so that I could light a candle and be alone to think of my father. When my bodyguard tried to come in with me, Abbot John pointed to the sky and said, "My boy, there is someone else inside protecting the king; you and I will wait for him outside." The fact of being received by the patriarch so early in in the visit was a very intense moment for me, both as a member of the Orthodox Church and as a Bulgarian. Even if I had seen many men of the cloth during my life, this meeting meant the return to normal. Not long after, in Sofia, in the vast Boyana Park, next to a beautiful tenth-century chapel covered in frescos, I was able to bow before the tomb of Queen Eleonore, the second wife of my grandfather, born Princess Reuss-Köstritz. My father was very fond of his stepmother. Her body had been exhumed, as had my father's, by the Communist authorities in the 1950s. A committee had subsequently taken the initiative to restore her tomb where it belonged. Numerous photos taken in the 1930s showed how her tomb had been renovated so that people could go there to pray. She had been the first queen of the "Third Kingdom," the name used for the period of Bulgarian history from the Liberation of 1878 until the fall of the monarchy in 1946.[2] When my grandmother, Maria Luisa of Bourbon-Parma, died, Bulgaria was still only an autonomous principality under Ottoman sovereignty. Queen Eleonore was for my father a true mother, giving him and his siblings the love that was lacking elsewhere, my grandfather always having maintained a certain distance from his four children. This courageous woman gave a lot to Bulgaria—a country she loved—working for numerous charities and always visiting the wounded, both from the Balkan Wars and from the First World War. My father spoke of his stepmother with great tenderness. She had been a nurse during the war between Japan and Russia and thought only of doing good for those around her. She spared no effort as a wife, her role as queen and "governess," according to the not very flattering term used by "The Monarch," her husband King Ferdinand. The marriage had been arranged by Grand Duchess Wladimir, née Princess of Mecklenburg, known in Paris for the magnificence of her jewels. It was only fair that I should restore her tomb in the place she herself had chosen for her burial. She still doesn't have a street named after her—as is the custom in other countries—and this seems quite unfair to me.

---

2. The "First Kingdom" dates from the seventh century until the Byzantine conquest in 1018, whereas the "Second Kingdom" lasted from 1186 to 1396, the beginning of the Ottoman period.

Indeed, I noticed that no Bulgarian sovereign from the sixth century on has his grave intact, with the exception of Prince Alexander of Battenberg's. I believe that we need to reflect on the meaning of this curious fact, one that I can't help but worry for my own future, should I in turn wish to be buried in Bulgaria.

But let us get back to my welcome. The clergy wanted to signal the importance of the "moral authority"—using the words of the spokesman of the Patriarchate—I could represent during the country's transition process. The Church holds an important place in our country. It served as a refuge for numerous families during the difficult years of the Communist regime. The evening before my departure I went to mass in the presence of Patriarch Maxim and Patriarch Paul of Serbia, there on an official visit. During the liturgy I recited the *credo*, symbol of Nicaea, a founding text for all Christian churches. This is a prerogative of the king, and I received the blessing from the two men, for whom I have a profound respect. Both of them belonged to the generation that lived through the war and died at over ninety years old, leaving a strong spiritual legacy. They had endured the same dangers as their fellow countrymen, yet maintaining intact the Orthodox tradition.

From the airport to the city, on this memorable May 25, 1996, we traveled through huge crowds. I remember the horizon packed with people. Although the distance is barely ten kilometers, our convoy took more than two hours to get to the center of town. In a typically "old school" attitude, the chauffeur had received instructions to drive us as quickly as possible to the Town Hall, to prevent me from being acclaimed by the crowd. They were afraid that I would linger with my sympathizers. I had to ask the security officer to kindly slow down so that I could greet them through the window, surely the least I could do. Those in charge of security even tried to insist on a different itinerary from the one planned. I refused: "Listen, I haven't been here for fifty years. The car is very comfortable; my wife and I can sleep here, but I insist that we take the route that was announced!" They understood.

There was already a large multitude along Constantinople Road, as the wide avenue that leads to the center of Sofia is called. Everyone was conscious that something important was happening. The spokesperson for the authorities, obviously not favorable to us, stated afterward that there were "only" five hundred thousand people. But five hundred thousand people represented half of the population of our capital. This turnout was not so bad for an exile. The prime minister, Jean Videnov, was at that moment on an official visit to Vietnam. There were some spiteful jokes about him in the press. The day after my departure, a cartoon showed him at the door of the plane that brought him back saying, "So, is he really gone?"

In the middle of the human crowds, the police intervened several times to open way for us, and even had to ask for reinforcements. Visibly, everyone was unable to cope, but I never felt in the least danger. On the contrary, I felt very well indeed. The public cheered "Si-me-on, Si-me-on," "We want our king, *Iskamesi tsaria,*" and "Simeon, he's our strength, our future." As security did not want me to open the car's sunroof, I got out of the car twice to use a microphone to thank people, and especially to ask them to allow us to move forward. It was a crazy scene: people were hanging from trees and off buses, which were at a standstill for the occasion, there were flags everywhere, and roses poured from every direction.

My wife thought I was out of my mind as I gave a running commentary about the route we would follow: "At such-and-such a crossroads, we'll take a right, then continue straight." "But how on earth do you know that?" she asked. Well, nothing had changed. Half a century later, and the town center had not been modified. I recognized the same buildings, the same avenues, the same parks. I remember the streets we took to go to the town hall when I was nine. All the memories came back little by little. The main street, the décor—everything was unchanged. The Communist period had frozen everything in time. What I realized later was that minds had also suffered from this "Ice Age," and there it was no longer a case of urban planning or architecture. Two generations had been exposed to brain wash by the regime. Among people we still knew—the children of those who had been shot after the Soviet coup d'état in 1944—there were those who had been discriminated against in the "new" Bulgaria. Life had played them a dirty trick, and I could not help but feel responsible. They were paying for the loyalty of their parents.

In that car, I was happy. The trip could have lasted for hours. But I was also frustrated because I couldn't reciprocate as I'd have liked to all the smiles and all the excited faces. I would have liked to understand better what was going on in their heads. Who was I really for them?

There was not a single moment when I thought an incident might take place, as some people might suppose. If there was going to be an assassination attempt, it would take place on foreign soil, not here in front of everyone. The crowd would have been unmanageable. We then passed near Alexander Nevsky; the bells were still ringing, and it was impressive. The sound of the great bell reached my ears, reminding me of the terrible day of my father's death in August 1943, the knelling of the bell whose sound is so characteristic that one can neither confuse it with another nor ever forget it. Until then, I had been a happy little prince, like in a fairy tale. I came of age at six, becoming king from one day to the next. My childhood had just ended. That is why I consider that I have lived twelve years more than my real age. I truly believe it. Even if my mother did everything she could to protect me, I was confronted with important responsibilities very early on.

The mayor of Sofia, Stefan Sofiyanski, a member of the Union of Free Democrats—an anti-Communist movement, in other words—received us, and I spent a long time waving at my fellow citizens from the little balcony on the second floor of the municipal building, a former out-building of the Royal Palace that lodged the famous *Intendance*. Everyone continued to cheer my name. I remember seeing crowd two Italian flags in the crowd with the Savoy coat of arms, certainly in tribute to my ancestors, one of which was carried by Camillo Zuccoli, who since then has become ambassador of the Order of Malta in Bulgaria. Even after the reception, the enthusiasm and intensity were such that I still couldn't believe it; people in the crowd wanted to carry me on their shoulders. We headed to the Hotel Intercontinental in the city heights. All I wanted was to find myself a bit of solitude, to digest such a demonstration of support. I wanted to talk about it with my wife, to hear her point of view. I was led to our room.

Down a long hallway; then the door opened and we set down our bags, and there I had my second shock after the one when we had landed: the shape of Mount Vitosha that dominates the plain of Sofia. I remembered it as if it were yesterday. The sight carried me back to a past that I had carefully buried under the years. Moved. Surprised. Touched. I was exhausted.

CHAPTER TWO

A Time for Homecoming

IN THE DAYS THAT FOLLOWED MY ARRIVAL, MEETINGS AND TOURS PILED up. While the essentials of the program had been organized with Margarita's and my agreement, I also liked letting myself be carried along by chance. I didn't want everything to go by in a whirl, since I didn't know at the time whether I would even be able to move back to Bulgaria one day. For the first time in ages, I allowed myself the right to enjoy a certain freedom. A rare feeling, I must admit, and one that did not last.

I had insisted on receiving alumni of the Military Academy the next day, those who had been the last to graduate under the monarchy. I wanted to meet with them before I met anyone else: it was important for me—a symbol, a form of gratitude that I owed them. Some had tears in their eyes, others had confidences to share, still others proudly wore their medals with the royal crown. Their representative, Officer Bankovski, solemnly presented me with his aide-de-camp saber, today exhibited with many other objects in our family museum in Vrana near where I live. Several of them had known my father and remembered him well, speaking of him with emotion. All were very elderly, since the last class to graduate was that of 1946.

Facing me were men who had come through the last half century with all of its turbulence: men who, after our departure and the hardening of the regime, were subjected to the opprobrium reserved for those "implicated" in the old regime—that is to say, that of my parents and myself. In the jargon of propaganda, the reigns of my father and my grandfather were referred to using the astonishing term "monarcho-fascism." Even now, I am still trying to understand the philosophical significance of such a gross misinterpretation, even if it was constantly repeated at the time and, alas, used again up until today by certain political commentators who wish to prove their point to me. If there is one truth I am convinced of, it is that the political system at the time of the monarchy had absolutely nothing in common with the totalitarian vision of society that came after us.

At the time, the young men who graduated from the Military Academy did not engage in politics since they were forbidden to do so. Since 1878, year of the Liberation of Bulgaria, officers constituted an elite. They were well educated and patriotic, and they often spoke foreign languages, having trained abroad, in France, Germany or Russia. They had chosen a military career to serve their country, and that was all there was to it. To condemn them in this way is a terrible injustice, as it is for many intellectuals, teachers and university professors. I tried to compensate for these sufferings to the extent I could, to heal the wounds of the past, with no thoughts of revenge. During the difficult period of the Second World War, when Bulgaria was coming under the joint pressure of Germany and the Soviet Union, the behavior of these men was exemplary. They had suffered terribly defending our borders. Even if it wasn't possible to make up for the decades of emptiness and abandonment, I felt that at that particular moment I had a role to play in that direction. A moral role, that of a stabilizer, showing the way to reconciliation and of memory at peace. History had already judged in a way those in government since 1944, and even if they have not been sentenced for their countless crimes, I did not intend to stir up grievances.

Still, in Sofia, and in the same spirit, I asked to meet the descendants of people who had worked at the palace. Their parents had certainly been shot during the early days of the coup d'état. Some of them were my age, and we shared childhood memories. About one hundred of them came to see me that day. Among them were the sons, daughters and sometimes even widows of those who had been executed at the same time as my Uncle Kyril, the regent. As I heard each of their names, I would see again the face of their relatives, individuals I had rubbed shoulders with at our house in Vrana, near Sofia, or at the Royal Palace in the city center. I tried to say something different to each of them, but it was not easy.

Sometimes the emotion was so intense the words would not come. We would look at each other, and that was enough.

These people had suffered because of "us." I could not be indifferent. The idea of sacrifice has become obsolete in our time, but these people had been prosecuted for a single, unique reason: their loyalty, or what used to be called a sense of honor. The "people's" trials had been expeditious, sometimes even nonexistent. Why bother with procedure when the verdict is made in advance? Can we even talk about justice in these circumstances? I am sensitive to the weight of words, and I don't like their misuse. Long after, senior party members bragged about participating in these murders. This was not justice meted out because of "social class," for the victims belonged to all levels of society, but indiscriminate, unforgivable crimes. I recognized the names of each one of them, for my mother had never stopped talking about them during our years in exile. The night after these meetings, I couldn't sleep. I was unable to relax and rest, even if I was only a child at the time of those sufferings.

I could have tried to forget everything, to pretend as if that life had not been my own. Yet I saw myself almost reincarnated in their faces, like ghosts unexpectedly coming out of the past. Neither they nor I ever imagined that we would see each other again. They were emerging from a long period of darkness, and I did not dare inquire too closely what had happened to them since the war, lest I remind them of their suffering, of lives ruined by those decades.

Each year since 1945, on February 1, the day of the executions, my mother had a requiem mass said in their honor, wherever we found ourselves. I attended it, whether in Estoril or Madrid. She had the priest read out the list of names of those who had been closest to my father. This mass was one of the rituals to which she was very attached, as was August 28, the day we commemorated the death of my father. These events marked the years of my youth, then those of my life as an adult. My mother felt in her heart the horror of those days. In our yearly litany, we mentioned only the names of those who were present at the palace and with whom we came into contact on a daily basis. I hope that those absent will forgive me. There were so many victims, it would not be possible to name each one of them.

Their descendants for the most part stayed in Bulgaria. They really had no other choice, enduring the fact of being the sons and daughters of those outlawed, an unbearable social sentence. The new system would not hold any consideration for them. Many were monarchists. But in the face of my necessarily conciliatory attitude with the ex-Communists, some gradually turned away from me: "We have nothing to do with your brother," some people annoyingly told my sister. This was tough to hear. They were disappointed that I wasn't settling scores more clearly with the "Reds." I can't hold it against them. The atmosphere was very anti-Communist in the 1990s, and you had to choose sides.

With hindsight, I understand their reaction. But given my position, I couldn't do otherwise. My role was not to despise part of the population, even if they themselves had not hesitated in doing so. I have carefully kept all my life the list of victims, some two hundred people executed in February 1945.

When I think of it, I remember a quote displayed in the military museum in Toledo under a painting representing the summary executions during the Civil War: "Spaniards, forgive, but do not forget!"

Repression was very severe during the months that followed the Soviet invasion and the seizing of power by the Bulgarian Communists in September 1944. Hundreds of people were assassinated, even priests by their altars, and thousands of people kidnapped, never to reappear. Near Samokov, for example, from the top of a rock cliff that I sometimes pass on my mountain walks, the mayor—a lawyer friend of my father—and other senior officials from the area were pushed into space the day after the coup d'état, with no trial whatsoever. Violence in its purest state. Unfortunately, in such chaotic moments, vendettas and the settling of accounts were fearsome. Human nature brings out its worst in such moments. Unleashed, the animal in us reveals itself. These tragedies made a huge impact on me and to this day explain why I hate and condemn violence so deeply.

What displeases me as well the bias found nowadays when providing a view on past events. The dead were not of a single political end. As far as Bulgaria is concerned, there were those who disappeared, and there were the people's courts. The number of executions was appalling. Numbers were published, but there are still discussions among historians as to their accuracy. When they are corrected, they always increase—never decrease. In the three years of terror, from 1944 to 1947, there were several tens of thousands of individuals who were shot by firing squads. They didn't hesitate to shoot my uncle even though he had assumed political responsibilities quite late, when he became one of the regents in 1943, after the death of my father. This is Marxism too, with the example of what it had already accomplished in Russia in the course of the Bolshevik Revolution. Only the naïve could have been surprised.

I have never understood this attitude. The methods have stayed the same since the Cheka and the pre-war Stalinist purges. It shouldn't be forgotten that not a single culprit was ever judged for these mass crimes. There was no Nuremberg for Communism. It is for this reason that Eastern countries have an amputated memory: Poland, the Baltic states, even Ukraine with its millions of victims from the 1932 famine . . . the suffering that our people endured—some passing directly from Nazism to Stalinism—has no equivalent in Western Europe. During the Cold War, the West did not know—or wish to know—about this suffering, or even recognize the price paid by populations to the most outrageous totalitarianisms. I think again of the Poles, who paid such a heavy price during the Second World War. We need only think of the Katyn massacre, in the spring of 1940: 22,000 officers, soldiers, students and professors, each with a bullet in the back of the neck, shot by NKVD henchmen! I also think of Alexander Solzhenitsyn, condemned in 1945 for "counter-revolutionary" activities, whose testimony on his life in the gulags I had read. At the same time, I couldn't help but think of my fellow countrymen who were subjected to a similar experience in Bulgaria, to the total indifference of the West. Silence is sometimes more painful than pain itself. I felt so powerless not to be able to do anything, I was enraged. But what could I do from my distant exile, except to constantly repeat the need for law and justice? I had testimony, firsthand sources in the form of Bulgarians who managed to flee and whom I would visit in refugee camps in Germany, Greece and Italy. But no one wanted to hear us. *Vox clamantis in deserto*: "A voice crying in the desert," that of Saint John the Baptist.

For little Bulgaria alone, historians count more than 130,000 victims. This is an enormous proportion for a country whose total population was estimated at seven million—equivalent to approximately one million victims for a population like that of France at the same time. Imagine the magnitude of such slaughter.

The archives of our countries are beginning to shed some light on these taboo subjects. How many people outside the countries under these regimes protected them? This needs to be talked about, too. I remember reading in the mid-1950s an article signed by Jean-Paul Sartre published in *Les Temps modernes*, in which he shamelessly affirmed, "The truth is that even the experience of a fact such as the horror of concentration camps does not determine policies." This was his way of trying to avoid condemning the Soviet Union at a time when the hell that hundreds of thousands of deported prisoners were experiencing in the gulags was already known. At this period, Soviet camps had been in existence almost thirty years. How could anyone state with any dignity that they didn't know? How can this be excused for political reasons? I still cannot understand how such bias could be tolerated by reputedly intelligent minds.

During these first days in Sofia, I saw one of our chauffeurs again, dear Sava, who had lived through the dark years. Of medium height, he had an ascetic face that made me think—I don't know why—of Ignatius of Loyola. How emotional when we met again! We fell into each other's arms. After my return, he came to see us regularly, with his granddaughter who helped him get around. He remembered all of the time we spent together, of the hours on the road to Tsarska or to the Rila Monastery, in the mountains. Despite the years, I was still the child-king for him. We were still in the period of the black and white photos I looked at over the years in our family albums, thinking of Bulgaria. He died not long after the arrival of the year 2000, over ninety years old. I was very fond of him.

In general, people who had worked at the palace were deemed "fascists," locked up or put under house arrest in the provinces. I can still picture the decorator-upholsterer—who was one of them—who my sister and I thought was wonderful because he could move from one draped window to another, never getting down from the ladder, which he moved like stilts. My aide-de-camp, Colonel Bardarov, was immediately deported and then allowed to work in a workshop making dolls. This was also the case for Simeon Groueff, older brother of Stephane Groueff, author of *Crown of Thorns*, a very beautiful book dedicated to the story of my father.[1] Their father had been shot in 1945 with the others since he was the head of the chancellery for King Boris. He was of a very gentle character, and I remember him well. Years later, in the Tintin comic *King Ottokar's Scepter*, I thought I recognized him in the role of the Chamberlain, with his square, beautifully trimmed and cared-for beard—a detail even more amusing when you know that Hergé apparently revealed to Albert, king of the Belgians, that Borduria was in reality Bulgaria! We have always been very close to the Groueff family. Stephane, who worked for twenty years for *Paris Match*, had left Bulgaria long before, and he came regularly to visit our mother in Portugal. But his older brother, Simeon, did not leave the country and was imprisoned and given a very rough time. Simeon traveled to Plovdiv to visit me. I remember the date: June 10, 1996. The man I saw coming toward me was so dried up and thin that I did not recognize him at first. Throughout our meeting, he couldn't stop crying. I remembered our childhood: even though he was older than I was, he used to come to the palace with his parents. "My world was here," he told me. "If everyone had left, there would have been no one to think differently." He was convinced that he had made the right decision—a position that did not lack panache despite all the sacrifices and was more than moving.

I could go on forever with examples, but I don't want to make the story of our homecoming, which was above all a happy time for us, too grim. However, I do want the truth to be told and want us at last to talk about this difficult period. My compatriots must learn what happened, the younger generation especially. In Sofia, in the main cemetery, I went to the stele dedicated to those shot on February 1, 1945, to meditate. I felt so terrible I have never been able to go back. One of my last prime ministers, for example, Ivan Bagrianov, was killed on that dreadful day. I

---

1. *Crown of Thorns: The Reign of King Boris III of Bulgaria, 1918–1943* (Lanham, MD: Madison Books, 1987).

remember the first time I received him, when I was only eight years old. On my first trip back, I met his son in Shumen.[2] He looked so much like his father that I recognized him immediately.

After September 1944, my mother and I received representatives of the new government at the palace at Vrana or at Tsarska, and I still remember the celebrated Kimon Georgiev, who had been involved in a plot against my father in May 1934. He found himself at the forefront of the Communist coup d'état of September 9, after which he became the last prime minister of the Kingdom of Bulgaria. A very intelligent man, he was one of those people who acted opportunistically rather than by real political convictions. The kind of person who turns up in revolutions and always know how to get the best for himself out of any situation. Just before our exile, it was he who handed over to my mother the list drawn up by the new regime of our private properties. The list used by the Constitutional Court in 1998 as a basis for the restitution of our family estates—but that is another subject, and one that I will save for later.

After these emotional moments, I wanted to explore the city a little, even if it was difficult to free myself from the program we had planned. Sofia for me was a springtime city, with its well-planned streets, and numerous squares and avenues. I could still smell the fragrance of the chestnut trees in the palace gardens on the rare occasions when I had accompanied my father there. These gardens no longer exist. In our childhood, my sister and I most often stayed at the residence in Vrana in the middle of a huge garden, a dozen or so kilometers from the town center. Today, I live there again, in this construction of composite styles, the creation of King Ferdinand. The presence of nature reassures me. I feel good there.

I have always found Sofia a pleasant city, one whose architecture somehow calls to mind a mixture of the styles of Vienna and Paris, a capital of uncommon charm, a city in Western Europe assembling a mosaic of different communities. A city above all that has succeeded in retaining its human scale. There was no massive destruction here, contrary to

---

2. Shumen is a beautiful city situated in northeast Bulgaria, which was important in the Middle Ages and continued to be so during the Ottoman period.

Bucharest: there, one fifth of the historic city was bulldozed to make way for the construction of President Ceausescu's palace.

I wanted to visit the schools, but the government prevented us from doing so. I don't know what they were afraid of. I had no bad intentions. I was awarded a *honoris causa* doctorate from the College of Sports in the presence of numerous students. I visited Saint Anne's Hospital with the interns for an unbelievable reception, a little bit in honor of my son Kubrat, who became a surgeon. Professor Alexander Chirkov welcomed me before the overflowing, enthusiastic audience: "Your Majesty, you are the only person capable of restoring social and political harmony, as well as hope, to Bulgaria." The political message was clear.

Lifted off my feet in an enormous crush of people at Saint Clement University, I thought my last hour had come. Foreign journalists were present, among them Stéphane Bern, who had covered the returns of my mother and sister for *Le Figaro*, and Ramón Pérez-Maura. The latter used the trip to Bulgaria to write his beautiful book, *El Rey posible* (The Possible King). On the cover, you see me on the first day of my return, my arms wide open, greeting the crowd from the balcony of the municipal headquarters in Sofia. I also remember that a German filmmaker accompanied us, planning to make a documentary film. The Spanish ambassador, Jorge Fuentes, had received instructions from the king to not let me out of his sight, the idea being that the presence of a foreign diplomat at my side would guarantee my freedom of movement. In Europe, the media gave my return massive coverage, as they had that of King Michael of Romania in 1992. Television cameras followed us everywhere, by car, by train, on foot. In Bulgaria, I was the headline story on the evening news. Everything I saw, did, or said needed to be known. Rare media coverage, and I'm not complaining.

In every corner of the country, the welcome was as exuberant and warm as the first days in Sofia. I understood rather quickly that my life was once again going to change. I felt that, almost at age sixty, my previous life was finished even though I hadn't yet decided to move back to Bulgaria, or even to get involved in politics. Quite simply, I wanted to see my country again. It was only later, in the years that followed that first trip, that I tried to get people used to my presence, as I had been advised to do by my uncle, Archduke Otto of Austria, known in politics as Dr. Otto von Habsburg, for whom I have always had great admiration: "Simeon, go in and come out." He was right. That's what I did, right up until my election. I went back four times for short, sporadic trips. In 1979, when he was elected to the European Parliament in the first elections held with direct universal suffrage, I sent him a congratulatory telegram. He answered immediately, saying that henceforth "my" Bulgaria—implying the free Bulgaria that I incarnated—would always have at least one vote in its favor in the assembly in Strasbourg. I was very touched by his support.

My trip continued with a new stopover point each day: "If I am able to experience these exceptional days, that means that Bulgaria is moving toward democracy," I declared during my first press conference in Sofia. There was no question of my saying anything more for the moment. I did not want to deliver a message that was too political. In each city, the crowds were there, thanks to the rumors that preceded us—a promising sign. People wanted to "see" the king. We had not expected this kind of reaction, a beautiful big surprise that did many people a lot of good. People were transformed; they followed the queen and me everywhere at each stop we made.

Over the following days, we crossed the region of Yambol, near the Toundja River, southeast of Sofia, in Thrace, a region known for the quality of its wines. Then to Stara Zagora, a city that, given its location, could have been our administrative capital. We visited a stud farm and a horse museum, in which I recognized numerous objects from the palace of my childhood. Should I claim them as my property? I thought not. Again, in the Museum of the City of Sofia, a few years later, I noticed the beautiful carriage facings that King Ferdinand had imported especially from France to embellish the royal barouche, as well as the desk that Queen Victoria had given him.

In Stara Zagora, a representative of the district turned out to wait for us, wishing us a good trip with great warmth. He was one of those royalists-at-heart who held it against me that I did not settle accounts with the Communists. There are many like him. Even if I understand their suffering, I can't help it—my humane principles prevent me from considering each former "Red" a criminal. I cannot do it. I am not easily manipulated. And even some politicians, having noisily declared themselves in favor of me, imagined that I would only play the role of a figurehead and were in fact only attempting to peacefully carry on with their backhanded little schemes.

I asked that we go by way of the pass at Shipka, perched at an altitude of more than one thousand five hundred meters, facing a superb panorama. It was there, during the summer of 1877, that four decisive battles led to our liberation from the Ottoman yoke. Russian troops, of several army corps composed of Finnish and Belarussians, backed by Romanian troops and battalions of Bulgarian ones, had crossed the Danube to carve out a route in the Balkans and topple the Turkish command. The battle was appalling, one of trenches and artillery in mountainous terrain. Cannons were fired by hand among the drifts of snow. In summer, the soldiers died from thirst and heat. The Russo-Turkish conflict ended the following year, in 1878, with the Treaty of San Stefano, a town near Istanbul, where the independence of the Principality of Bulgaria was recognized. It is for this reason that Shipka remains an important spot in our collective memory. A memorial that can be spotted from the air, a tower framed by four cannons, was built during my father's time to commemorate these confrontations. Below is a very beautiful, typically Russian church that was also built at the time and then restored for the visit of President Vladimir Putin for the 125th anniversary of the Liberation. This is a place that I like going back to for its natural beauty and its symbolism. From the Plain of Thrace, you can see the golden onion domes of the church in the distance.

I understood much later that the hope that I had stirred up during those memorable days went well beyond my possibilities as a simple mortal. There was a messianic—God forgive me—side to the welcome I was given. With hindsight, I still break out in a cold sweat. Everyone was waiting for things to change from one day to the next. But the time of great disappointments arrived fast, with each person having his own idea of the changes I should make. And it was not possible for me to instantly bring Bulgaria out of the rut it had been left in. I had the power, but not the means. Politicians like making promises they know quite well they can't keep. But voters are not fooled. I never wanted to give in to this sort of complacency.

Despite everything, many people hoped that both pensions and salaries could rise at the same time. It did not happen, and it became "Simeon's fault," and mine alone, even as I was fighting to have foreign investment capital for Bulgaria! There is sometimes a tendency to forget. Others thought that I should immediately restore the monarchy. Each one had his own firmly held ideas, and tensions ran very high.

In Burgas, our large commercial port on the Black Sea, the population was overexcited at my arrival. There was some debate among my staff whether I should go to the town hall first or visit the port and its industrial installations. For me, there was no question of my visiting a town without first meeting with the authorities—that was the very least of common courtesy. So off we went to the town hall. Part of the public was very clearly favorable to me, against the Communist mayor and the holdovers from the regime; the other side demonstrated their feelings against me just as loudly. The words were harsh, the slogans unambiguous. Each side had mobilized its henchmen. The mayor, Ioan Kostadinov, received me at the top of the immense stairway of his town hall; then, in the Meeting Room, he gave me an icon of Saint Nicolas. The noise coming from outside was such that he proposed that I go out on the balcony to wave to "my people," as he said to me. "Mayor," I said to him, "I don't think it's ethical given your political party; I'll greet them below as I leave." He looked very astonished at my answer; maybe he thought I was going to take advantage of the platform to address the crowd. We thus went down together, finding ourselves in the middle of the general confusion, facing groups ready to beat each other up with their bare hands. We were stuck. Looking for an honorable solution, I took his arm and held it high, saying loudly that this was the image of Bulgaria that I wanted to see: a reunited, peaceful country!

*

I am convinced that the memory of my father contributed greatly to the warmth of these reunions. I understood it immediately. He had been very popular in his time, and people hadn't forgotten him despite the years of disinformation. The older generation was still there to bear witness. All remembered the years between the wars as a period when the country was at peace with itself, despite international tensions and the coups d'état that my father had to contend with. King Boris was nothing like the potentate described afterward in books. It's always easy to rewrite history to your own advantage when there is no one around to challenge your version.

Whenever I arrived in a town, the march from "Simeon the Great"—as he presented himself before the gates of Constantinople—was always played for me. The notes would come back to me: a patriotic march from the time of my childhood, an anthem that had lived through the various governments until now. The Church, of course, was present throughout the trip, as were monarchist organizations, but also thousands of unknown people who had come out spontaneously to meet me. Each day was a victory. I spoke, I listened, people asked me questions and we exchanged ideas freely. The police no longer knew what to do. Some of them went so far as to join in with the crowds cheering me. Everywhere, even in the most remote places, I found the same enthusiasm.

At Plovdiv, I realized that I had to be really cautious, as the crowd was absolutely out of control. This city, with its ancient, prestigious past, is a little jewel of Ottoman architecture. In the main square, full to bursting, thousands of people had gathered in terrible heat. With my wife Margarita, I appeared on the balcony of our hotel several times, facing a tightly packed crowd overflowing with joy. I can still picture the ambulances waiting to intervene in case people fainted. Spas Garnevsky, the mayor at the time, delivered an enthusiastic speech in my favor. People cheered, "We want our king!" time and again.

"Here you must be very careful" was my innermost thought. Even a benign incident could cause the crowd to get out of hand, turning into a mob. I could feel tremendous energy, and I understood the intoxication that such a spectacle produces in a speaker, but I didn't want to give into voicing populist slogans that could have had dramatic consequences. It was important to avoid frightening the neo-Communist government. After all, I was there as a visitor, with no official invitation or specific approval from the authorities; it was pointless to risk being declared persona non grata. As I began my speech, I was thinking that if I let myself go like the mayor, it was possible that the crowd would "march" on Sofia. The government was fragile; the air was electric. The mayor had not led me to anticipate the tone of his speech. I thus began hoping to calm people down: "My dear compatriots, we are touched by your welcome. . . . Being back with you after all these years of absence . . ." But my tone was different from his, calmer, monotonous. People calmed down. I was reassured—I distrust crowds, suffering from agoraphobia myself. Finally, everything turned out well, with no fighting and no overreactions. Looking back, I don't regret my decision; I acted by instinct. Such an audience, thrown against a police force that was not used to containing that sort of demonstration in a peaceful way, could have led to bloodshed. It was impossible to imagine such a happy return linked to a tragedy.

That evening, I attended a performance of *Carmina Burana*, in a magnificent Roman amphitheater, accompanied by the philharmonic orchestras of Sofia and Plovdiv. The next day we went to pray at the tomb of my grandmother, Maria Luisa of Bourbon-Parma, in the Catholic church of Saint Louis. Her recumbent statue in Carrara marble is really marvelous. My mother later quoted a maxim taken from one of her letters: "How lovely it is to give happiness, and even lovelier to receive it one's self." Under the Communist regime, the church had been closed and a large wooden crate placed over the sculpture to hide it from the eyes of the public, and this in fact had protected it from potential damage. In Sofia, after the fall of the Communists, "Marshal Tolbukhin" Street had had its name changed to "Maria-Luisa." My grandfather Ferdinand died in Coburg, in our family fief. The idea of bringing his remains back to Bulgaria to be buried next to his first wife is spoken of regularly, but it hasn't been done yet.

We then went to the nearby monastery at Bachkovo,[3] where our welcome included following the miraculous icon of the Holy Virgin in procession. The first patriarch of the modern-day Bulgarian Church was named Kyril, and the holy man is buried here, in a place symbolic for Bulgarian identity. The father-abbot of the convent, Bishop Naum, was an eccentric who said anything that came to mind, a somewhat

---

3. The foundation of this monastery goes back more than a thousand years at a point to the south of Plovdiv, at the edge of the Rhodope Mountains.

comical situation for a man of his rank! We lunched in the refectory on a huge slab of pink marble. The presence of the monks in such a beautiful setting showed how some institutions had stood the test of time, despite the difficult years.

I also experienced a wonderful episode on a train. In the 1980s, in Madrid, I had noticed in my mail a letter in very beautiful calligraphy written by a young man in a refugee camp in Italy. As it happened, I needed a new secretary. Why not invite him to come? Intelligent and resourceful, Augustin Peychinov came to work in my office for six months. He had then left for the United States, where he had made a fortune. A few years later, I received a letter from him in which he warmly thanked me for what (little, to my mind) I had done at the time to help him. And now we were meeting up again on this trip. To thank me, he booked several cars on the train from Sofia to Pleven—better known as Plevna—on the way to the Black Sea. This town was the headquarters for the War of Liberation, where Russians and Turks had locked in bitter confrontation. Wounded, the pasha of the Ottoman army had surrendered with dignity at the end of the battle. Those few hours in the train were impressive, for we went through extremely remote countryside. People lined the tracks so that they could throw flowers at us. In the stations, people poured out to meet us with cheers. I remember one elderly man who ran alongside yelling, "Long live the king, long live the king . . ." He was wearing a military cap from the 1950s, with a great big red star on it! Another one of those out-of-time historical moments that never cease to surprise me.

Rail engineers came to see me especially because of my father's love of trains: they called him "king of the railroad." At his funeral, in 1943, a delegation carried his coffin for part of the long procession.

At Varna, the great seaside city on the Black Sea and one of the last stops on this journey worthy of an epic, my wife was given a horse as a present. Near the famous city aquarium, I was shown a marble plaque dating from 1910, given by King Ferdinand, where he had carved, "Bulgarians, Love the Sea, Take Care of Your Coasts." An environmentalist ahead of his time! We contemplated the beaches of yellow sand, the superb coastline. Suddenly, I recognized the very characteristic smell of its algae, an odor I had smelled for the first time at age three.

Not wanting to appear too attached to material goods, or nostalgic for a bygone era, I hadn't wanted to visit our house at Euxinograd,[4] which looks like a French château. The widow of the property manager, whom my sister and I had known when we were children, was very sad about this decision. I now regret that my scruples made me so self-conscious. When I hear all the slander about me, including the accusation that my only goal in coming back to Bulgaria was to get back my estates, I understand to what point subtlety is never understood. It's my great mistake.

We stayed two nights at the seaside, on the famous coast with its golden sands. I needed a bit of time to breathe. We made some daytrips in the surroundings, a thousand things a day to see, to do, to be given. What remained of the Bulgaria I had left? What were the next generations—those who had grown up under Communism—thinking? I studied my fellow countrymen to know their feelings and, above all, to understand *them*. It would have been pretentious of me to want to impose my point of view as the only one. We are in a period of democracy and open debate of ideas. I am not forgetting my background, either, or the way I was raised, which always taught me to respect others. Even if Voltaire was rather sarcastic at the time with the German principalities, from which we Saxe-Coburgs come, I like reading his letters and reflecting on his thoughts. I also appreciate Montesquieu and his sense of measure. Above all, I believe in freedom of expression and competition between sound ideas.

*

In exile, I never ceased to act in favor of Bulgaria, in the largest sense of the word. Despite the obstacles, I watched with interest all that was happening inside the country. From 1989 on, I paid even closer attention.

The Bulgarian people cannot be mobilized as easily as one might think. It takes a lot of work—a political lesson it might be well to spread elsewhere. In Madrid, I met with many contacts and gathered information. I was at the center of these conversations, since my compatriots wanted to know what I was planning on doing. After 1989, the meetings

---

4. It was my grandfather who had given it this name, after the Greek "Pont Euxin Sea," the former name of these fringes of the Black Sea.

increased, especially with Bulgarians—but this time they were not just exiles like me: many of them came from Bulgaria itself.

I knew people active in politics in the country, but not only them: some—whose names I will not mention—had already come to see me in secret, in "Coburg's Lair," as Communist propaganda snidely called the house I had lived in since 1946. I had done my homework—accumulated piles of files in my office, collected hundreds of hours of interviews and information on people, the state of the country, and its economy. I am not a holder of grudges. Even Communists came to see me. And I was nowhere near the end of my surprises.

After visiting Plovdiv, Todor Zhivkov himself proposed that we meet. I couldn't believe my ears: in 1996, he was still alive, the all-powerful chief who had governed Bulgaria with an iron hand for several decades. The old man, a native of Pravets, was under house arrest while awaiting trial. A first request had been delivered to me by the head of my security, who knew him; I received the second from a general in the Bulgarian security services on the eve of the last day of my trip. Faithful to my convictions—I had already taken enormous trouble not to anathematize partisans of the former regime in general—I felt that it was impossible for me to meet him. My supporters would not have understood. Seeing Zhivkov one-to-one in the climate of exasperation that existed was not conceivable, even if I must admit that I was tempted to actually meet someone who had done us so much harm. He had imposed the Sovietization of the country by force and, in the 1980s, had launched a movement to persecute our Turkish-speaking minority. Still, I was bothered because I didn't want to offend him. An idea came me: "I don't think it is polite to visit a former chief of state on the last day of my visit," he was told. I suggested that I would prefer to visit him the first day of my next trip, on condition that he serve me the twelve-year-old whisky that he kept for his friends, a detail I had read in an article on him—an elegant manner to kick the ball when you can't score. Apparently, the old dictator appreciated the response. Already ill, he died in August 1998, a year and a half after our exchange, so I never met with him. I admit, though, that I am the first to practice deliberate forgetfulness; I really don't have a choice—otherwise we'd all die sour and bitter.

Todor Zhivkov remains the symbol of a system to which we were subjected for over thirty years. The decades of the 1970s and 1980s were very wearing for Bulgarians. Even as conditions improved for other socialist countries, in our country, on the contrary, life became harsher. When, by accident, I bumped into compatriots abroad, they were very frightened about being denounced when they returned. Most often, their families were held as hostages to guarantee that they returned to the country. Each time, their reactions dismayed me, so unthinkable they were in Western Europe, where freedom was such a given for us. No one could imagine the dark time out of which a country like Bulgaria was emerging after forty-five years of a totalitarian regime. After my return, I felt that people were still frightened to talk about their traumatizing experiences. Some spoke about their time in work camps. Two camps with most sinister reputations had marked everyone's minds with sadness: Belene, situated on an island in the Danube near the Romanian border, and Lovech, near a stone quarry. The latter, active from 1959 to 1962, incarnated terror: torture was practiced there on a wide scale, as was enslavement of prisoners and starvation. Starting in 1961, women were sent to a separate camp in Skravena, where they also crushed stone.

It is said that in the 1960s, the International Committee of the Red Cross numbered concentration camps in Bulgaria at 110, an enormous number for a country of its size. These "residences for reform through work," as the government called them, were created by decree in the first months of 1945. I still see quite clearly the map that I found so shocking. When they talked about them, the still-frightened survivors stood close and whispered in my ear.

How can such a traumatic past be managed? The book by Tzvetan Todorov, *Au nom du peuple*, which presents the testimony of the survivors, is revealing. It is painful for me to dive into it once again. The author reminds us how when prisoners were freed, they were forced to sign a statement in which they promised to say nothing of what they had seen during their incarceration. If they broke their word, they were accused of spreading "rumors." It is for this reason that for twenty or thirty years after the events, these poor people did not dare talk about what they had lived through. Reading Todorov, I was profoundly impressed by his great humanism. His analysis is powerful: "All totalitarianism is thus Manichaeism, dividing the world into two mutually exclusive camps, the good and the bad, its goal being the annihilation of the latter. . . . It should not be forgotten that Lenin, Stalin and Hitler were sought after and loved by the crowds," he wrote in *Mémoires du mal, tentation du bien*. For me, there is no difference between various totalitarianisms: they are all horrendous and all the same in the eyes of History. I am incapable of differentiating between them.

First as secretary general, then as prime minister, and finally as president of the Supreme Council, Zhivkov changed the constitution twice in his favor to stay in power. In the middle of the 1970s, in a speech that has remained famous, he even proclaimed that one of his objectives was for Bulgaria to become the sixteenth Soviet Republic. This sparked quite an outcry despite the country's allegiance to the Soviet Union. The "Romanian barrier"—that country with Latin roots—protected us in a certain way from that project becoming reality, as did the cynicism of Soviet leaders, who had understood that this sort of *Anschluss* was no longer possible in Europe. Besides, the Russians had no interest, given that the Cold War was ending and relations with the West were warming.

We Bulgarians were convinced that the West wanted nothing to do with us and that, in fact, the only great powers courting us were Germany and Russia. Small countries are always looking to be protected. We shouldn't be judged for this situation; History looms behind it. Our affinity to our Russian "Uncle Ivan" is tenacious: our languages, our alphabet, and our religion make us close, as do our Slav roots. But, thank God, we became members of the European Union. Given the crises we are going through at present, I believe that nostalgia for "the good old days" of Communism—when things were, of course, much easier—could otherwise already have submerged us. It's easy to idealize. After fifty years of ideological occupation and indoctrination, the idea had the time to sink deep into people's minds. "Does freedom have a price for you?" I asked one day in a public debate.

*

On June 7, Professor Axinia Djourova, a great Byzantine scholar and passionate lover of history, visited me. I had read several of her articles in scientific reviews. The history of the Eastern Roman Empire has always fascinated me, especially as Constantine had for a time envisaged installing his new Rome on the site of present-day Sofia, before settling on the tip of the Bosphorus, which became Istanbul. I was delighted to host her. A very interesting woman, whose father, curiously, had been Zhivkov's closest friend. For over twenty years, General Dobri Djourov held the job of minister of defense. Although I had never thought that one day I would be speaking with this sort of person, the meeting was very cordial.

In a similar way, I also met the granddaughter of Todor Zhivkov, Jenny Zhivkova, who after 1991 was elected member of Parliament for three terms. Her mother, Ludmila, the dictator's beloved daughter, had studied at Oxford and became minister of culture in the final days of the regime. A sad story, for she died mysteriously at the age of thirty-eight. It was she who saved many of the icons that form our national heritage by having the state store them in the crypt of Alexander Nevsky, where they are on view to the public. It is said that highly ranked officials of the *nomenklatura* were beginning to sell them abroad. She was very influential, but not a Russophile, which greatly annoyed Moscow. In 1981, during the commemoration of the thirteen hundred years since the founding of Bulgaria's "First Kingdom," the Russians reduced their delegation to a minimum as a sign of displeasure. After the death of his darling daughter, Zhivkov was a broken man, never the same again. Her death has remained an enigma, as has the death of my father.

Later, when we had moved back, Jenny Zhivkova came to visit me at Tsarska, a family house that Zhivkov was very fond of and had taken over for his personal use. "This was his favorite spot," she told me, indicating a spot on the terrace of the first floor where I myself like to get away to quietly read or to smoke. The house had remained in good shape during the years of my absence, unlike the Vrana Palace: I found it empty and abandoned, with a leaking roof, cracked walls and overgrown grounds. I asked her how it had been possible to preserve Tsarska. "You know, we didn't have a revolution like in Russia," she said in her quiet voice, "my grandfather had respect for the past." I was surprised by her answer: his regime had done so much to erase memory and, in fact, History. I would later find in the house greeting cards on the walls—written in French—from my aunts Eudoxia and Nadezhda, addressed to my grandfather: "This modest little bird brings you, dear Papa, all good wishes from your little queen," wrote the latter. It was as if time had stopped and my parents had just walked out the door. I understood that Zhivkov had continued to enjoy the royal surroundings of the house: he used it for his hunting parties.[5]

There were many meetings: I also had the pleasure of meeting an old leader, a steadfast politician who had opposed the Communist regime, Dr. Peter Dertliev. I made the trip to see him, out of respect for his age. He did not want to come to my hotel, as it might have been interpreted as a form of submission. We thus met up in a Sofia pastry shop to share strawberries and cream.

This politician, who had suffered the consequences of his political dissidence heavily, had proven his courage. I wanted to show him that I did not have institutional prejudices and that I respected the fact that, as a believer in the republic, he had never betrayed his ideals. That is just what I told him, quite simply, and he couldn't help the tears that came to his eyes. He was perhaps one of those contacts who could have helped me be understood beyond my circle of faithful supporters, an opening toward republicans, but we were coming from far apart.

Zhelyu Zhelev, the first democratically elected president of the country—that is, after 1989—hosted Margarita and me for lunch at his official residence, Villa Kalina. He and his wife were extremely friendly. Under the Communists, Zhelev had been interned in a village and forbidden to travel to Sofia for having written a famous book, *Fascism*, which was in fact a veiled critique of the regime. The censorship had understood the hidden meaning, and the book was banned, confiscated and removed from bookstores. In some way, this conferred legitimacy on him. Later, the book was republished and Zhelev was finally able to

---

5. He is known for having shot the largest stag ever in Europe.

say what he thought in the preface, speaking of "absolute coincidence of two variations of the totalitarian regime, the fascist version and ours, the communist." We stayed on good terms and, despite our different visions, I have kept all of my respect for him. I remember that during one of our conversations about the previous regime, he wisely noted that before turning the page, it was necessary to have read it thoroughly—meaning that we needed to understand the rise of totalitarianism so as not to fall back into another form of it.

CHAPTER THREE

The Creation of a Kingdom

THE FORMATION OF MODERN BULGARIA MUST BE SITUATED IN THE context of the weakening of the Ottoman Empire, the "sick man of Europe." The vast Turkish Empire, which ruled immense territories from the Balkans to the deserts of Arabia and Yemen, was, in the last quarter of the nineteenth century, no longer able to hold itself together despite the considerable force that it still represented on three continents. The independence of Greece in 1821 marked an important defeat, a signal of freedom retrieved for the peoples under Ottoman domination, including southeastern Europe.

In Istanbul, whenever I visited the ecumenical patriarch, His Holiness Bartholomew—the primate of the Orthodox world—in the Phanar section on the banks of the Golden Horn, I couldn't help but think of this important chapter in history. I paused every time before the closed gate of the former entrance to the palace, where the patriarch of the period had been hanged in retaliation. The gate has remained closed ever since as a sign of mourning. The sultans of Istanbul had tried hard to rally, but History was not moving in their favor. The century of Suleiman the Magnificent and his conquests had been over for a long time. The Empire was showing symptoms of decadence, and national declarations of independence only accelerated it. The century was changing, and enormous upheavals were on the way.

Serbia and Montenegro obtained their autonomy; then it was Romania's turn, under the Treaty of Paris in 1856 and thanks to the support of Napoleon III. The suzerainty of Istanbul was now only nominal and distant. Multiethnic empires would now give way to nations, with the fate of the Ottomans foreshadowing, as I see it, the breakup of the Austro-Hungarian Empire in Central Europe. It was the end of an era, as if Europe were throwing off its old clothes to put on newer ones. We were entering into modernity and the time of nations. There was no reason for Bulgarians to be left out any longer. In their turn, they would take advantage of this wind of revolt led by intellectuals, men of the church, and an industrial bourgeoisie, all used to traveling around Europe. For them, the backwardness of the country was more than obvious. Many young Bulgarians had gone to study in Vienna since the end of the eighteenth century. This period of transition remains known as the Bulgarian Renaissance, with the birth of a patriotic feeling.

But the road to independence from the first revolutionary committee created by Vasil Levski, our national hero, was long and perilous. Ottoman reaction was violent and ended in the massacre of several thousand people all over the country between April and May 1876. Against the Krupp cannons of the Turkish army, our resistance could offer no adequate opposition. Our fighters demanded equality in civil rights for all of Bulgaria's inhabitants, whatever their origins. There were even Turks who joined in the revolt. In my archives, I found a copy of a revolutionary declaration dating from 1875, addressed to the Turkish and Bulgarian populations: "Very much to the contrary, we must hold out a fraternal hand to them, and lend them aid and protection should they be persecuted by the government for having shown sympathy to our people's movement. The honor, property and lives of peaceful Turks must be as precious and sacred [to us] as they are to themselves." I find this text important, for it shows above all that Bulgarians were strangers to "racism," and this may also explain the protection of our Jewish nationals during the Second World War. The country has never been extremely nationalistic, and I believe this to be an important feature of the nature of the Bulgarian people.

This fit of violence by the Ottomans caused a government crisis in Istanbul, for the massacres created a considerable stir internationally, reaching as far as Russia, England and the United States. In France, the words spoken on August 2, 1876, by Victor Hugo to the Chambre des Députés in Paris—but addressed to the conscience of Europe—were recalled: "A nation has been assassinated. Where? In Europe. Were there witnesses? A single witness: the entire world. Do governments see it? No . . . When will the martyrdom of this heroic little nation end? It is time for civilization to mount an impressive defense."[1]

In parallel to this Ottoman decline—I've always held that violence is an indication of weakness—the increase in power of Russia must be considered, and it partly explains our current situation. Since the fall of the Khanate of the Golden Horde—the descendants of Genghis Khan—and the storming of Kazan by Ivan the Terrible in the middle of the sixteenth century, the Russian Empire has attempted to consolidate its territory by every means possible. Russian troops were to be found as far away as Siberia and Central Asia. The country gnawed away at Turkish territories on every side, in Crimea and in the Caucasus, but also through the Balkans, finding ways to extend its influence. The two empires constantly confronted one another over a vast band of territories to the north of the Black Sea, over a landscape of steppes facilitating incursions, raids, and huge hordes of invaders.

Another expression of the Russian policy of expansion lives in its attraction to warm seas—that is, the Mediterranean and thus the Strait of the Bosphorus. Anything that brought Russians closer to Istanbul was up for grabs. Since its fall in 1453, this millennial and twice-over imperial city has constantly fed fantasy. Called Constantinople at the time of Rome's empire in the Orient, as well as "Byzantium," we have always called it Tsarigrad in Bulgarian, meaning "City of Kings." Well before the Ottomans seized it, Simeon I, a Bulgarian sovereign in the ninth century, had already attempted to conquer it: "As a name he had Symeon and his country, one of mountains with thick forests and plains where the sun turned the harvests golden as far as you could see, was called Bulgaria," wrote a respected historian of my acquaintance[2] about this great king.

Until the two Balkan Wars, the desire to take Istanbul was shared by all belligerents, not only Greeks and Bulgarians but also the Allies who occupied it after 1918. King Ferdinand, my grandfather, had had his

---

1. Victor Hugo, *Actes et paroles depuis l'exil, 1876–1880*, Œuvres complètes, volume 3 (Paris: Hetzel, 1880).
2. Gérard Sergheraert, *Syméon le Grand (893–927)* (Paris: Éditions Maisonneuve, 1960).

wife, Maria Luisa, dressed as a Byzantine empress in a celebrated portrait by the Czech painter Ian Murkvichka, invited to stay in Sofia to be the official painter of the army. The closeness of the Russians with the Bulgarian people—a population speaking a Slavic language and of Orthodox faith—constituted in their eyes a terrific foothold in the Balkans. Russia, having always presented itself as the protector of Slav peoples, decided to respond to Ottoman violence.

It is for these reasons that after the massacres of 1876, the Russians came to our assistance. Bulgaria, which hadn't enjoyed independence for centuries, would be reborn from its ashes. I have already quoted the terrible battles of Shipka Pass; I must also mention the heroic crossing of the Danube by the Russian troops and the siege of Plevna, where, with Romanian, Serbian and Bulgarian contingents, they won a series of victories leading to autonomy in 1878. European powers quickly intervened diplomatically, and particularly England, which did not want to see Russia take on too much relevance. The question of the Orient had already become part of the political landscape with the Crimean War.[3]

I am struck by the fact that the more one tries to bury History, the more it comes back like a boomerang. I have always thought that Russia belongs culturally to Europe, perhaps not to its politics—though that could also be debated—but the Europe of Dante and Tolstoy, Voltaire and Dostoyevsky. It was in no one's interest to break up the Ottoman Empire. In Greece, the English were very powerful. The Russians and the English confronted each other in Central Asia around the borders of Afghanistan. London kept track of the Russian policy of expansion and did all that it could to contain it. The two empires stared at one another like dogs ready to fight. Military operations ended with the taking of Andrianople—Edirne today in Turkey—and the Treaty of San Stefano, then that of Berlin in 1883, which determined the division of the Balkans and the creation of the Principality of Bulgaria.

---

3. In 1854, the English, the French, and the Ottomans united militarily against Russian expansionism, leading to the terrible siege of Sebastopol, which lasted more than eight months. The port was important because it sheltered a portion of the fleet, and it has since been restored to Russia.

*

After the Ottoman occupation, which lasted five centuries, no one in Bulgaria could claim lineage or historical superiority. There were no families whose line went back to the ancient sovereigns who had sufficient claim to demand recognition. During the Turkish period, births were rarely recorded in the *rayas*—the "subjugated" territories. Land was divided up, and no archives existed (or only those that monasteries rarely were able to keep). The idea of importing a neutral individual of royal blood from abroad was quickly adopted by young nations. This prince would place himself above local rivalries, an altogether healthy way of solving problems. Only the royal families of Serbia and the future small kingdom of Montenegro were originally from their respective countries.

Prestige, first of all, counted for much, followed by a European air and, above all, an absence of any links with local feudal groups that would create clans and supporters. Reclaiming ancient titles was difficult given the absence of archives. This way of proceeding was convenient. The great powers would be satisfied, as there was the possibility of placing their own candidates.

Over just a few years, Europe witnessed the hatching out of new countries born up on a huge wave of cultural energy and the desire to make up for lost time. Royal families, however, were often denigrated, accused—with a reek of xenophobia—of being "foreigners": Danish in Greece, German in Bulgaria and in Romania. But this was the only solution to ensure that these countries would not immediately start up civil wars. In addition, royal families were rarely native to a single country, with roots spreading out a little everywhere.

This idea went hand in hand with that of international recognition. When my grandfather traveled through Europe, he was received everywhere, Paris included, and was a worthy representative of his adoptive country. Thanks to him, Bulgaria was no longer a remote, unknown province, and it took up its place on the map of the modern world. All these princes spoke several languages, incarnating Europe themselves. This is a little what happened when I represented the candidature of my country for membership in the European Union: European leaders knew me or had heard of me, and their curiosity about me preceded me. Often, I could speak to each of them in his own language—in French, English, German, Italian, or Spanish. A century and a half later, the logic remained the same, that of trust. I can truly say that it was a great help.

Imagine the time necessary for any Bulgarian personality around 1878 to understand European politics, to be received and listened to. Parting with the Ottoman Empire meant being modern, evolving after centuries of stagnation. Bulgarians who had been able to study in Romania and Vienna were well in advance of their fellow countrymen. They were respected, but the habit of despising whatever seemed superior already existed: "It's not because he is more educated that he can give himself airs." At the time, the republican view was not very widespread. I continue this tradition in a certain way. Even if I am third-generation Bulgarian, my name remains attached to the history of Europe, and it would be pointless to pretend otherwise. As prime minister, I benefited from this aura across most chancelleries and the European Commission. I was not the unknown head of the executive of post-Communist Bulgaria; I was "King Simeon," and that opened numerous doors for us.

But let's get back to the nineteenth century: Though the Principality of Bulgaria had de facto autonomy, it remained a vassal and dependent on the High Porte, otherwise known as Istanbul. The prince of the new political entity also had to keep Russia happy. It was for these reasons that it wasn't easy to find a suitor who could satisfy all parties. First there was the question of origins: he couldn't be related to a royal family that was too important—Austrian, English or French. Then there was religion: the Catholic Church was not very inclined to accept the conversion of one of its flock, as this was still seen as heresy.

For Romania, the choice of a German prince of Hohenzollern became the obvious solution rather quickly. In 1866, he was elected by plebiscite, and Charles I made a triumphal entry in Bucharest under the name of Carol. In Bucharest, a city that I have loved for its charming architecture and wide streets since the first time I visited it, his equestrian statue sits imposingly in the city center—contrary to Sofia, where my grandfather is represented nowhere.

As for Bulgaria, the "Liberator Tsar"—as we call Alexander II of Russia—imposed Prince Alexander of Battenberg, related to the Russian imperial family through his aunt, the Tsarina Maria Alexandrovna, herself of German origin, from Hesse. The Saxe-Coburgs had already had access to the thrones of England, Belgium and Portugal. The young Battenberg was thus sent to Sofia as a kind of loyal supporter of Russia and established himself there with a modest court. Six years after his accession, an uprising occurred in Eastern Rumelia—Thrace—to dislodge the Turks. The prince agreed to take them under his protection, resulting in a war with Serbia in which Bulgarian troops managed to heroically turn them back at Slivnitsa, near Sofia. But very quickly relations with Russia went downhill, with Battenberg seeking to mark his independence from his relative, Tsar Alexander III. He had cause to regret it, for Russian officers kidnapped him to force his abdication in 1886. An English historian of the time referred to it as "the first political kidnapping."

Despite his short reign, we Bulgarians have kept a very good memory of him. Battenberg organized the country, putting an army and an administration in place. It was also he who had the former Turkish *konak* replaced by the royal palace in Sofia, embellished later by my grandfather Ferdinand, and today the Museum of Fine Arts. Prince Alexander ended in life as a general in the Austrian army and would never see Bulgaria again. But in accordance with the will he left, my grandfather had his remains brought back from Vienna to be buried in a mausoleum built for the occasion. He is still there, in the middle of a small garden, facing the large monument in Sofia dedicated to the Soviet army. I find this rather ironic, for it is the only royal grave remaining intact in our country. He is a well-loved character in my family and my mother was very sympathetic to the man, who had the reputation of being brilliant and courageous. Queen Victoria liked him enormously—from this came a quarrel with Russia when, out of jealousy, he was forced by Alexander III to abdicate. A person who curiously escaped the ideological censure of the Communist regime, for his name still stands in the official chronology of Bulgarian history, contrary to our dynasty, which is only mentioned in offensive terms. It was only in 2008, in Tarnovo, that the name of King Ferdinand was mentioned for the first time in an official speech by the president of the Republic, Georgi Parvanov. The speech was to celebrate the one hundredth anniversary of the proclamation of our independence. "You see, it just goes to show you have to know how to wait to be recognized for the good you have done," said my wife when we got back from the ceremony, with her usual sense of humor and good sense. My thought was that this would also be the case before anyone admitted my role in favor of our entry into the European Union.

The destiny of the Battenberg family is interesting and merits some explanation. In my life, I have come across a number of colorful descendants of this lineage. Originally, it was a morganatic[4] branch of the House of Hesse. All the men had the reputation of being very handsome.

One of Alexander's brothers, Henry of Battenberg, married the youngest daughter of Queen Victoria, Princess Beatrice of Great Britain. Together, they had four children, including the future queen of Spain, Victoria Eugenie, wife of King Alphonse XIII, the grandfather of Juan Carlos. Another brother, Prince Louis of Battenberg, married a granddaughter of Queen Victoria—Princess Victoria of Hesse—and became English. His military career took him to the prestigious post of first lord of the Admiralty, but, as he was of German origin, he was relieved of his duties in 1917. This injustice was the sorrow of his life.

His son, who had always been outraged by this humiliation—he would not hear of anyone questioning the loyalty of his father—in his turn made his career in the English navy, ending as first lord of the Admiralty under the Anglicized name of Mountbatten. We all know his story: he became the last viceroy of India, a war hero in the Mediterranean against the Germans and in Burma against the Japanese—hence his title, *Mountbatten of Burma*—before being assassinated by the IRA in 1979 in Donegal Bay in Ireland. I can still see in my mind his official photograph taken by Allan Warren, the photo of the royal family and of *Swinging London*. His death was a tragedy for England and

---

4. Marriage between people of different social ranks.

for the royal family, as well as being hugely negative for the Irish cause, for he was much loved and two young people were killed at the same time, one of them his fourteen-year-old grandson. Moreover, he was the only member of the royal family who had relatives in continental Europe. This is noticeable when the isolationist tendency of the English is taken into account.

He was flamboyant, combining the innate class of a breed on the way to becoming extinct and the spirit of adventure that could still be experienced at the time. In this sense, he and my grandfather Ferdinand resembled each other; both of them lived as if they were on stage. Mountbatten loved being observed, and the people he met with were fascinated—or perhaps *mesmerized* is the better word. He left no one indifferent. In his household, the staff was made up of former soldiers from the army who worshiped him with unfailing admiration. Nothing stopped him, neither ambition nor charm. A character from a novel whom I was lucky enough to see several times at family or official meetings in London.

Lord Mountbatten had an imposing presence, and he impressed me by the number of decorations he wore on his uniform. I was only a young man, but he treated me with consideration. He traveled frequently and liked to visit his extended family to spend time with them. Each time he went to Canada, my sister would tell me about their meetings. He always asked to see her children, whom he adored. In Spain, I remember having seen him when he visited the royal palace in Madrid to see the room he had lived in as a young man again. We discovered at the moment of his tragic end that he had prepared all the details of his funeral—a state ceremony: the list of guests, the protocol to be respected, the music and the anthems he wanted us to sing. I attended it, seeing a large part of the family and the representatives of each of the countries of the Commonwealth, and even the British Empire, in those sad circumstances.

His sister Aunt Alice, who married Prince Andrew of Greece, was the mother of the duke of Edinburgh, husband of Queen Elizabeth II. I remember having crossed her path several times in family reunions. Aunt Alice fascinated me by her very royal demeanor—that and the fact that she dressed as an Orthodox nun, having withdrawn to live in a monastery for a time.

*

After the abdication of Prince Alexander, Bulgaria was governed for a time by regency, one composed of three people, of which the principal one was Stefan Stambolov. If I pause over him, it is because he took part in the Movement for National Liberation. A native of Tarnovo, he later sat in the Bulgarian National Assembly, the Sobranje, becoming head of the Liberals. Somewhat anti-Russian, he was my grandfather's prime minister for several years up to 1890 and was sometimes known as the "Bulgarian Bismarck" in some Western chancelleries.

In 1886, each of the Powers had its candidate, but they couldn't come to an agreement between them on the name of a prince for Bulgaria. As circumstances would have it, the candidature of Prince Ferdinand was brought forward after the retraction of several others. My grandfather had the advantage of being young, ambitious, related with royal families, wealthy and, above all, the adored son of Clémentine of Orléans, the youngest daughter of King Louis Philippe who, according to family legend, helped in making the decision. The older brother of my grandfather, Philippe, had inherited from his father the Koháry titles and estates and had to manage immense tracks of land in Austria-Hungary. Our ancestor Maria Antónia of Koháry was the sole heir of Prince Franz Joseph of Koháry, owner of vast estates, and some historians use Coburg-Koháry to identify our branch of the family. Their 80,000 hectares constituted the third largest fortune in the Empire. The other brother of my grandfather, Augustus, married the daughter of the emperor of Brazil, Dom Pedro, and was raised to the rank of Brazilian admiral while another of his sisters-in-law married an Orléans, the Count of Eu, giving birth to descendants including my aunt, the Countess of Paris.[5] The brothers-in-law did not get along.

The Coburgs we are talking about formed a younger branch of the family. They lived in Vienna, where they built a magnificent palace over which Clémentine, my great-grandmother, reigned. The elders of the Coburg family, including Prince Albert, Victoria's husband, had reigned over England and Belgium since 1831 with Leopold I. Louis

---

5. It is customary in our family to call someone "aunt" or "uncle" if the person belongs to the preceding generation, even if genealogy shows that the generation is not accurate.

Philippe had requested that he marry Louise, since Leopold had been England's candidate.

My grandfather understood immediately where his interests lay. The Bulgarian delegation offered him the crown—which he accepted—but without the Powers really choosing him. Ferdinand was proud to be related to the House of France. A young prince and officer in the Austrian army related to most of the great families and very cultivated for all his youth, he could have led a carefree life. But this would have been without taking into consideration his mother's ambition and the particular affection she had for her youngest son.

Clémentine of Orléans was an outstanding character with a great capacity to influence the Europe of her times. I have always found it unfair that she be perceived as a forlorn princess who spent her life making a king of her youngest son. She deserves much more esteem. Whole chapters in her life are ignored, even though she was very open minded for the period. I want to focus a little on her because she mattered in our family, as in Bulgaria, where she made numerous trips—only the country of her son was able to replace France in her heart.

Clémentine was the youngest of the Orléans children, the last daughter of Louis Philippe, King of the French. Born in 1817, her title was Mademoiselle de Beaujolais. At a ball at the Tuileries Palace around 1829, she was so ravishingly beautiful and graceful that King Charles X, taking her by the hand, led her to the Duke of Orléans, the future Louis Philippe, and pronounced, "My dear cousin, were I forty years younger I would ask you for your daughter's hand to make her queen of France!"

She received an excellent education, rather liberal and open to the arts. The Orléans children did not live cut off from the rest of the world. She had Jules Michelet as a private tutor and met Victor Hugo at gatherings in her parents' home, whom he knew well. She gave her opinion on everything. At a dinner at Versailles in 1836, seated next to Minister Adolphe Thiers, she did not hesitate to discuss politics directly with him.

Her beauty inspired many artists, among them great painters like Ary Scheffer and the celebrated Winterhalter. On the Place de la Concorde, her father had her represented in 1835 on one of the small pavilions at the angles of the square—Gabriel's sentry boxes—in a statue symbolizing the city of Lille. I wonder whether any Parisians walking across this beautiful square nowadays know it.

When she was twenty, a husband had to be found. Her father is said to have declared, "Clémentine is ambitious, she wants to be a queen." So they began by looking at the Habsburgs, but unsuccessfully, as the latter balked at a marriage with the Orléans, still considered usurpers. This seems to me quite unfair when you know that Louis Philippe gave eighteen years of peace to France and to Europe, allowing the beginning of a period of great prosperity. Another request apparently arrived at the Tuileries, that of a young Bavarian who had in 1833 become king of the Hellenes.[6] But Queen Maria Amalia was not very enthusiastic at the idea of seeing any of her descendants becoming Orthodox. Then came the idea of marriage with the crown prince of Bavaria, this time a Catholic. However, Germany and Prussia were opposed for political reasons, remembering what happened when Bavaria allied itself with the France of Napoleon.

Finally, Clémentine married Augustus of Saxe-Coburg, who had a solid family background. After their marriage, the latter became Royal Highness in France by decree of Louis Philippe, a decision that Queen Victoria approved. Louis Philippe showed himself to be very sensitive to his daughter's position at the court of Vienna and to the financial aspects of this union. But, quite simply, I believe that beyond all the political calculations plotted at the time back and forth between the courts of Europe, Clémentine fell in love with her husband. What followed in their life easily proves it: "Each year, we loved each other more. He gave me thirty-eight years of perfect happiness," she wrote to her faithful friend Queen Victoria after the death of Augustus.[7]

They were married at the Château de Saint Cloud, residence of the Orléans family, in April 1843. Numerous personalities attended the cer-

---

6. King Otto remained in Athens only a few years, soon replaced by a young Danish prince who reigned under the name of George I and whose descendants occupied the throne of Greece until King Constantine II in 1973.
7. The quotes from Clémentine of Orléans are taken from the book by Olivier Defrance, *La Médicis des Coburg, Clémentine of Orléans* (Brussels: Éditions Racine, 2007).

emony: the French sovereigns; Prince Ferdinand of Saxe-Coburg and his youngest son Leopold; the King of the Belgians; Queen Marie-Christine of Spain; the Duke and Duchess de Nemours; the Duke de Montpensier; Madame Adelaide, the sister of Louis Philippe who never married; Prince Alexander of Wüttemberg and Prince Ernest of Saxe-Coburg, the patriarch of the family. The Château de Saint Cloud, alas, burned down in 1870. In 1892, Clémentine bought the pediment from the ruins that were being cleared away to have it placed in the gardens at Euxinograd in Bulgaria. "This is a souvenir from the château belonging to Monsieur, head of our branch of the family, where I got married," she wrote. "Monsieur" was the brother of Louis XIV, founder of the Orléans branch.

The young couple settled in Coburg, bastion of her new family in southeast Germany. Luther had lived for a time in the city. The two of them at first lived in a small palace in the center of town, far from the pomp of French castles. Clémentine seemed to have grown used to it, and her husband spent a large part of his day hunting, a tradition firmly rooted in my family over the ages. It would seem that I did not inherit the virus, for it has been a very long time since I have hunted. Clémentine simply did not understand this passion: she was more interested in theater and literature, much like my wife and my daughter Kalina. My great-grandmother also drew very well; I have some of her sketches. She also tried to learn German, but the couple's usual language all of their life together remained French, and it was also used to communicate with their son and grandchildren. Her entourage was French speaking. Of course, my great-grandparents made frequent trips to Paris, where Clémentine stayed at the Tuileries Palace. As he grew older, I believe that Louis Philippe, my dear ancestor, tended to shut himself away in an ivory tower, for only international politics interested him. I have a feeling that this quality is a constant among statesmen at the height of their power. His downfall was very sad: he died of fatigue after a few years of exile in England.

In our family, we frequently remember a famous anecdote, one in which Clémentine was watching from the windows of the Tuileries in 1848, her father in his lieutenant-general uniform passing the troops in review that had remained loyal to him even as the noise of the rioters approached. The children had been sent to hide in the attics: this was the end of the July Monarchy. Queen Maria Amalia had told her husband not to sign the act of abdication: "We must die here," she said to him with panache, thus saving the family's honor. She had the sturdy character of the Bourbon-Sicily family! The wind of rebellion blew across all of Europe, shaking up Vienna a few weeks later.

"Clem," as some members of the family called her, only slowly got over the death of her father, to whom she was very attached. Aunt Eudoxia said that Clémentine was his favorite. She remained a very thoughtful and affectionate mother: "Family, the only thing that I possess," she wrote to her friend Victoria. This was even more true since, after his decree banishing the Orléans, the future Napoleon III (*l'Aigle*) had all of the family's property in France confiscated—the *"premier vol de l'aigle,"* according to a contemporary politician. Since the word *vol* has two meanings in French, this statement can be translated as "the first flight of the Eagle" or "the first theft of the Eagle."

*

My grandfather Ferdinand was born in February 1861. Clémentine was then forty-three, old in those days to bear a child. "Ferdinand is still my tyrant. I am crazier than ever about him," she wrote to her brother, the duke of Aumale. Stylish, she continued to follow fashion and ordered her outfits from Paris. Portraits of her show the fine looks of a determined woman, and she retained her gravitas right up to her death. I believe her personality was infinitely stronger than that of her husband, who, I must admit, doesn't really show up much in the history of the country, since The Monarch acceded to the Principality of Bulgaria after his death. In Coburg, the sarcophagus of Augustus was sculpted in Carrara marble by the French artist Aimé Millet. The deceased was represented there in his uniform of an Austrian general, his cavalry sword in his hand.

Princess Clémentine spent a lot of time with little Ferdinand; her other children were already married. He traveled with her all over Europe and to Brazil, there discovering a passion for ornithology with his older brother. In Russia, he went to Moscow in 1881 for the crowning of Tsar Alexander III; in Spain, he met the royal family, and in Belgium, his first cousin, Leopold II. Everything interested him, and his curiosity was insatiable: the arts, politics, the economy, geography and hunting. Then came the question of the new kingdoms in Eastern Europe. He seethed with impatience, dreaming of finding a role worthy of his talents. With his mother, he closely followed contemporary politics. The regents no longer knew what to do.

At last, my grandfather received the Bulgarian delegation and accepted the reign on principle, but he asked as a precondition that his candidacy be recognized by the great powers, including Russia and Austria-Hungary. Stoilov, one of the members of the delegation, insistently explained again to the new prince that it was impossible to obtain prior sign-off from Russia in these conditions. Ferdinand then responded that he would accept if the Bulgarian regents officially offered him the throne, with a vote in parliament. "My son Ferdinand did not propose himself as a candidate for Bulgaria. The Bulgarian delegates asked him with insistence to accept the proposition, and many others like them wanted it and still want it!" noted Clémentine. During this time, in Bulgaria, the situation was unstable, with the Russians threatening the fragile state. But on April 28, 1887, a telegram informed Ferdinand that he was being offered the crown. On July 3 of the same year, in the ancient Bulgarian capital of Tarnovo, the Sobranje—the National Assembly—proclaimed him prince of Bulgaria. On August 1, at the age of twenty-six, the young Ferdinand set foot on Bulgarian soil, discovering his country for the first time.

His mother, Princess Clémentine, very quickly joined him: in November, she took the express train from Vienna and arrived in Belgrade where the king of Serbia received her in a manner worthy of her rank. The next day, she discovered her son's new kingdom. She was welcomed by Stambolov, who had become prime minister in the meantime. At the palace in Sofia, she wrote to her brother, the duke of Aumale, "The white dining room is quite beautiful. Military music played during the meal. After dinner, social circle. Almost everyone speaks French and I rarely had to call on an interpreter." But she knew that the task awaiting Ferdinand was going to be difficult. The country was poor, its economy based on subsistence agriculture, and the pro-Russian party acted behind the scenes to destabilize it. She asked her nephew the Count of Paris to propose names of people who could help her son in his task. This is how Count Robert of Bourboulon appeared in the history of Bulgaria, becoming the talented chronicler of the years of instauration. The young Quai d'Orsay diplomat, whose family served the French royal family, became my grandfather's secretary, beginning in 1887. His very charming letters contain many witty descriptions of our country, the mysteries of the new power, "snapshots" of life at court, promenades, landscapes, the people he met and above all the central figure that was my grandfather: "A kind of its own, I have no fear of saying it, a truly unusual personality!" For me they are the Bulgarian equivalent of the letters of the Marquis of Custine for Russia.

Abroad, Alexander III was furious. He refused to recognize my grandfather, using the pretext that he had remained Catholic—the child having been baptized automatically in the tradition of the two royal families. The Russians applied pressure, to the extent of threatening to find another dynasty. Everyone was frightened that the country would find itself destabilized again. In order for Russia to finally recognize the independent state of Bulgaria, it was necessary to wait for my father's admission to the Orthodox faith. Princess Clémentine was chosen to be his godmother.[8] It was also Clémentine, for my grandmother was ill, who appeared on the balcony of the princely palace in Sofia to present the heir, titled prince of Tarnovo, to the cheering Bulgarians. Grand Duke Michael Alexandrovich came to Sofia to represent the tsar.

My great-grandmother came regularly to visit Bulgaria, to Sofia and the rest of the country, Plovdiv among other cities. That was where the infantry regiment named after her was stationed, as the photographs of the superb album that I found accidentally in an antiques shop in Vienna show. This is a box-album, finely worked and decorated with fleur-de-lys with her initial, a Cyrillic *K*, covered in pale blue velvet. In a photo taken at a picnic, she is seen posing next to the officers of her son and daughter-in-law, holding my father, the future King Boris, in her arms.

---

8. Whereas the duke of Aumale, her brother, was the godfather of my Uncle Kyril, whose name was that of one of the two venerated saints of Bulgaria, Cyril and Methodius. In 1985, His Holiness John Paul II proclaimed the two brothers patron saints of Europe.

Taken around 1895, the picture is an important one for me, for it shows the three generations that preceded me, all together on Bulgarian soil.

Clémentine described Plovdiv in letters that I found in the Orléans collection of documents at Chantilly: "This Oriental city, with its bazaar, its old-style Turks in large turbans walking in the streets as well as veiled Turkish women, is quite a novelty. Its location is picturesque. . . . There is a lot of Greco-Bulgarian society and it is friendly. I was covered with gifts, all of them made locally!" In general, she felt quite happy there. She was acclaimed wherever she went: "I am very popular there, especially with the army, which flatters me greatly." "I am a soldier at heart," she wrote elsewhere. Another photo shows her at our house at Tsarska, a part of which had just been built by my grandfather who loved staying there.

Princess Clémentine remains for me a founding presence of our family in Bulgaria; we owe a vision of Europe to her that brought much to the expansion of the country. She brought in talents from abroad. While I mentioned Bourboulon, my thoughts also go to the celebrated Baron Hirsch who worked for the railways, and to others, among them a young Frenchwoman who was responsible for the education of the princely children: Madame de Grenaud married a Bulgarian, and I got to know her granddaughter.

As a woman who had a mind for business, Clémentine realized how much Bulgaria would need money. She managed her fortune herself, which was quite uncommon during this period. She invested four million gold francs to underwrite the construction of the railway that would cross Bulgaria and open the country to the outside world. The Orient Express was to link "Vienna to Constantinople, the Atlantic to the Bosphorus! . . . Brilliant ending of the first year of sovereignty of my dear son!" she wrote.

The Bulgarians greatly appreciated her. For them, she became *Baba Klementina*, "Granny Clémentine," an affectionate name for a grandmother in the country. Family being important in our culture, they adopted her as their queen mother. Her stays lasted longer; she would come several months a year, keeping up with her charities to finance hospitals and schools, for which she enlisted the help of other royal families, including her old friend Victoria. Her brother Aumale, a historian who no longer left the Château de Chantilly, nicknamed her "Clémentine de' Medici." Even when tired and very elderly, she never renounced her trips to Bulgaria, which she liked to say did her enormous good. She loved spending time with her grandchildren—Boris, Kyril, Eudoxia and Nadezhda—and dedicated what was left of her strength to them, taking them on trips around Europe as soon as summer approached. They enjoyed, I was told, the human warmth of the old lady with so many tales to tell.

She passed away in 1907 at the age of ninety and by the Hofburg, the royal palace in Vienna; her funeral brought together the princes and princesses of the Europe of yesteryear, one that would go through profound upheaval. After the religious ceremony and various pleasantries, she was buried in Coburg next to her dear husband, Augustus. As an oration, her son Ferdinand had inscribed at the foot of her sarcophagus, "King's daughter, no queen herself, yet now King's mother." I've always thought that the nineteenth century, and with it the old world, lasted up until the First World War.

CHAPTER FOUR

The Thread of History

ONE OF MY LIFETIME REGRETS IS NOT HAVING MET MY GRANDFATHER Ferdinand. My father succeeded him at the end of the war, in 1918, under the name of Boris III, when he was only a young man of not quite twenty-five. After his abdication, King Ferdinand lived at his residence in Coburg and died there in 1948, well after the deaths of his two sons. As the father of a family in my turn, and even a grandfather several times over, I can only imagine the terrible suffering he must have gone through on learning of the deaths of his children. What a tragic destiny! My grandfather wrote, understandably, that he had been spared nothing. Surviving his two sons was a profoundly painful experience, like that of seeing his country crushed by the Soviets. I don't know exactly when he saw his children together for the last time.

My mother went to see him in Coburg a few months before his death in 1948, when we were already living in Egypt. She had refused to have me accompany her, Coburg being located only ten minutes from the German Democratic Republic border. She did not want to take any risks, particularly that of being kidnapped. We had just barely emerged from hell, with no desire to return. In Sofia, we had seen what people were capable of doing. Never during the half-century of my exile did I forget how lucky I was to be free. My sister and I were sent to await our mother in Switzerland, in Villars-sur-Ollon at the home of Queen Geraldine of Albania, who was from a prominent Hungarian family, and whom we had known since Alexandria, where King Zog was also in exile. Our trip had begun with our departure from Egypt. It was a long trip by boat to

Marseille, and then by train and over the roads of a still very damaged Europe, especially in Germany, where communications systems continued to be bad. My mother saw The Monarch one last time; he was already ill then. He had seen so much: the splendor of the palace of Coburg in Vienna, at the time of the Austro-Hungarian Empire, and then the convulsions of a Europe at war, devoured by ideologies.

What did they say to each other? It was a cordial meeting according to her. Their relationship had never been too warm, remaining quite formal, as The Monarch had not always been very nice to my father. But I never dared venture onto the field of the complicated father-son relationship. The two of them had quite different personalities, the one all reserved and discreet, the other flamboyant. But they also had very strong points in common: a constant concern for the public interest, a sense of duty, and a passion for nature. These were not hollow words in the circumstances they experienced—each of them lived through a world war as head of state, even if my father did not live to see the end of the Second World War or the Soviet invasion.

My mother must have suffered from this distance between father and son, especially when seeing that their relationship became poorer and poorer. The way she was raised meant she had to treat my grandfather with deference, but that didn't keep her from having an opinion. Of course, she fought for my father and, when things were going badly, never hesitated to say that it was The Monarch's fault. As in every family, there were unspoken resentments and misunderstandings that went back for ages and never quite disappeared.

My mother was big-hearted. I think my father had a need to assert himself, to show clearly that his was not the more interventionist mentality of his father. Despite his education as crown prince, with good teachers, my father had to assume the throne at a very early age and grow up more quickly than other young people his age, traveling to the front to inspect the troops when he was just out of adolescence.

My parents were married in 1930 in Assisi, Italy, in the presence of King Ferdinand—there is a photo showing the two kings of the Bulgarians side-by-side. My father had wanted to get married for a long time. His two sisters had approached several royal courts with the idea of finding "the right girl" for their brother. While the shine of the Bulgarian crown was not at its best at that time, my father's personality won approval, and everyone was full of esteem and affection for him. It was at a reception that my parents met each other, two years before their marriage. Princess Giovanna was favorable to the approaches of young King Boris, while King Victor Emmanuel considered him a desirable son-in-law. My mother had brown eyes and black hair, with a lively way of expressing herself. He was twelve years older and reassured her. She fell madly in love with him. They were made to understand each other for a lifetime. This is rare.

After the wedding, the couple left for Burgas, in Bulgaria, aboard a ship that had been completely renovated for the occasion, the *Ferdinand I*. My mother told me how surprised she was when she saw children pouring water on the red carpet that had been laid down for them on the dock. The custom was explained to her: "May the young couple glide over everything as over water," says an old adage. There was a grand nuptial ceremony in Alexander Nevsky and, according to the newspapers of the time, the population was very enthusiastic. At the beginning, Mama was horrified that Papa didn't shave every day, that he had so many different kinds of friends—writers and other good friends from all different backgrounds who came to the household—a shock for her, coming from Rome and its strict court protocol. It must be understood that my father had been a bachelor for a long time. But she never complained about anything.

During autumn 1931, the young royal couple traveled to Italy, Switzerland and Germany. My mother was very religious. When she had typhoid at the age of twelve, she had promised to become a Franciscan tertiary if she recovered—hence her devotion to Francis of Assisi. She had asked to be married in Assisi because she did not want to upset the Vatican with a grand wedding in Rome, since my father was Orthodox. She remained Catholic, which was why a chaplain came on Sundays to say mass for her. At Vrana, The Monarch had a small chapel on the ground floor, even having a large cushion placed next to his prie-dieu for his basset hound. In the basement of the house, there was a fairly spacious Orthodox chapel where we sheltered during the bombings—before having a bunker built in due time in 1941.

Whenever they were in Western Europe, they went to visit The Monarch. One of these visits took place in 1938, following my birth. I believe this was their last one before the war.

The Monarch wrote to me in pencil, I don't know why, in his very beautiful handwriting, "Sire and dear grandson," to which I responded (in diplomatic French, of course), "Your Majesty and dearly loved grandfather." We respected all the forms and customs of the period. My memory of these writing exercises is painful: during them our mother would dictate what we had to say to each other. If we made a mistake, we had to start all over again. There was no question of doing it any differently. I was then seven or eight, so that was nearly seventy years ago. I know that my mother wrote to him regularly as well.

I heard my grandfather spoken about a lot, his portraits and photographs were everywhere in the house. I couldn't help contemplating them with admiration. My father told anecdotes about him. He seemed like a character out of a legend from long ago. My sister and I placed him very high up in our childish imaginations. We then lived in the palace at Vrana, the house he had had built at great expense at the beginning of last century. The memory of him was omnipresent, as was the case at Tsarska in the forest, too. Papa had kept his room there intact after his departure on October 3, 1918. Maria Luisa and I would go there in secret; nothing had changed. The bed was there; even his pens were still in place on the desk, as if he had left the evening before and was going to come back any minute. I remember that there were even some dead flowers that hadn't been cleared away. The room only became a bedroom again after the RAF bombings of the Second World War, when we needed more room because part of the house had burned. This is the room that I now occupy at Vrana.

I myself have always enjoyed writing very much. I am making up for lost time, first of all with this book, then with the historical foundation we have created in Sofia, whose purpose is the organization of my grandfather's archives from Coburg and making them available to the public. Those of my father were seized by the state after our departure. Little by little, I'm bringing back to the country a great number of boxes from Madrid, with the archives I have of fifty years of correspondence, as well as objects and paintings, so as to gather together our family memories in the same place.

*

Bulgaria is a country to which King Ferdinand soon became attached. From the moment of his arrival he felt at home, as if the landscapes were an extension of the ones in Central Europe that he already knew well. I believe he had a taste for adventure. He truly did all that he could in the course of the roughly thirty years of his reign to put Bulgaria on the rails of the modern world. Except for a few manufactures, industry for all intents and purposes did not exist, nor did large-scale trade. The time had come to prepare a new generation of Bulgarian executives and entrepreneurs. The outcome of his venture was not a safe bet, either from the point of view of the Great Powers or from that of the internal politics that preoccupied him so much.

The Austrians, in any case, were satisfied with him, for he had been an officer in the Imperial Army. The Tsar of All Russia was convinced that he had been taken for a ride and refused to recognize him for religious reasons. My grandfather Ferdinand remained Catholic all his life. He had to constantly maintain a balance between the Austrian Empire, the Ottoman Empire and the Russian one, which saw itself as guardian.

The Monarch played an important role in the construction of contemporary Bulgaria. He never ceased wanting the country to benefit from his education and his intellectual openness, and his curiosity about science and progress. He created numerous institutes and universities, like those he had seen abroad. After his accession to the throne in 1887, he established the first state medical school and the first archeological museum. He also used his own funds to send numerous young Bulgarians to be educated in Europe in foreign languages, law, and medicine, or to enroll in officer training schools, and many other areas that now seem obvious to us. The country was avid for openness and encounter. In addition to guaranteeing the loan for the construction of the railways, Princess Clémentine bought the first Bulgarian locomotive for the Orient Express.

But King Ferdinand was also an authoritarian, subject to fits of violence despite his keen intelligence. He did not make only friends during his reign, regularly crossing swords with a very solid political opposition. Some understanding of him can be had by reading the letters of Bourboulon, who refers to the relief at court in Sofia when the king would leave to visit foreign countries. His rages were famous, and the court feared but one thing: that he would return early! He had the "Orléans fidgets," and wherever he went, he sent threatening telegrams to show that he continued to follow the affairs of the palace closely. The dates of his departures for Hungary, for Vienna, for Bayreuth, Coburg, and elsewhere in Europe to attend political or family meetings, or to hunt, were carefully kept secrets. He was deeply intuitive and saw himself as a modern sovereign in many ways, taking inspiration from both Louis XIV for the splendor and Colbert for his reforms. He himself had created the ceremonial system that focused on him, drawing at once from protocol in Vienna, from the French royal family, and from what he had observed in Spain. At their most formal, his valets were dressed in a uniform inspired by the century of Louis the Great. After the Liberation of 1878, Prince Alexander had considered that it was pointless to create titles in a social system that was basically rather democratic and rural.[1] Why begin again to confer the sorts of distinctions that might stir up jealousy? My grandfather followed Alexander's suit, and the only titles that existed were those of the royal family.

His resemblance to his Bourbon ancestors flattered him enormously: he had the nose, the light-colored eyes, the sensitivity, and above all the fanciful imagination. Raised by a mother who adulated him, he apparently complained constantly of a thousand little aches and pains and took medicine all the time. He was always up on the latest treatments and had an irrational fear of germs, carrying a tin box full of pills with him, which he would offer to his visitors. He was also very superstitious and believed in the evil eye: this was not a bad thing in Bulgaria, where these sorts of beliefs were widely held. The Monarch was quite taken by "spirits" and invoked them with amusement; he had a collection of masks and mortuary relics. He kept a whole series of them at Vrana, which my mother and my aunt destroyed before we left, for fear the new

---

1. Titles existed in Bulgarian history, the Boyars, but these were forgotten over the five centuries of Ottoman presence.

regime would use them against us. While being very religious, Papa was superstitious too, but not as much as my Aunt Eudoxia. She told me that she never went anywhere without her good luck charms to protect the "eyes" that people wear here.

The Monarch's French was elegant and very forthright, since the Orléans have never been strangers to stinging witticisms or salacious jokes. I sometimes still laugh at them with my cousins when we see each other at weddings or funerals. To make up for it, King Ferdinand was careful to maintain the rigorous etiquette that corresponded to the way he saw his position, a way of making an impression à l'orientale. He loved jewels and wore his decorations with ostentation, prompting Princess Pauline Metternich, the granddaughter of the famous chancellor, to wittily remark, "When you don't see Ferdinand I, you hear him." He had all the grandeur of a Renaissance prince. It is hardly surprising that my father adopted the opposite attitude, preferring discretion to what he took to be showing off. I think that, having been a witness to all sorts of scenes during his childhood, he often did the exact opposite of what his father had done. Just before the official dinners they had to attend, it was my grandfather's habit to have his children served the same meal as a sort of dress rehearsal. In this way, he could be certain that they would use the right silverware and that they would be so full that they wouldn't throw themselves on the food!

Over his decades in power, King Ferdinand accomplished many things. He cannot be reduced to the role of warmonger that history has assigned him. As of 1903, he led the government toward one centered on his position, and Bulgaria became a power in the Balkans. But it was only in 1908 that the prince declared the country independent, taking advantage of the Young Turks takeover in Istanbul and of a new wind of freedom. No one could resist him. At this point he became king, without any form of subjection other than the duties he owed to his people. Ferdinand launched wide-reaching projects to develop infrastructure: the construction of roads and railroads, the paving of sidewalks, the opening of ports, and even the planting of walnut trees along roads to provide both shade and nuts, as well as developing a postal service. He thought out all the details. To open up his country, he pressured his contacts in

Europe to get them interested in investing in Bulgaria. I would do a bit of the same thing a century later.

My grandfather was conscious that his position gave him a destiny to which he was well suited. It seems to me that everyone got something out of this combination, which worked well despite the criticism and the dark legends. The Monarch was undeniably charismatic, as we say now. So, I find it difficult to blame him *a posteriori* for what he had been chosen to do. It was the Balkan Wars that clouded his track record. But to understand those conflicts, they must be put in context, including the aspirations of the population. I admit recriminations against his foreign policy only to a certain point, even if it had grave consequences for the country. Something Churchill said comes to mind: "You have enemies? Good. That means that you were committed to something at some point in your life."

*

Each nation was trying to ensure its freshly acquired sovereignty, trying to find its bearings in the uncertainty that follow the end of empires. Where were our borders? Should we go back to ancient history—our frontiers during the Middle Ages—or rather gather together people who spoke the same language? Answering these questions was not all that obvious in the nineteenth century. This is not an attempt to remake history, but to understand it. A little humility is necessary. We were emerging from nearly five hundred years of Ottoman presence in our country. The maneuverings of the Great Powers had to be considered, since each had its own agenda for partitioning, and this can't be forgotten. It is always simple to reinterpret events one hundred years later, but I don't think that King Ferdinand could have made the decision to take Bulgaria to war against its neighbors all by himself. He was intelligent and very knowledgeable about history, despite "dreaming of Byzantium," as he is popularly caricatured. It was not like him to throw himself into the lion's jaw. Expansionist ideas for a Greater Bulgaria were very widespread at the time; there was even talk of the Bulgaria of Simeon the Great, who had attempted to capture Constantinople. I do not share this point of view, and that is why nationalists do not like me: each country's space must be respected—this is how people search for an ideal together. One of the ideas held that we needed to extend our borders to "the White Sea," the Aegean—hence the attempt to march against Istanbul or Salonika.

Since Catherine the Great, the Russians have also dreamed of access to the sea, not wanting to be only an Asian power but also a European one. We see today more than ever how important this question is and how the geopolitical aspirations remain constant over time. It is for this reason that I have always thought that as far as international politics are concerned, it behooves us to know History above anything else. But I was able to realize, in the course of my own political mandate, that this sentiment (really an obvious fact) is not shared by everyone.

Myths are created and repeated over and over until they end up as truth. A Spanish saying claims that "victory has a thousand godfathers and defeat is an orphan." My grandfather could not have started those wars from personal ambitions, nor because he was "German," as I sometimes still read. These are platitudes that were consciously introduced into history books and are still defended by reputable historians. How, in the nineteenth century, would it have been possible for a king to trigger such momentous events singlehandedly? A king in the Middle Ages, perhaps—and even so—but a king from the period of the Balkan Wars? He gets up one morning and says, "Let's go"? No, he'd have had to explore the mood, the circumstances, his people; sound his army, his officers, his diplomats; and then, in the end, things happen and go on happening. Even for the worst kinds. It is never only with a drawn sword that you start a conflict. This type of malevolent rubbish annoys me, but, alas, this is the manner in which the reign of my grandfather is often summarized.

Ferdinand distrusted Kaiser Wilhelm and vice versa. Monarchial Europe did not like the German sovereign. This did not prevent the alliance of our two countries during the First World War. I believe The Monarch also distrusted the excessive influence of the Russians. "From Russia, you never knew what to expect, from Germany, you knew it would be disagreeable,"[2] wrote Bourboulon. But it was not possible for a country like ours to remain strictly neutral. The same dilemma was faced in 1939 by my father, who tried until the end to maintain Bulgaria's neutrality.

---

2. Comte de Bourboulon, *Ephémérides de Bulgarie, 1887–1913*, typed document (Private Archive).

In the course of the turmoil of the first worldwide conflict, the head of the House of France, the Duke of Orléans, attempted to convince King Ferdinand to break the alliance with Germany through diplomatic action. These two cousins had known each other for a long time. The duke had been invited to carry out this approach by the French Republic, which nevertheless treated him as an exile, refusing to let the oldest members of the family serve in the army. My grandfather's decision had not yet been made, but the attempt failed, causing a breach between the two branches of the family—a stain on our family's past that only the diplomacy and good will of my father finally managed to resolve over the course of several visits. I read in the memoirs of Raymond Poincaré that he, too, had approached the king of the Belgians—also a Saxe-Coburg—to ask him to intercede with my grandfather.

During the war and in face of the slaughter, a similar attempt took place to establish a separate peace with the emperor of Austria, led by the princes of Bourbon-Parma, Xavier and Sixtus, brothers of my grandmother Maria Luisa, who were fighting in the Belgian army. Empress Zita of Austria was their sister. Clemenceau did not want peace too rapidly, as he wanted Austria-Hungary to be annihilated and dismembered. King Ferdinand had to exile himself in 1918 after our military defeat. His authority and prestige had been seriously undermined, and he could no longer reign. He understood that only his departure could ensure that his dynasty would be maintained. Best to wisely step aside and leave the throne to Prince Boris.

The Monarch abdicated in good and due form, without being forced. But he had doubts about the abilities of his son, as happens when one generation hands over power to another. Wasted scruples: Boris III would be a good king for Bulgaria, a man worthy of his duties, an admirable and attentive father to my sister and me. King Ferdinand thus took his superb train one last time, departing from Kazichene accompanied by his two daughters and Prince Kyril, leaving the reins of power to my father. The Monarch withdrew to his properties in Coburg and would never see Bulgaria again.

In 1978, I organized a high mass in Coburg for the thirtieth anniversary of his death. Lectures about him were organized—on botany and ornithology (which were his passion), on Bulgaria and his political actions. This was a first, as no one had spoken of him for decades. After his departure, he threw himself wholeheartedly into his pet hobbies: hunting, travel and nature. The huge ornithological collection that he willed to the town of Coburg remains one of the largest in Europe. After 1918, he took up traveling again, bringing back new birds and plants, especially from Brazil, where he made a long visit. In Bulgaria, he had created a zoological garden and a natural history museum modeled after the one in Paris. At Vrana, I still carefully tend to the *alpineum* that he left there, as he did in each one of his houses. His own father, Prince Augustus of Saxe-Coburg, had been a patron and art lover, a protector of the sciences, as well as of the Artist's House of Vienna. At Coburg Palace, he received researchers and lead the classification of the archives of the Koháry family.

My Württemberg cousins were there on this important day for the family. We found ourselves in the crypt of the Church of Saint Augustine, facing the recumbent statues of our great-grandparents and the sarcophagus of King Ferdinand, covered with the Bulgarian flag. He had expressed the desire to be taken back to Bulgaria. I am hoping that we will manage to eliminate the obstacles and one day bring him back to Sofia.

My father was afraid of this authoritarian character. As a child, he avoided confrontations and was careful not to commit a blunder that was likely to irritate the mood of the great man. The Monarch demanded a great deal from him, as he did from everyone he worked with. My father did not have an easy life; nothing he did was ever good enough. Despite his exile, I know that The Monarch continued his interest in the politics of the kingdom. My father and he had a very odd relationship, one I have never been able to understand. Perhaps my father needed to assert himself? My Aunt Eudoxia, who adored her brother, nonetheless found it very hard of him not to allow the exile to visit Bulgaria. We could see him, but only abroad. My birth, for example, would have been a beautiful occasion to invite him to Sofia to see his grandson and thus display the three generations of our family together. But it was not possible.

King Ferdinand wrote very moving texts on Bulgaria, the country he had served—words of affection, of frustration, and also of regret. He wanted to "finish his days in the country that he had loved so much and for which he had worked so hard." I don't know whether Papa was frightened of him, if he held his very strict upbringing against him, or if he was afraid his father would interfere. With age, The Monarch's faults did not improve, and some of his letters have a threatening tone that exhausted my father. I believe that the personal mixed with the political.

After 1918, then, my father found himself alone, managing unspeakable difficulties: an atmosphere of insurrection and troops returning in chaos. Papa bore a complicated legacy on his shoulders. When I mull over his early reign, the words of André Malraux come to me: "It is difficult to be a man." There are more enviable destinies than being the sovereign of a country in collapse at the age of twenty-four. He was by himself until the return of his sister Eudoxia, who became a sort of first lady until he got married. My Aunt Eudoxia played an important role in Bulgaria. She was born there and spoke Bulgarian to perfection. She was popular, very energetic, with a strong character. I adored her. I sometimes wonder how my father managed alone for several years, with no family and no wife at his side, until she came back. We mustn't forget that his mother, Princess Maria Luisa, died very young, after the birth of my Aunt Nadezhda, leaving the little children alone and distraught. Despite his age—he was five—my father remembered her death and the last words she had whispered to him on her deathbed: "My son, be good. Try to be an exemplary sovereign." I am certain that he did his best his whole life to live up to this maternal legacy. She was not yet thirty, and the fate of this grandmother has always touched us deeply.

I know that my father stayed in contact with the aged count Bourboulon, who had been King Ferdinand's advisor and confidant during his youth. The latter even stayed as a guest at the palace in 1928, the tenth anniversary of my father's accession to the throne. They must have talked a lot about politics. Unlike his own father, the young Boris adopted a modest profile. The nineteenth century, with certain delusions of grandeur, was most assuredly over. According to his tutor, Constant Schaufelberger, sometimes he and his brother called the palace a "prison" and complained of the severity of The Monarch: "They had no friends, no comrades of their age, except on very rare and brief occasions—visits of cousins, young foreign highnesses, or relations with the children of diplomats, or high-placed bureaucrats," he wrote in his memoirs.[3] My father, however, proved later to be very sociable, always going spontaneously toward others, as this was the natural inclination of his heart. Fortunately, the two brothers went on trips, including one in 1911 that took them to Istanbul and Smyrna, and during which they went off on hiking expeditions for whole days in Anatolia. Prince Boris even went to England to represent his father at the crowning of George V, then to Paris—a town he adored exploring alone and incognito—for official meetings, and finally to Turin to attend the funeral services of the old queen Maria Pia of Portugal, who had been born princess of Savoy. The same year, he was invited by his godfather Nicolas II to Kiev to observe military maneuvers, and one evening at the opera, he witnessed the assassination of Prime Minister Stolypin, who was shot twice before the eyes of the imperial family. Attempts at murder are also part of the apprenticeship for the job of sovereign.

When Prince Boris came of age, in 1912, my grandfather decided to organize grand celebrations in his honor. The Monarch received the greats of Europe, come to Sofia to see the tsar of the Bulgarians, who wanted to play some sort of leadership role in the Balkans. Prince Boris showed himself to be equal to the ceremonies, military parades and dinners, which lasted several days, fearing his father's disappointment above all. In his turn, Kaiser Wilhelm invited the two brothers to participate in the maneuvers of the German army, and they came back impressed. Then came the time of the wars, when they followed the army from Salonika, a city that Ferdinand wanted to seize from the Ottomans. My father represented the king on the front in Thrace. He was even under enemy fire, on the front line with the soldiers during the Battle of Roupel. During these battles, especially those of the 1913 Second Balkan War, my father was liaison officer with headquarters. It was as a simple lieutenant that he followed the retreat of our troops, sharing with them their humilia-

---

3. Constant Schaufelberger, *La destinée tragique d'un roi: La vie et le règne de Boris III, roi des Bulgarians (1894–1918–1943)* (Uppsala: Boktryckeri Aktiebolag, 1952).

tion and anger. The situation was very grave; my father proved to be up to what was expected of him in those perilous conditions. I think that it was from this experience that he drew his profound disgust at war, an additional explanation for his attitude after 1939.

During the first eight years of his reign, he did not leave Bulgaria; it was not until 1926 that he began to travel again, renewing contact with the West and pleading the cause of his country. He received foreign journalists in Sofia, surprising them with the finesse of his analyses and especially his lucidity. He always favored personal contact, and he met with many people (a thing I also do). He did not hesitate to invite people to dine with him, compatriots as well as foreigners passing through. "I am the rare bird of the country," he once said dryly to a cousin who was visiting. Court ceremony was reduced to a minimum at the time. Staff was not very plentiful and the large reception rooms were rarely opened. For several years, he corresponded only indirectly with the family in Coburg. He was extremely cautious about everything concerning his father, for after his abdication The Monarch crystallized much of his resentment on his son. Politicians had made him the scapegoat for all the difficulties of the country. This was easy: he had no way of defending himself. King Boris communicated with him using his sisters as intermediaries or The Monarch's aide-de-camp, General Peter Gantchev, who had followed him in his withdrawal to Coburg. The prime minister, Alexander Stamboliyski, a former journalist who had clashed with my grandfather more than once, even wanted to pass a law forbidding all Bulgarians from writing or visiting him. It was only after 1930 and his wedding that my father resumed regular exchanges with him. But it was not easy nonetheless.

The archives of Purvan Draganov, our ambassador to Vienna, Berlin and Madrid, in the 1930s and 1940s, now repatriated to Vrana, are full of letters addressed by my grandfather to his son. The Monarch often appears angry with him for his attitude, accusing him of being disrespectful and, most important in his view, of preventing him from returning to "the country I created and which owes me everything."

My father took advantage of his isolation from the outside world to crisscross all of Bulgaria, from the Danube to the Maritsa, from the Black Sea to the Rhodope Mountains. He traveled to villages on horseback or on foot, visited monasteries and met his subjects. Bulgarians are very hospitable and can show astonishing generosity. He sometimes would even stay overnight with people when it was too late to return. It was in this way that he built his enormous popularity. He wanted to demonstrate that he was completely dedicated to his work and his people, within the limits of his position as a constitutional monarch.

It must be remembered that Bulgaria was occupied, the army discontented, and subject to huge financial sanctions to force it to pay the costs of a lost war. The debt had become considerable. Not much was left of the family fortune, as The Monarch had spent a great deal of it on Bulgaria. My father was even obliged to sell the wines from the Euxinograd property. (I feel compelled to open a rapid parenthesis here to note the unfortunate tendency of certain heads of state to export funds from their countries rather than importing them. The international press reminds us regularly of these misdemeanors.)

My father also saw Monsignor Roncalli fairly regularly, future Pope and Saint John XXIII, who was at the time the apostolic envoy of the Vatican to Bulgaria. The two would go on walking tours and visits of historical sites. The vast properties that he held in the Austro-Hungarian Empire had disappeared with the end of the Habsburg monarchy. I believe that Uncle Kyril attempted to reclaim a few bits and pieces from the Czech government, which had nationalized it all. During this time, my Aunt Nadezhda married Duke Albrecht Eugen of Württemberg, and her sister, my Aunt Eudoxia, decided to return to Sofia and her brother. My Uncle Kyril remained a bachelor. During the summer of 1926, a first trip to Europe was planned for my father. He first went to Switzerland, to Zurich, a city he always liked visiting during his travels. He made the Baur au Lac Hotel his headquarters. In Geneva, he visited the League of Nations and had discussions with Henri Bergson, Nobel Prize for Literature, and with Albert Einstein. He passed through Paris, where he placed a wreath at the Tomb of the Unknown Soldier with President Raymond Poincaré, despite an insulting article in *Humanité* about the "Bloody Tsar," and then went to England, where George V received him at Balmoral to hunt grouse, and finally moved on to Italy, where he became acquainted with my other grandfather, King Victor Emmanuel, and the pomp of the Roman court. During the trip, which he got in the habit of making every year, he always went to Coburg to pay his respects to his father. His activities were numerous. In Sofia, I read in the memoirs of the celebrated actress Cécile Sorel that he had attended a performance she had given of *Misanthrope* in the 1920s.

Little by little and against all predictions, my father got back on his feet again, successfully countering plans for a Bolshevik revolution and fencing the Agrarian Party, who wanted to instaure an authoritarian Republic. The political independence of a country like Bulgaria was difficult to maintain, given its position on the borders of Russian and German influence, Communism versus Nazism, with each having its henchmen in Bulgaria interested in destabilizing the country. We were young—politically speaking—without any real track record in democracy, and no history to use as a reference. My father governed with common sense and the principles of an education taught by rather liberal-minded tutors. The question was not to find the best solution but the least bad. The governing style of King Boris seemed well balanced, and he did not hesitate to commit himself personally.

My father was from many points of view one of the relevant politicians of the twentieth century: his premature death transformed the tragic into the forgotten. In 1922, he suffered a first attempt at a takeover of power by the Communists, inspired by the coup led by Béla Kun in Hungary in 1919; then the following year, in reaction, there was a coup d'état from forces on the nationalist right. He did not share their views, but he had to deal with these extreme ideologies, managing as well as possible the large gap between them to prevent a civil war. In April 1925, he narrowly escaped an assassination attempt in which his chauffeur, an assistant from the Museum of Natural History, and a gamekeeper were killed. A few days later, dynamite was detonated in the dome of the Cathedral of Saint Nedelya in Sofia, killing 213 people and wounding 500 as it fell on the public gathered for the funeral service for General Konstantin Georgiev, assassinated by revolutionaries. My father, who had stubbornly attended the funeral of his chauffeur, arrived late and was thus spared. The series of political crimes continued. A sovereign never sleeps "on a bed of roses," as we say in Bulgaria: the assassination of Alexander of Yugoslavia in Marseille in 1934 was an example. Two weeks before, he had come to Sofia on an official visit, and my father was then already very worried about his security. The two sovereigns got along well.

Despite this context of violence, my father remained faithful to his principles and rejected many death sentences issued by his government. He skillfully waited for official holidays to commute them. The repression of 1923 had been severe, bringing about a first wave of emigration in leftist circles. I know that King Boris disapproved of the methods used by the Tsankov government. He even spared Communist leader Georgi Dimitrov, who took advantage of it to flee to Moscow, actively participating in Stalin's purges. Then, in 1933, he was accused of being one of the authors of the Reichstag fire, and my father saved him a second time, from the hands of Hitler: "You are not going to condemn this man, who, as you know better than I, is not guilty of the fire." Of course, Dimitrov showed no gratitude and, after Sofia was taken over thanks to the Red Army, was the one who orchestrated the 1944 massacres, particularly having the three regents executed after their appearance before the "People's Tribunal."[4] A photo of my uncle taken at the time shows, for the last time, the tired features of an utterly demoralized man. These figures were the first expiatory victims of a dictatorship that would last until the fall of the wall in 1989.

But let's rewind the film a little, as we say. In those years of trouble and uncertainty, my birth was an occasion for calm and national unity. I was born June 16, 1937, the year my father tried to reestablish the Constitution. He knew very well that if the monarchy fell, the two extremes would collide. He had just come back from a long trip through Europe during which he had tried to convince the English and the French of the good intentions of Bulgaria. He was opposed to an alliance with the Axis and wanted to promote peace in his country and in the region, having himself lived through the throes of the First World War and its poisonous division of neighbors. "In union, there is strength" is today our national motto. Chosen by my grandfather, it is inscribed on the

---

4. After a rapprochement with Yugoslavia, Dimitrov became suspect in the eyes of Stalin. He died in 1949 in a rather strange manner in a hospital in Russia. In the center of Sofia, a mausoleum reproducing Lenin's on Red Square was built to him, but it has now been destroyed.

pediment of the National Assembly building. The divisions among the peoples of southeastern Europe have always attracted the worst of calamities. His principal idea was to remain neutral, working and attracting investments to develop our natural resources.

At the announcement of my birth, the country was jubilant. Popular enthusiasm went beyond anything imaginable. My father felt that it would not last. "The Monarch asked the impossible of his people . . . in my case, my people ask the impossible from me," he noted with some bitterness. My sister Maria Luisa was four years older than me, and, when she was born, Queen Elena of Italy had made the trip to Sofia. She has a very clear memory of the moment when my birth was announced. Perched on her pony, she was delighted to have a little brother because she felt quite lonely. I came seven years after their marriage. The future of the dynasty was at stake.

The cannons from the batteries placed at the foot of Mount Vitosha began firing. The crowds remained silent until the twenty-first gun salute, the number used to announce the birth of a girl. The officer consciously paused a few seconds, then continued to a hundred and one, the number heralding an heir to the throne. Joy exploded throughout the city. People got to think of something other than their everyday problems, ignoring the black clouds gathering over our little country.

I was born in a hospital in town—not at the palace, as was the tradition. Since my mother had had a difficult delivery with my sister, the doctors requested that this time the birth take place in a medical environment—a sign of progress. Only a few hours after my birth, the queen—poor thing—was transported by ambulance to the palace, to counter any possible rumors of the substitution of another child. The crowd went wild. There were three days of parades and receptions. A U.S. television channel even came to cover the news, filming footage that I saw much, much later: my parents appearing on the balcony, as the crowd chanted, "Si-me-on, Si-me-on." The name Simeon means "he who is a wish fulfilled" in Hebrew and refers to the king of our First Kingdom, Simeon the Great. In Bulgaria, tradition is that the first boy be given the name of his grandfather; however, my family did not follow it. My mother wanted me to be called Borislav, a glorification of Boris in reference to the given name of my father, since my sister already had that of our grandmother, Princess Maria Luisa. But that day, outside the Royal Palace, people decided otherwise. I became "Simeon."

My father and the Holy Synod appointed the metropolitan,[5] Simeon of Varna, an elderly man with a strong personality, to baptize me in the palace chapel. My godfather was General Danail Nikolaev, a national hero, born in 1852, who in his youth had taken part in the War of Independence. When I mention his name to my compatriots, they can't believe their ears, whereas I have a memory of him in a white uniform leaning heavily on a cane and of my father offering his arm as they left parliament. He died soon after.

---

5. A highly placed dignitary in the Orthodox Church.

CHAPTER FIVE

The Pains of Childhood

MY FATHER DIED IN THE MIDDLE OF THE WAR, TOTALLY UNEXPECTEDLY. The reasons for his death have never been clarified. Upon his return from Rastenburg, after a final meeting with Hitler on the question the engagement of the Bulgarian army on the Eastern front, he came directly to Tsarska to rest. With his brother, he climbed Mount Musala, the highest summit in the Balkan Peninsula, and it was during this hike that, as later mentioned by his aide-de-camp, the king stopped above an abyss, staring at it for long minutes. This story gave rise to rumors of suicide, but I believe that those were part of misleadings. My father was much too religious to consider such an option. In his mental universe, there was no room for that kind of escape. Duty is a sacred value for us. The next day he went stag hunting, using the age-old technique of silently stalking the animal during its bell. Once home, he received several ministers, including the minister of war, General Mikhov, for an audience that lasted two hours. On Monday morning, he returned to his office in Sofia, working with Pavel Groueff, his principal private secretary. It was after he had lunched with the architect Yordan Sévov, in charge of construction on our properties—and also the architect of Atatürk's palace in Ankara—that he began to feel ill. The same evening, he called his sister Eudoxia, who was just back from Euxinograd, and complained to her of heaviness in his chest. He died the following Saturday, August 28, a hot summer day.

Returning to Tsarska in the late 1990s for the first time since those years of horror, the emotion I felt had a peculiar taste, that of the last moments I spent with my father. In my turn, like him and like King Ferdinand, I am very happy in this house. Going there in summer was very special. When I entered the large room on the ground floor, I smelled the odors of my childhood, and a fire crackled in the fireplace. My wife and I were expected. In the bedrooms, not much had changed: the decoration was still the same (contrary to Vrana, left in a state of neglect). I went into the room where I had seen my father for the last time. As there was no one else present, I shed a tear.

We had all seen him when he came back from Hitler's headquarters, the *Wolfsschanze*, or "Wolf's Lair." We all went together to see the Führer's personal plane that had flown him back, and that was leaving again, piloted by the Luftwaffe Colonel Franz Bauer. I remember it very well: it was at the airport not far from Sofia, and a very exciting event for me. The pilots had removed the machine guns from their glass-canopied bubbles to fill them with watermelons and melons. There was not much to eat in Germany in 1943. They also took back tobacco and the many kinds of fruit that our country abounded in. We saluted the colonel and returned to Vrana. My father went back to Sofia to work. His trip to Silesia had lasted only three days, but he was deeply distressed by the meeting. His discussions with Hitler had been stormy: My father had begun by refusing to let our Jewish compatriots be touched or to send Bulgarian troops to the Eastern front. This was a very serious affront at a critical moment for the Wehrmacht. The outcome of the Battle of Stalingrad was very recent. Bulgaria had at its disposal dozens of intact divisions that, without doubt, would have helped the German army. But the king was firmly opposed to this plan, just as he had already refused to participate in the campaigns against Yugoslavia and Greece. Thus, not a single Bulgarian soldier was sent to the Russian front. My father told the Führer "that our people would not have marched against Uncle Ivan, who had liberated us from the Ottomans." Our army had a very good reputation, and it was for this reason that Hitler wanted it. The king's secretary, Stanislav Balan, who made the trip with him and saw him come out of this meeting, reported later that the face of the "chief" was livid. After our departure from Bulgaria, he was placed under house arrest; much later, in the 1970s, he managed to travel to France, where I met him in Ferney-Voltaire, and this is where he shared this detail with me.

For his part, Hitler was afraid that my father would want to quit the war, as Italy would soon do. He suspected an alliance in this direction between the two royal families. Some people said that my father had signed his death warrant in opposing the Nazis in this way, but caution must be exercised on this question. King Boris was unfairly accused of collaborating with them, when on the contrary he was fighting to save his seven million countrymen.

In 1941, when the Germans arrived at our border of the Danube, having crushed Yugoslavia, my father chose not to resist: he was convinced that we would be crushed in our turn, and Sofia erased from the map. I remember going out to the big road in front of Vrana and seeing the German troops pass. I observed practically the same scene with the Russian troops in September 1944. Opposition would have had as direct consequence the deaths of several thousands, followed by a painful occupation. We would have lost the war twice over, first against the Germans and above all against the Russians, who would have invaded us as they did with Poland, rather than entering as "liberators." My father remained at the head of the country until the end.

King Boris did all that he could to delay the signature of the Tripartite Pact, resisting the influence of his prime minister, a supporter of Germany, and the birds of bad omen. Bulgaria did not carry much weight in this battle of titans. My father understood it all too well. Basically, we were only a pawn on the vast chessboard of Operation Barbarossa. As long as the German-Soviet pact held, Bulgaria could remain neutral; afterward, nothing was impossible. Surprisingly, the kingdom had always kept up diplomatic relations with the Soviet Union. So, claiming that my father "collaborated" because the dynasty was of German origin or because it was said that Hitler admired him—when in fact he despised the institution that we represented—or because in a photo he was smiling as he greeted the chancellor, is not acceptable. History deserves a bit more subtlety and seriousness.

Indeed, I find that a minimum of courtesy was mandatory, even if my father had an aversion to Hitler. He called him "the huge nasty swine" in private and was as suspicious of him "as the devil is of incense." When he was summoned to the headquarters at Rastenburg, he refused the first date proposed, deciding to go two days later as a way of marking his territory. While he had had to meet with Hitler in Berchtesgaden in the company of other disreputable individuals like Joachim von Ribbentrop and Martin Bormann, it was to negotiate the survival of his country. From the moment Hitler took power, my father had understood the nihilism of the Nazi regime and the danger it represented. Let us not forget that a large part of the resistance to these deadly ideas in Germany came from conservative Catholic groups. Our legation in Berlin warned my father that his sister Nadezhda, wife of Duke Albrecht of Württemberg, did not mince words about Hitler, not hesitating to say what she thought in public, and this was of course not looked on favorably by the regime.

In Sofia, the first doctors able to examine my father diagnosed a "blocked" heart, or a form of angina pectoris, resulting from enormous stress, we would say now. My father was only forty-nine years old. He was healthy and a great walker. While he sometimes complained of sciatica, it never went further than that. He didn't share King Ferdinand's habit of complaining easily. He liked taking the waters in Bulgaria and vitamins and tonics. During the war, my grandfather Victor Emmanuel of Italy managed to send them to him, via Switzerland. An after-the-fact rumor, in which Joseph Goebbels participated, saw this as a means of poisoning him. The idea seems to me quite ludicrous. It was also said that the English had killed him using curare, and the English accused the Nazis of having poisoned him on the plane using his oxygen mask. As for Goebbels, he started an even baser story: that my Aunt Mafalda (who, according to him, was in Sofia at the time) had poisoned him! In fact, she came—and I am a witness to this—only for my father's burial.

Each one put the responsibility for his death on someone else. This was ridiculous. According to the toxicologists I have been able to consult over the years, slow-acting poisons did not yet exist at the time.

The Italian newspapers also recounted that Papa died during the flight and that his lifeless body had been removed from the plane. In the 1950s, a journalist from the *Figaro* wrote an article favorable to my father, attempting to explain the rapidity of his death. I also met her, and she came to see my mother in Madrid to interview her. Then the story fell into oblivion. His death remains a mystery. King Boris loved mushrooms, and my daughter Kalina, when she came to live in Bulgaria for a time, asked me whether we knew the menu for the last lunch he had eaten with the architect. I had no idea, and nothing was found on the subject. It is true that it would have been easy to introduce a poisonous *Amanita*. My father was taken with vomiting, and then convulsions, accompanied by fever. His red blood cells exploded. These are the symptoms of an intoxication that blocks liver function, such as the ones mentioned in the summary report on the autopsy. No one ever made any reference to it, neither in our entourage nor my mother or my aunt or the doctors. Still, it must be admitted: the architect Sévov who shared the meal with my father was not taken ill.

Just after his death pangs began, the Germans sent specialists on the nervous system to Sofia to care for him. They even requisitioned an airplane to come to Bulgaria, which, during war, was quite a feat. There were two professors, one Viennese, the other a Berliner. The Austrian committed suicide before the end of the war. They came with my father's German doctor, Professor Rudolf Sajitz, and then left. The final medical report speaks of a severe left coronary embolism, signed by only the eleven Bulgarian doctors. After the war, Sajitz came to live in Madrid, where we saw him, taking up his function as family doctor again. He was even present for the birth of our oldest son Kardam in 1962. Once in his office, my sister asked, "Tell me, what do you know about the death of Papa?" "Princess, I gave my word that I would never speak about it." To whom? To Hitler? They were all dead. "Please, I beg you, don't insist." It seems quite odd, to say the least. Perhaps my father died a natural death, but there is still a probability that it was a crime. Our doctor carried his secret to the grave.

I continue to be haunted by doubt, I must admit. I think about it sometimes. I would have liked to know, not for vengeance but to render justice to my father. He had no reason to die so quickly and so young. My Aunt Eudoxia wrote in her notebook, "The Nazis burned his lungs." The pilot of the German plane located by my sister after the war, Hans Bauer—he had been in captivity in Russia—confirmed to her that it was impossible that the king was poisoned during the flight: "Princess, my copilot and I would never have let those pigs, SS or Gestapo, get near the plane, even less to enter it." Much later, I came to have doubts about the role of the Soviets in his death. If my father had succeeded in getting us out of the war, the Russians wouldn't have had a pretext for "liberating" us, thus taking over Bulgaria the way they did. One day, in Moscow, passing in front of Lubyanka—the prison run by the KGB—I thought to myself that the answer to our questions might well be found inside that building. My father was a serious obstacle in their path, both by the strength of his character and by his immense popularity. Two years after the death of King Boris, they were in our country! I talked over the question with Yevgeny Primakov, a former highly placed agent of the KGB, whom I met with three times, but, obviously, nothing came out of it. A charming man, who spoke impeccable English, as well as Iraqi Arabic. I leave it to historians to do their job and leave no stone unturned.

It is then mostly through echoes that I know my father, especially through the stories told by my mother, and through the advisors and officers who had rubbed shoulders with him and whom I was able to locate afterward. Numerous popular legends still circulate about him. As my mother deified him, the image I had of him was quite wonderful. I have a few memories of the period, especially at Tsarska, where my sister and I went in winter to ski, as well as for a part of summer. My mother didn't like the house, which had been designed by The Monarch, a sort of vast chalet such as is found in *Mitteleuropa*. A remote spot, high in altitude, situated near a large forest of conifers where the sun quickly sets in the afternoon, a spot for hunting and long walks. When I see the mist come down in autumn, I always think of my mother. "That hole," she used to say. It was everything she didn't like. Proximity to the Black Sea and its sunny shores was better suited to her Mediterranean nature. She had spent her childhood in Italy, in the various history-filled properties belonging to the Savoy family, each spot more enjoyable than the others. So, in August, when we went to Tsarska, she took advantage of the time to go to Italy for a few weeks when she would stay with her large family, while we stayed alone with our father, Uncle Kyril and Aunt Eudoxia. During the rare days of vacation that he took, my father would come there to rest, spending time in the open air and seeing his children; then he would leave as quickly as he had come, going back to Sofia in his car, which he loved driving himself. Since the beginning of the war, his get-aways became less frequent, but they were never interrupted. When we were in Sofia, at the Vrana estate, he went every morning to the Royal Palace, in the center of town, and returned late every night.

We didn't see much of him. This is how children were brought up at the time, of course, but also and above all, due to the difficult circumstances the country was going through. Bulgaria joined the Axis forces in 1941, forced by the presence of the German army posted at our borders. We had a small dining room where my sister and I ate in the evening with our German nannies. Our parents would come to spend a few moments with us, and even then not every day. Papa spent long hours at the office: he had audiences, receptions and diplomats to receive, especially in these long years full of crises and war. He had to make important decisions for the future of Bulgaria, meanwhile subject to enormous pressure. "My generals are Germanophiles, my diplomats Anglophiles; the Queen is Italophile and my people Russophile. I am the only Bulgarophile," he used to say with a certain irony. *Se non è vero è ben trovato* ("Even if not true, it's nicely put").

Despite everything, politics were dropped at the threshold of the door to our home. His moments with us were happy, a privilege. A sort of parenthesis for him in the middle of the storm, perhaps. He would come to the room where we were playing, sit with us with our two dachshunds near him, and ask us questions. Sometimes he drew locomotives with us and had quite a talent for drawing. We even have two or three watercolors done by him—a talent that he probably inherited from his grandmother Clémentine, who left some very beautiful drawings. I remember having seen him one day in uniform after coming back from an official celebration where formal uniforms were required. I was very impressed. At Tsarska, we walked together in the woods; he would hold my hand. He was happy to wear a soft hat, as fashion demanded at the time—it was not done to appear bare headed—and, furthermore, he had turned bald at a young age, as I did in turn as well. One particular walk stays in my head, that on Mount Mourgash, not far from Sofia, which culminated at an altitude of just over one thousand six hundred meters. This was the last excursion that we made together, shortly before his death. I was then six. I would like to do the same walk with my children again after all these years. When flying out of Sofia, toward the East, it is easy to see. It is not very high, but it is an important place for me. Each time I go near it, I think of that last moment together when my short little legs tried to follow my father's long mountain strides.

But I know that he had memorable fits of anger too. Perhaps it was a character trait that he had in common with his father, The Omnipotent Monarch? When he lost his temper, he often used bad language in Turkish, which he spoke very well. He also mastered Hungarian, English, French, Italian and German. However, he did not speak Russian, though he knew a little Albanian. I never knew why, since there was never a large Albanian population in Bulgaria. In Vrana, in the kitchen where he would often go before official dinners to oversee the preparations, I heard him call the chief pastry cook a "camel brain" in German! The latter had put too much salt in the ice cream machine, and a salty sorbet had been served to the guests. As a child, I was thrilled to hear him use such an expression.

My mother used to say that my father was very demanding about details, as I am too. His colleagues spoke to me of his enormous capacity for work, his courtesy, his talent for listening. He succeeded in maintaining himself at the head of the country since 1918. He did a good job of calming things down and keeping on the course that he had set, successful at diplomatically asserting himself. He never wanted to give in on what seemed the most important to him: peace and independence. After the two coups d'état, he could have turned into a dictator—this is precisely what some hoped he would do—but he was wary: it was not in his character, even if after 1934 the constitution was suspended for a time. My father had the last word on all decisions. The ideas held by the Berlin regime did not influence our country much. Racism is not in our mentality, for Bulgaria itself has served as a passageway and been occupied by different civilizations. He never aspired to lead with an iron hand, in a period when this style was practiced. One day, in Borovets, while out walking, he said to me, "You're about to see a former prime minister, an old man, take a good look at his eyes: they're yellow!" And there he was, coming toward us, greeting us ceremoniously. I later learned that this was Alexander Tsankov, the one who had been so severe in repressing the first Communist uprising. I still remember his eyes. The position of a democratic king in that context was a difficult one to be in. We must not judge the period with our own ideas and comfort level. The peace that we enjoy today was bought at a high price, and many sacrificed themselves for us.

The greatest joy that I shared with my father was our hikes. We would go to the mountains and camp out in a tent. A few guards followed us, but no one else. A bit higher in the mountains than Tsarska, at Sarigöl, there is a pleasant hunting lodge built by The Monarch, at an altitude of almost two thousand meters. Papa adored the spot, and let us come with him, mounted on the backs of mules. He would happily walk along, wearing the baggy trousers of the period and his hobnailed mountain boots; I remember it well. One day he told us to pay attention to an approaching storm, so as not to attract "balls" of lightning. My sister and I were scared to death. And we were right: once during a storm in these mountains, in air that was full of static electricity, we saw a blue glow around my Uncle Kyril's ice ax! We climbed on our mules and quickly decamped.

At Vrana, I can still see my father sitting and watching us at length. He was always well, if unpretentiously, dressed, often in the same suit. His mustache impressed me: it was very black and thick. I rarely attended official events with him. When that was the case, my sister and I were dressed in consequence, to be presented to the guests before being sent to bed.

On Epiphany, there was a buffet for the military, and I was overjoyed at being able to have hard-boiled eggs stuffed with Russian salad: this is my version of Proust's madeleine. A most "glorious" memory, having the right to eat the same food as my father's officers! I was also absolutely delighted when I was allowed to attend the Royal Guard practicing gymnastics and shooting in the park. I was proud of the privilege.

My parents spoke French to each other so that we wouldn't understand them. With my father, our discussions were in Bulgarian. We called him "Papa." I remember one January 6 in Sofia, when Santa Claus arrived with a big hamper on his back. He was pulling a little stuffed elephant behind him; it looked very big to me. I was extremely impressed because Santa Claus always knew when we were naughty. How was it possible? My father told us that he had a telephone in his office that he could use to speak directly to him. In fact, our Santa was a very old servant from the days of The Monarch who did a wonderful job playing the role for us.

As soon as he had a free moment, Papa would come to get us to take a walk or to show us the plants in the garden. Under the trees, he would point out the spots where elves lived, or fairies, explaining that they ate only certain plants. He always had a spade on him, to dig up plants in case he found any that he hadn't yet recorded. He had inherited his father's passion for botany, a Saxe-Coburg atavism. His love for nature was very intense.

Animals were just as important for him: he had a dog, a dachshund called Johnny that my mother had bought at Harrods in London. When he would come home from work, he would ask, "Where are the children?" and Johnny would set off to find us on the grounds. We liked playing near a small lake, in a spot where the bushes had made a little shelter, just right for the stories we made up. My mother would join us with her lady-in-waiting; both of them would knit. We also had our own little garden plot where we would plant flowers and vegetables, particularly carrots, with the help of the gardener. There were small streams here and there, and we got it into our heads that there were pearls in them. I believe that all in all, we found exactly one freshwater shell! My mother was dreadfully afraid that we would get typhoid playing in the mud.

My sister and I got up to all kinds of mischief—we were very close. As she was four years older than I was, Maria Luisa always looked out for me. And as a daughter, she was also very close to my father.

Before Christmas, the two nannies would allow us to make special Christmas cookies. Sometimes Papa would come and sit with us to taste them. He loved the local food—bean soup, for instance. Its recipe remains the same to this day and continues to satisfy my guests' appetites.

We felt so important when we were near him! He was attentive and warm, and we enjoyed being together. We thought that he had nothing else to do but to be with us. He also took us to church, but as we couldn't remain standing for the whole of an Orthodox mass, we would arrive only for the credo. Next to him, we kissed the cross and the hand of the officiating priest. But our greatest joy was to ride in the car with him, driving to town or to the monastery at Rila in his convertible Packard, with him at the wheel.

Other children our age sometimes came to play with us on Sunday. For us, these were privileged moments, for we didn't go to school—the teachers came to the palace to give us lessons. During her visit in 1991, my sister located the woman who taught her Bulgarian, the teacher who taught her to read and write. She died soon after. We were in separate classes. After 1944, the nature of our education changed. We learned Soviet songs, and I would have begun to study Russian if we had remained, like little Pioneers. Our former teachers were changed, relegated to less important roles. The three new regents imposed on us decided everything for us. My mother was unable to fight this interference by herself. When the subjects were history and literature, the content of the courses became ideological.

The ritual of our days was unchanging. In the morning, as soon as we were dressed, we would go to greet our mother, who would be drinking her *caffè latte* and having her hair done in her rooms. We would kiss her and then go to our classes. Sometimes in the afternoon we would go to hear her play the cello, but she preferred playing Bulgarian airs for us on the accordion, which was more amusing for us. As for my father, we would also go to give him a kiss in the breakfast room as he was having his breakfast in a part of the house that I am today restoring. I can still see him enjoying his lime blossom tea with his dog under the table. My father then would go to Sofia, to his office in the palace, or receive at home, as I do myself today in turn, in the same room on the ground floor.

We did not eat with our parents. My mother had her own activities and spent time doing charity work during the day. Her dowry was used entirely to construct a sanatorium, in the city of Tryavna, for children with lung conditions. At that time, it was the largest establishment of the kind on the Balkan Peninsula. I went there myself ten years ago and saw that a large plaque had been put up in her memory. She would have been touched.

My mother had learned Bulgarian in only a few years and spoke it to perfection—with no accent. In exile, she continued to use it. She took courses in the morning and the afternoon—out of love, it is certain. When she arrived in Sofia, she was only twenty-two and quickly became more Bulgarian than the Bulgarians. When she said "our country" or "my country," it was not Italy she was speaking of but in fact Bulgaria, even though she stayed there only sixteen years: the happiest years of her life, but also the hardest.

We made only brief stays in Sofia. In the summer, we were at Tsarska, and in the autumn, at Euxinograd by the Black Sea. It all depended on what our mother wanted and especially on the circumstances. One day in summer 1939, the war broke out. My sister remembers it: we mounted horses at Tsarska and rode to Sarigöl. Papa announced to us that a war had begun: "Good people, innocent people, are going to be attacked, crushed." This was the beginning of the invasion of Poland . . . and so it was that war entered into our childhood world.

At the moment of my father's death, we were at Tsarska in the company of our nannies, who never left us. The first, Hildegard Schmoll, stayed with us for ten years. She called me her "sparrow." In 1944, my mother made her leave after the arrival of the Red Army, since, as a German, she was running a great risk. Her train was bombed in Yugoslavia, but she arrived safe and sound. The second, Annelise Wilhelm, also had to leave Bulgaria. She lived to an advanced age. We were very close to them, for they took care of us every day. They told us that our father was sick, but no more than that.

I think I remember that on the day of his death, a Saturday, my sister and I were playing together in one of the meadows that surrounded the house. Our nannies had told us that the radio wasn't working to hide the news bulletins from us. We had done little drawings to be taken to our father. Before returning to Sofia, he had come to our playroom to give us a kiss: "I'll see you tonight," he had told us, thinking he would have time to do the round trip in a single day. And he did not return.

Mama only learned of the seriousness of his condition on Wednesday, poor thing. Each time we spoke of him, the eyes of the nanny would fill with tears, which we didn't understand. She already knew of his probable death.

On Sunday, my Aunt Eudoxia arrived from Sofia. Dressed in black, she announced the sad news: "Papa is no more!" It was a terrible shock. I didn't understand right away what had happened. We left with her for the palace. At the entry to town, black flags hung at windows and balconies. At the palace, we were reunited with our mother, already dressed in black as well and trying, with difficulty, to smile at us. She took us by our hands and led us to the chapel where the body was on view. Maria Luisa and I kissed his wide, cold forehead and then left. This is when I noticed that people were using the term "Your Majesty" to address me—in other words, in the way they had addressed my father.

It was unbelievable for us that he went so quickly. He was just like always, full of energy and drive. "I'll see you tonight" were the last words he said to us. The memory of this day is particularly painful for me. He had been embalmed, and I had to kiss him a second time in the Cathedral of Alexander Nevsky, where his body was displayed on a raised catafalque. Funerary columns draped in dark cloth and burning incense had been installed in the streets. Mama wept, and so did my aunt. My Uncle Kyril had a black armband, and the whole Royal Guard was in mourning.

Ever since those days, I have loathed black, all the more so as my mother wore a black veil for a long time afterward, only taking it off when we got on the boat for Egypt. After that, she only wore it for the requiem mass for King Boris each August 28.

The whole funeral ceremony was filmed by the newsreels of the period. I had the opportunity to see the original of the film where I appear with a black armband coming out of the church. My mother spared us the long funeral procession to the Rila Monastery, which she judged too distressing for us. It was her decision. There she was at thirty-nine, a young widow. Another life began for us all, a tapestry of sadness and uncertainty.

In the streets of Sofia, thousands of people wept. We were swept up in this wave of emotion. The population's grief was stunning, touching, unforgettable. We stayed at Vrana during the day. Since then, I have had an almost unmanageable phobia in the presence of a dead body. I have never forgotten viewing the remains, the icy forehead and hands that I had to kiss. This experience has stayed with me. In Madrid, I almost fainted at the sight of the body of a friend, and another time before the first cousin of my wife. I couldn't look at them; I was shaking. This phobia has never left me; the emotion is indelible. I didn't even want to see my mother on her deathbed. "I cannot," I said simply to my sister, preferring to remember her as she was when she was alive.

*

Very quickly my entourage behaved toward me as they would have with an adult. People addressed me in the same way they would have addressed my father. This had a strange effect on me: the formal aspect of it made my behavior change. I had to receive "grown-ups"; my mother underlined each time that I had to act "properly," which was hard for a child. Parading in front of me were military men, people from the court, and ministers curious to meet me. There was even an American colonel, Mr. Baldridge, chief of the Allied Mission in Bulgaria,[1] coming to see us in his full-dress uniform. It was for him that I learned my first words in English, for I had to say, "How do you do, sir?" From a sack that he wore slung across his shoulder, he took out Lucky Strike cigarettes for my mother—who didn't like American tobacco because it was too aromatic—and, for my sister and me, chewing gum that tasted of cloves and sour candies in the form of buoys called Life Savers. We chewed so much that the next day we had sore jaws—to the point that Mama thought we had caught the mumps!

The time came for the 1944 New Year festivities. The queen had me dressed in a naval uniform to receive the members of parliament who came to Vrana to present their good wishes to the "little king." When they saw me come in with my mother holding me by the hand, there was not a dry eye. They were very moved, I believe. As crown prince, I had had to sign photos for the graduating classes of the military academy. This was hard for me, as I had to use calligraphy. My signature was the long "Simeon Prince of Tarnovo"; after the death of my father, it

---

1. Baldridge's daughter, Tish, held an important job in the Nixon administration.

became "Simeon II," shorter and simpler for the child that I was. Here, from my point of view, is a modest reminiscence about my new position. Signatures on official documents, however, were the responsibility of the Counsel on which my Uncle Kyril sat.

My father had died before having designated a regency or even guardians for his minor children, two prerogatives reserved for him by the Constitution. My mother could not, according to this same Constitution, have any political role. Given the exceptional circumstances, the choice of Prince Kyril emerged naturally. Two other regents had to be named: these were Prime Minister Bogdan Filov and the war minister, General Mikhov. The latter, loyal to my father, would be shot with the others.

I was very fond of our uncle, who was always cheerful around us. In the face of adversity, my aunt always said that he was unable to take things as a tragedy and apt to "open the Orléans umbrella of indifference." We were the only family he had. For us, he was an "old bachelor" who lived independently, in the shadow of our father, whom he tried to help as best he could. Still, he had his own friends and circle. Before deciding to return to Bulgaria, around 1927, my uncle had traveled abroad, leading the life of enjoyment of a young prince of the time. After the long interruption that had begun in 1918, the two brothers apparently were intensely happy to be together again.

It was at my father's death that Uncle Kyril truly came into our lives—alas, to leave again all too rapidly. He played with us. Sometimes he let us ride in the sidecar of his motorcycle, a huge treat for us. Once, at the monastery at Rila, with the help of a monk who was a very good fisherman, he taught me to catch trout with flies in the stream that flowed alongside the monastery. I have good memories of him—a child's memories. I am far from being able to analyze his personality, which I would only be able to reconstitute by repeating what I was told afterward. He had been general inspector of the artillery and years later was able, at the appropriate time, to assume his duty of sacrifice. He had never been involved in politics before, and this was true for the whole of the royal family except for the sovereign. My Aunt Eudoxia said that he died "for Simeon," since shoving the child-king that I was against a wall to be shot would have been quite an atrocity.

*

The period between the death of my father and our departure from Bulgaria was marked by Allied bombings of Sofia. The greater part of the city was damaged. The air raids terrified us. Several times we finished our nights in the bunker at the foot of the castle, where we would wait for hours for the alert to end. I would take a small flashlight with me and we would go down with the nannies.

The intensity of the bombing of January 10, 1944, was appalling. This was a daylight attack and I remember having seen formations of hundreds of American B-17 bombers and fighter jets coming from Sicily passing over us to drop their bomb load on Sofia. I am sure that my contemporaries have a very distinct memory of it. We heard the muffled sound of the bombs. In town, everything was in ruins, the streets strewn with bodies. Two different bombings succeeded one another: the first destroyed the electricity network and the warning systems, the second occurred when these same planes made the return trip from Romania where they had gone to destroy the oil fields.

Vrana was hit in the night of March 24, 1944, the day we were deliberately targeted by the Royal Air Force. The house burned and the corner tower fell down. It had had a beautiful clock that was never put back in place. Five hundred and some incendiary bombs were dropped on the palace, as well as eleven eight-hundred-kilo bombs. I will never forget that long night. The bunker shook and the noise was unbearable. We thought we were all going to die. My mother, dressed in black and her rosary in her hand, remained impassive. She dominated her feelings with admirable strength.

Later, one of the craters formed quite near the palace—a good ten meters in diameter—once filled by rising ground water, was transformed into a pond baptized "Lake Churchill"! Also, my mother had the rose bushes replaced by potato plants, so that potatoes could be distributed to families who had fled town.

For me, the bombing of the palace was meant to demoralize us: indeed, there was no military objective nearby—there was only our residence.

A little before dawn, as the house had burned, we left for Tsarska. After Samokov, the snow prevented us from continuing by car, so we were transferred to a sleigh, each of us enveloped in sheepskins. Tsarska had not been bombed, as the house had been cleverly camouflaged by the Germans. This trip was quite an event for us, as we did not have the same perception of danger as the adults. My uncle stayed at Vrana to take charge of the situation.

On March 30, bombs rained on Sofia again. Our chauffeur at the time reports the story well in his family memoirs. In town, there was no water, no electricity. The victims numbered in the hundreds. At the all clear, the queen rushed to visit the hospitals in town. Our mother went to see everyone she could, smiling angelically at them and talking with them to reassure them. She endeavored to share their suffering. The people who accompanied her told us all she had done afterward. She was incredible and spontaneous and as modest as ever. In these cases, it was her heart that spoke.

*

The day after the Communist coup d'état on September 9, 1944, the three regents were taken to Moscow, along with a few other dignitaries. They were interrogated before being brought back in January 1945 to appear before a "people's tribunal." This was, of course, a grotesque and evil farce. In the courtroom, people chanted, "Death to him, death to him," as if in a scene from the French Revolution. My uncle showed himself enormously courageous, not losing his sense of humor even in this atrocious situation. Having been condemned to death, and seeing the minister of the interior, whose given name was "Peter" and who was also going to be shot, he said to him, "Minister, I believe that tomorrow we will be meeting your namesake." In the trucks taking them to the scene of their execution, he apparently ordered them all to sing the royal anthem. We heard his sentence announced on the radio. A terrible shock. My mother immediately asked for permission for us all to go to say goodbye to them, but it was refused. A little after midnight, they were shot at the edge of a crater left by an American bomb. We think we know where this sinister spot is to be found, but it was obliterated intentionally from the memory of the people of Sofia.

The bodies of the more or less one hundred people shot were then thrown into a ditch. The minister of health, a renowned doctor at the time, Professor Stanishev, asked to be shot last so that he could verify that everyone was clinically dead. He was then shot in turn! No one was spared. The barbarity of people so full of hate needs to be noted. The Central Committee had put out a circular calling for all nests of "fascist resistance" to be liquidated and "counter-revolutionaries" exterminated. It is said that my uncle gave the tobacco pouch that he always carried to one of his executioners. The prince was forty-five years old. All were accused of high treason, even though my father and his government had resisted sending Bulgarian troops against the Russians right up to the end.

As for my Aunt Eudoxia, whom we called "Koka," she had deliberately moved away from the court so as to give the queen free rein in her management of the house. She lived in an independent villa a little way outside Sofia. In October 1944, on her way to mass at the Catholic Church of Saint Joseph, she was arrested by the militia and then imprisoned as the sister of King Boris. When the regents were deported to the Soviet Union, my mother wrote to King George VI to beg him to intervene in favor of our prisoners, since the Allied Commission still carried a lot of weight in Bulgaria. She never received an answer. I believe that she never forgave this act, no more than she did the manner in which the Duke of Aosta, her much-beloved cousin and husband of Anne of France, was treated by the English after the defeat in Ethiopia. She never wanted to go to London again.

In the 1980s, during a visit to Balmoral, in Scotland, I mustered up my courage to speak about this incident to Queen Elizabeth. We were walking in her splendid garden in front of the castle before lunch. The weather was beautiful and hot: "Lilibeth, there is something that has weighed on me for a long time: did you ever hear anything about this letter?" and I explained what had happened. After listening to me, the queen talked about my parents visiting Balmoral in 1936 and showed me their signature in her guest book. She then explained that all correspondence concerning any royal family is kept in the archives of Windsor Castle, not those of the Foreign Office. She suggested that I contact the curator, who was a great help, even if we never found the least trace of the letter. This means that it never reached the king and was most probably intercepted on the way. By whom? I still wonder. Yet another mystery of the war and that atrocious period.

After the execution of our uncle, the situation went downhill. We moved around very little, our life was concentrated around Sofia and especially Vrana. We now had the militia, the police of the new regime, to guard us. When we played in the park, there was always an officer in charge of shadowing us, machine gun quite visible. This gave me an extremely unpleasant feeling. In the evening, as something of a distraction, my sister and I would be taken to a bridge near the station where we would watch the trains pass. Once an obviously very drunk soldier fired on our car, but no damage was done, thanks to its reinforced armor plating.[2] As for the queen, she used her prerogatives to continue her visits to hospitals and orphanages. She did her best to be seen in public, despite the aides-de-camp of the new power who accompanied her everywhere.

Times were difficult for everyone. Suspicion was everywhere. Rather than protecting us, the security measures forced on us were there to isolate us. I understood what was going on, for even if Mama wanted to spare us from all the pain, we heard the news on the radio—the announcements of executions, propaganda, the waves of lies and grotesque calumny. My mother never showed evidence of weakness, but I know she was very frightened that they would take us to Russia and never stopped dreading it. We were fully aware about the fact that the world around us was disappearing.

I remember one day when, having refused to receive Marshal Tolbukhin at Vrana, she sent us upstairs. In fact, the commander of Soviet troops in Bulgaria had been based in Sofia for over a year and didn't realize that the royal family still lived in the residence. Through the window, we saw the car arrive: in it, a Russian colonel holding a bouquet in his hand as if it were a saber. He handed it to my aide-de-camp, Colonel

---

2. The car weighed five tons. After the war, it sat at the bottom of the park at Vrana. Imagine my surprise when, in the 1970s, I ran across it through a Spanish friend who had seen it in Las Vegas, on the upstairs floor of a casino, bearing the label "Armored car of King of Bulgaria."

Stefanov, who later told us that he apologized: he thought he was visiting a museum. Over time, we teased our mother about it, since she was probably one of the rare women to have ever received a bouquet from a Soviet marshal.

A few weeks after the coup d'état, while we were still at Tsarska, we received the visit of the new regents. I remember very clearly how I was dressed—it was the first time I had worn long pants—and the manner in which I addressed them. I can see the irruption in our living room of partisans armed with machine guns with belts of ammunition. Each of these representatives of the people arrived in a car escorted by a large contingent of guards, all of them wearing red handkerchiefs knotted around their throats. The first regents before then, including my uncle, used to travel all three in the same automobile. After only a few months, I had an idea of how procedures had changed. The principal regent, Todor Pavlov—the Communist ideologist—had the nerve to offer his condolences to my mother for the executions, the height of cynicism for me. So as not to betray her emotion, she gripped her hands so tightly that she warped a ring she was wearing. Her self-control was impressive.

"The king and I wish to leave Bulgaria *ipso facto*," she said. "Your Majesty, that is your right, but the little king must remain here; otherwise, there will be civil war." We thus remained until the famous referendum of September 1946. This was the beginning for all of us of a long journey, an exile that taught us many things. In the course of half a century, I've often reflected on the grief of the banished. What bothers me is that often the sole commiseration for the unhappiness of exiles is for those on one side only.

CHAPTER SIX

Exile

THE MEMORY OF OUR FIRST WEEKS OF EXILE IS FAR FROM SAD. MY SIS-
ter and I did not completely realize the drama that had taken place. The
word *exile* had no meaning for us. We were not even conscious that we
were leaving forever. We knew that we were about to undertake a long
trip, of course, but we had no idea of the size of what was at stake, or of
the difficulty that this meant for our young mother. The referendum of
September 8 had resulted in a 95.4 percent vote in favor of the People's
Republic. Not only was it rigged, but the vote was null and void, as it
was held under the occupation of foreign troops, those of the Soviets.
The monarchy was abolished. It was time to go. The Bulgarian Central
Committee had apparently even received an instruction from Moscow to
be careful with the "little boy," avoiding anyone in Bulgaria who might
want to eliminate us, since it would have given a poor image of the new
regime abroad. But there was nothing to it, at least as far as I know.

The queen had prepared the ground by finding a place for us to go.
It was complicated, since the war had cut communications between the
royal families in Europe. One beautiful morning, in great agitation and
after having informed the new authorities, she told us, "We're leaving the
day after tomorrow"—September 16. The plan was that we would travel
by train to Istanbul and then embark for Alexandria, Egypt, where her
parents awaited us, having themselves gone into exile not long before. At
the agreed time, we got into the car to go to the station in Kazichene,
quite close to Vrana, where a pavilion had been specially built by my
grandfather. We had been forbidden to leave from the center of Sofia to

avoid demonstrations in our favor. In front of the palace, a small unit of the Royal Guard presented arms to us. I can still picture the wide avenue of plane trees as it paraded past us in the warm light of that autumn afternoon. We had been cloistered many months: even if we could hear from people and receive visitors, we were not free to move around. The only exception was August 28, when we had at least been able to go to the monastery at Rila for the mass commemorating my father. The execution of my uncle and the close members of our entourage had been a serious blow to our morale. Little by little, the house was being emptied of its inhabitants.

Thus, we packed our suitcases. Among other things, my sister took a small stuffed bear that she still has. On the front steps of Vrana, the staff and those who had been allowed to stay on the property had come to say their goodbyes. Some were very emotional, others in tears, not knowing what was going to happen to them. They were far from imagining that their ordeal had only just begun. One of them, a tractor driver, Vlado, known to be a member of the Communist Party, kneeled: "Forgive me, we never believed it would come to this." We also kissed our two dogs; then someone took them from us. The scene was heart-breaking. We were put into the bullet-proof Mercedes. In this dire moment, my Aunt Eudoxia, referring to Louis XVI, said to my mother, "It's the flight to Varennes." My sister and I didn't know what it meant, but Mama turned white.

At the station, I believe I saw Russian soldiers, not Bulgarian. After greeting the handful of people present, including the regent Venelin Ganev, I remember that I became frightened. As we stepped up into the train, I had a feeling that they were going to shoot us in the back—I don't know why. The train had been specially put together and was made of a locomotive and three cars. We left around four o'clock in the afternoon. My last memories of Bulgaria are of the smell of our forests.

We were to cross Bulgaria and Turkish Thrace overnight, waking up in Istanbul. Paradox of history, it was the section of the Orient Express financed by my great-grandmother, Princess Clémentine, that allowed us to leave the country safe and sound. A few days before, the minister of foreign affairs had proposed to my mother that we embark directly from the port of Varna on a liner leaving three weeks later but that stopped in Odessa before going on to Istanbul and Egypt. In spite of its being more convenient, she refused the offer because the stopover in the Soviet Union might have meant running a risk. In 1946, the memory of Ekaterinburg and the massacre of the Russian imperial family was still very present.

In a nearby station, although the train had barely set off, I remember hearing a desperate cry from outside, one that wrenched my heart: "*Simeontcho*, who are you leaving us to?"[1] I understood then that I was leaving for good. The sorrow was very much present, but I felt a whiff of adventure in this departure. My mother had told me that we were going to Egypt and, as was normal for a boy of nine, I could already see myself conversing with the pharaohs from the top of the pyramids. Despite all the emotional upheaval, we fell asleep rather quickly. In the middle of the night, the train stopped at the Turkish border. We didn't understand why, and our mother was very worried. She was afraid they were taking us back to Sofia. A general who had participated in the coup and had become the head of my military bureau was accompanying us. He came to tell us that the driver refused to go any farther, as he did not want to be the man who had taken the king out of the country. My father had always loved the railway workers and, respected by this group, had become an honorary member of their union. When we took drives with him, we would stop at railroad crossings, and when a train would pass, the driver often blew his whistle to greet us. I never knew what happened to the driver in question. You'd have needed a certain courage to stand up to the authorities like that because you could be deported for much less. The poor man surely paid dearly for his loyalty.

We had to wait for a Turkish locomotive to be warmed up to take us to the banks of the Bosphorus. The next morning, we left the train at Sirkeci Station, at the foot of the former *saray* of the sultans, under the flashbulbs of the international press awaiting us. My mother was still wearing her long black veil. She had dressed me with care: short grey pants, coat and tie. She held each of us by the hand. The Italian ambassador to Turkey came to

---

1. *Simeontcho* is the affectionate diminutive of my given name in Bulgarian: "My little Simeon."

greet us, and we traveled by car to the port. That very evening, September 17, we were already on the ship.

I had no memory of Istanbul except of the silhouettes of domes and minarets fading in the distance. My sister and I stayed on the bridge to see this scenery. There was a new moon in the evening sky.

Our baggage was limited. My mother would have liked to bring more mementos, things that were dear to her, but the authorities told us it was complicated. We were informed that the rest of our personal possessions—among them objects that she had brought from Italy just after her marriage—would be sent to us in our new place of residence. They consisted of paintings, books and family bibelots. Of course, nothing was ever sent to us. We were told that if we preferred the exchange value, the Communist government would indemnify us, but we did not accept this offer. Before we left, our mother had given away a great many objects and clothes—including her collection of national costumes today exhibited in museums in Sofia—and gifts to the city hospitals.

It had occurred to her to have a complete service of our porcelain dishes packed to go with us, and I still use them in Madrid. The palace kitchen had taken the initiative of preparing us two crates full of pots and pans, and even canned goods and jam, rather than our family paintings. They would indeed have been more useful, but upon our arrival in Alexandria, a crane unloading one of them slipped and the contents ended up smashed on the pier, to the joy of the dockers unloading it, who were able to take advantage of the food.

When we left, Communist propaganda had the nerve to leak to the international press that we had received no less than twenty million dollars to cover the costs of my education, and the Bulgarian legation in Cairo was delighted to spread this false bit of news. This was very harmful to us, as in reality we had nothing. As a settlement, we had received two hundred dollars per person. This was, in fact, the first time I had seen American dollar bills. I had completely forgotten the myth of the false indemnity until 1959. That particular day, in New York, during an interview televised live on NBC, the star journalist, who had recently interviewed Fidel Castro, brought up the question on air again—with a certain irony—catching me off guard. I answered her that this was totally unfounded because (a) I doubted that in 1946 Bulgaria even had two million in cash at its disposal, (b) the money would have been tainted, since stolen from the people, and (c) with the twenty million dollars, I could have bought the whole government and would not be having the pleasure today of having to answer the type of question she was asking. And that was it. The Embassy of the People's Republic of Bulgaria immediately complained to the State Department as well as to the television station—with no result, of course.

Two political commissioners accompanied us all the way to our final destination, Alexandria, to make sure that we did not get off the ship before that. One of these men had fought in the Spanish Civil War. I remember that he carried a miniature chess set in his pocket that he had made himself. He had fixed a system of nails under the pieces so that we could also play in bad weather. At the end of the trip, he gave it to me. I lost it at some point, but I still remember its little red cardboard box.

The other commissioner became an ambassador afterward. I came across his name again in Syria, in 1964, but didn't see him for obvious political reasons. I was there to visit the monastery of Saint Simeon Stylites near Aleppo. Then I saw him again in New York, during a large reception organized by one of my compatriots in the early 1990s. He was introduced to me as Mr. Stefanov, but I immediately recognized him by his floppy mustache. I thought it was kinder of me to address him as "Mister Ambassador" rather than "Comrade Commissioner," but I still hadn't forgotten.

Our trip lasted twelve days. The Turkish captain had given us his cabin—I remember his name: Adnan Ülgütsen. The ship was a small cargo belonging to the Turkish national company and it was called the *Aksu*, and we were the only passengers on board. The crew members loaded and unloaded the ship at the various ports of Turkey and the Eastern Mediterranean. I asked permission to go on the bridge to be able to study these operations carefully, as I was fascinated. At each stop, the authorities were very considerate to us: the governor, or perhaps the mayor, received us or sometimes came on board. The mayor of Antalya gave us enormous melons and bananas, a fruit that I had never tasted before, like the guavas that I discovered later in Egypt.

We spent a lot of time walking on the bridge looking at the coastline so that we wouldn't miss anything. I was fascinated by the new smells carried on the winds and by the Mediterranean, which I was discovering for the first time. At Larnaca, while cargo was being off loaded, we were able to go ashore to stretch our legs and have a walk around town. We subsequently traveled on to Beirut and then Haifa, where we arrived in the middle of a riot against the English—serious enough that we were not able to dock. This was the beginning of serious troubles in Palestine, just before the creation of the State of Israel. From there we arrived at Port-Said, the city at the entrance of the Suez Canal, leading toward the Red Sea and the Indian Ocean. My Aunt Eudoxia left us at this port of call, for she had found a connection to Marseille; from there, she wanted to travel on to her Württemberg sister in Germany. For my aunt, leaving Bulgaria meant that life was over. There was nothing else for her. Red Bulgaria was no longer hers. The deaths of her two brothers, like her detention in horrifying conditions, sorely afflicted her. Her pain was indelible.

Two days later, we disembarked at Alexandria. Their mission accomplished, the two political commissioners returned to Bulgaria. Thereafter, we no longer had any official contact with the People's Republic until 1989. In propaganda terms, we had become pariahs, to be avoided like the devil.

The presence of the Italian royal family in Egypt was the principal reason for my mother's choice. The fact that we were in the immediate postwar years did not work in our favor. We were coming from a country that had been part of the Axis and was now occupied by the Soviets. Finding a country willing to host us was not obvious. At our arrival, we were met by a representative of King Farouk, but above all by my mother's family: my grandfather, the old king, Victor Emmanuel III of Italy, and my grandmother Elena, as well as my mother's older sister, Yolanda, married to an officer in the Italian cavalry, Carlo Calvi, Count of Bergolo.

We called our grandmother "Nonna." She was extremely kind and sweet, very Slav, being a native of Montenegro. Grandmamma Elena had never shown a preference among her eighteen grandchildren, so that each of us was convinced that he was quite unique. My mother did exactly the same thing with my children and my nephews and nieces: everyone wondered who the favorite was.

In keeping with protocol, my grandfather had demanded that I travel with him in his car. I was quite overawed. I didn't know him, having only seen him once, in Italy, at the age of two! I was very anxious. We made the trip from the port to the Hôtel Méditerranée, where we were staying temporarily.

Later, he said to my mother, "Giovanna, you did a good job teaching Simeon Italian." Thinking he was making fun of her, Mama apologized: "I wasn't able to do any better because of the circumstances." But I had gotten along very well, studiously focusing to put all the words I knew in Italian into the same sentence!

My grandparents had been living in Alexandria for several months. The king had abdicated in favor of his son, my Uncle Umberto, who ascended the throne before the referendum on June 2, 1946, which would proclaim the Republic. Afterward, his presence on Italian soil was forbidden, as was that of all the male members of the royal family. My uncle had gone to Portugal, where he awaited the queen, Marie-José, and their four children. My grandfather sincerely thought that his departure would help his son reestablish the political situation, a bit like my grandfather Ferdinand had done in leaving Bulgaria to leave my father a free hand, but it was simply not the case. By experience, I can say that a king is often the last fuse before the whole circuit blows. That Victor Emmanuel fled in haste is simply a legend, made up from beginning to end by Italian Communists and Republicans, with no basis in truth.

My grandfather liked to joke with us, even though he was still rather strict. He had an unbelievably ugly little dog, Diana, that we played with. He took us fishing with our grandmother, Nonna, in Lake Mariout, toward the Nile Delta, or in the port of Alexandria, at the very spot where years later traces of the famous library and rich statuary would be discovered only a few meters from the surface. We would go there with Salvatore, the Italian chauffeur who was a Levantine Egyptian. Sometimes we would also fish in the wide canal, among half-naked men who pulled feluccas with a sort of bridle around their heads. Once, a poor fellow whose legs were hidden under a cover came in a little wagon to ask for charity. Then we saw him later, standing up and whistling, his wagon tucked under his arm. "That will teach you to be too generous," Salvatore allowed himself to say to my grandmother, whose generosity was reputed—but who also had a sense of humor.

The Hôtel Méditerranée was located on the celebrated coast road of the Alexandria corniche. The first morning, when the waiter came into my room wearing the traditional djellaba and a turban, he said "*Za'yek*" to me, which in Egyptian means "How are you?" But in Bulgarian, *zaek* means "rabbit"! "Why is this person saying rabbit to me?" I wondered. Sometimes under the windows, we would see trucks go past transporting prisoners of war, survivors of the Battle of El Alamein.

We stayed at the hotel for a few weeks, time enough for my mother to find the house we rented. It was situated just behind the summer residence of the English High Commissioner and belonged to an Italo-Maltese family called Limongelli. It was a very pleasant two-story villa with a little garden in front. Our neighborhood was on a hill. At the corner, we had Copt neighbors, the Khayat family. During the war, they had had Churchill as a guest and had played a role against the Germans. They gave big parties, with a tent set up in their garden, and afterward would send us big platters of sweet pastries. We went past their house whenever we went down to take the tram.

At home, we formed an astonishing community, a sort of miniature Bulgaria in exile. In addition to the three of us, there were the two Petrov sisters, my mother's companions; Colonel Malchev, serving as an aide-de-camp—he was the last officer to command the Guard before the coup d'état—along with his wife and two children; and four members of the palace staff who had been authorized to leave with us.

I was enrolled at Victoria College, even if I did not yet know a word of English. My sister was sent to Sacred Heart, for girls only and run by Irish nuns.

The experience at Victoria College was a novelty for me, for up to then I had only had private lessons. I found myself in the middle of a large institution of six hundred children. They were all polyglot, and it was very hard at the beginning. Fortunately, my Calvi cousin, Pier Francesco—three years older than I and a forceful, generous personality—took me under his protective wing. I didn't yet know how to defend myself, but I soon learned. He was the only boy in his family, a bit of a rebel and had already been expelled from another school in Alexandria. Around age eighteen, he began to flirt with the ladies—successfully. One day, the husband of one of them gave him a serious thrashing. Grandmamma and I were fishing when we saw his little car coming back from Cairo. As he was bleeding and had lost two teeth, he came up with a story about some Bedouins who had beat him up. My grandmother didn't believe a single word of his story. Much later, he confided the truth of his adventure to me.

At Victoria, the institution was thoroughly English. On Sundays, we sang Anglican hymns, and that is why I know them well. I was still able to sing them at the wedding of Prince William in 2011. School for me was synonymous with being equal; I was no longer king but one student among all the others. There were the sons of big shots—Greeks, Armenians and large, influential Jewish families, and so on. Bulgaria? No one even knew where it was.

Most of the students were boarders. I was a day boy, going home for the night. At the beginning, King Farouk lent us a car, and it would come for me each day. It was a sedan, bright red with black mudguards, the palace colors, and conspicuous from miles away. It was in this style that I arrived at school, and I can tell you, the effect was guaranteed! Later, feeling that we should not take too much advantage of such favors, my mother decided to give it back, much to my regret.

In the evenings, I came home on foot or in the tram with a friend who had a Bulgarian nanny. I remember that when she saw me, Sonka wanted at all costs to kiss me! At home, we ate dinner as a family. Often, we would listen to Ravel's *Boléro*, one of the only records we possessed, on the gramophone we had been able to bring with us.

Alexandria was an international, fascinating city. Ancient Egyptians were never attracted by the sea, preferring to let the Phoenicians, who were excellent sailors, take care of roving around the oceans. Postwar Greek families were the height of chic and distinction. In this regard, the novels by Lawrence Durrell (*The Alexandria Quartet*) delighted me. As we were children, his descriptions of decadence did not make much of an impression on us. For me, Alexandria was an immense playground, full of discoveries to be made. Egypt was redeveloping in those postwar years: the country was going full speed ahead, and the people we met, such as the parents of my friends at school, were all fully committed to the new economic expansion. The years of hardship and fear were truly over. A child doesn't see things in the same way. Everyone was forging ahead, until the Suez Crisis caused a huge change. Most of the royal courts were accused of excesses, and this was the case for King Farouk, who was vilified for any difficulties. But these accusations were untrue. I cannot stand the preachings of prophets of the past—it's much too easy to criticize after the fact. Most royal courts finally had normal lives, like all families. In Alexandria, our existence was certainly not very lavish, since fishing parties with my grandmother were the only excesses of my tender youth—if you can use the word "tender," given what I had lived through.

At school, the young sons of the future Gulf States made quite an impression on me. Today they are billionaires, but at the time they preferred sleeping on the floor to sleeping in their beds. They were from Abu Dhabi, Sharjah, Dubai, and so on, territories under British administration known by the name of *Trucial States*. Among the boys were Egyptians, of course, but also Jordanians, Saudis, Lebanese, Libyans, Syrians, Iraqis, Maltese, Italians, a few English—including one of the descendants of Howard Carter, the man who discovered Tutankhamun's tomb—the sons of Armenians who had made a fortune in tobacco, a few French boys, and some children of diplomats. There were a great number of different religious communities and Eastern Christians, each with their own services and churches—Orthodox, Catholic Armenians, Greeks, Melkites, and especially Copts.

In this theatrical setting, I saw myself as the young Frederic II discovering the Orient and its bazaars. This was an extraordinary, cosmopolite society, made up of elites who greatly enjoyed finding themselves in each other's company in Alexandria. Old Greeks said that they were "going to Egypt" when they traveled to Cairo. For them, Alexandria was still a Hellenic colony dating from the time of Alexander the Great. Straight from Bulgaria, I suddenly found myself thrown into a wildly multicolored, interesting world. Everyone tolerated everyone else. People were at ease in several languages and cultures. Above all, I was struck by the beauty of this city with its jacarandas[2] and flamboyants.[3] On a trip several years later to Mozambique, I would discover these same characteristic trees. I remember the unique smells, the narrow streets, the crowds, the *dondurma* sellers, the people who sold sweet syrup from under immense silver cloches, vendors selling grilled ears of corn or peanuts—the discovery of new tastes. I didn't go into town alone, but with a friend, Sameh Aboulela. Europeans were advised to avoid the old section of Alexandria: it was *off limits*. You still found English soldiers stationed there at the time. When I go to Switzerland to the home of our dear friend Catherine Aga Khan, a Greek born in Alexandria, we talk nostalgically of our memories of this lost world.

It was also at Victoria College that I met the future King Hussein of Jordan and began a long friendship. We were in the same class. I would also get to know Sadiq al-Mahdi, future prime minister of Sudan in the 1970s, as well as the members of the royal families of Libya and Iraq. King Faisal of Iraq was also there: he was a few years ahead of me.

Our school had the reputation of being the best in the Near East. At the time, England, France and the United States were too far away for anyone to envisage going to school there, as it would have meant taking a ship and leaving a child to board for a whole year—there were not yet regular flights on airlines. I remember really well the huge BOAC hydroplanes[4] that landed on the Nile in route for the Far East. The desert princes sent their children to the Victoria in Cairo or to the one in Alexandria. The teachers were all hand picked in England for their competence and their pedagogical skills. English was the required language for courses. Among ourselves, however, we spoke just about any imaginable language except English. I even learned a little Arabic during those years, along with Latin, which my mother made me take, thinking it would be more useful! As for her, she had begun to learn the Turkish that some members of the Egyptian Royal Family spoke at court, as did the exiled members of the Ottoman imperial House of Osman whom she enjoyed meeting. I am also thinking of the older Egyptian families—the Toussoun

---

2. Originally from South America, this tree can grow to fifteen meters and has very beautiful flowers.
3. A tree with red flowers, originally from Madagascar.
4. This was the British Overseas Airways Corporation, which before was called Imperial Airways.

princes, for example, related to the Khedives, themselves of Turkish or Albanian origin. My mother numbered among their closest friends, as with Prince Said Toussoun, who considerately invited us to the family's numerous estates, of which one at Aboukir (Abu Qir).

We quickly got our bearings in the country. On Sundays, we went to Grandmama's, who lived in a very pretty villa, "Jela," the diminutive of Elena in Montenegrin—a less than forty-minute walk from our house. There we joined our cousins in the big garden. We adored playing with them or playing soccer in the streets with little hellions our age. Many years after, during the Crans-Montana Economic Symposium when I was prime minister, the Palestinian delegate, Saeb Erekat, reminded me that he was one of my friends back then!

We also went to Agami, to a beach where the water was turquoise and the sand white. These were the first times we swam in the sea, and a great joy. Today, the city of Alexandria has spread out so much that this is practically a section of it, whereas then it was quite an expedition to get there. I went to Cairo once or twice when I had whooping cough. I had been prescribed bedrest at a higher altitude by the doctor. So, I found myself at Mena House, perched forty-two meters above the sea, facing the Cheops pyramid! I remember, too, the Sphinx and the museum, and going to Luxor by train; crossing the Nile in a felucca comes back to me, and a camel ride and a long hot visit to the Valley of Kings.

In Alexandria, my mother had to make ends meet as best she could. We were hardly rolling in money, for we had no income. Our mother had sold some jewelry to the famous jewelers of Alexandria, the firms of Horowitz and Youssoufian. Years later, I would study the sales catalogs hoping to find a brooch with hearts in rubies, which she really loved and I wanted to get back for her—alas, without success. We also had brought with us some items in silver, one of which was a set of figures around the fountain at the Piazza Navona, which some Italian friends had given her for her marriage, but she never had the heart to sell it. She loved to knit the skeins of wool given to her by my grandmother. The latter, so as not to give offense, used to hide a twenty-pound note inside, and we would discover it with great joy as the wool unraveled. My mother also organized little charity bazaars to come to the aid of Bulgarians who, like us, had found refuge in Egypt, people who had disembarked from boats and found themselves with nothing, or who had been there before the Bulgarian coup d'état and could no longer return to the country. After 1944, there was a large wave of emigration from Bulgaria, primarily to the United States, Canada and Australia, but also to Egypt. We also knew three or four families who were long established and very successful. This was the case for a family that was originally from Macedonia, who owned a large pastry shop in Cairo. Their children, who were our age, became friends with whom we could speak Bulgarian. When Nasser came to power, these people lost everything, as did the Armenian families who had moved to Egypt from Bulgaria, where their parents had moved after the massacres of 1915 in Eastern Turkey.

My mother was of an infinite kindness, but she was also very strict. We were required to be perfect in what was expected of us. This was non-negotiable: if not, it was the chop. No exceptions. Much later, in Portugal, when she was working with a dozen charities—the Parish of Saint Anthony, the Society of St. Francis de Sales, the nuns at Mafra—she put me in charge of managing her accounts. Unhappy with the allowance I gave her, she asked me for ten thousand *escudos* more per month and wouldn't tell me what the money was for. It was obvious to me that it was for other charities. Since then, I have always made sure that I have change on me, in case I come across someone begging, and this is often the case today.

Fortunately, she put me in charge of her purse strings; otherwise she'd have ended up ruined. She hosted and financially supported a whole group of ladies in exile: Hungarians, Bulgarians—ladies from families known in "society" but destitute, for whom she prepared sumptuous tea parties. Everyone was a subject of commiseration: a "poor him" here, a "poor her" there. Everyone was forgiven. One day when we were all together in the garden in Madrid, our friend the journalist Stephane Groueff teasingly said to her, "Majesty, I think you would even be capable of saying *Bédniat Stalin*" ("That poor Stalin" in Bulgarian).

*

A few weeks after our arrival, my mother was received by King Farouk at Montazah Palace, an immense Italian-style villa set down at the far end of town in a magnificent park. Afterward, she would see him at official receptions, where she would also come across the Turkish princesses whom she was particularly fond of. The Ras El-Tin Palace, a royal residence, was near the port, where his celebrated yacht, *Mahroussa*, lay at anchor; this was the same vessel on which he would be forced to leave Egypt a few years later. Because of my young age, I never had the opportunity to see Farouk during our stay. I only met him in exile, at the same time as the other members of his family. A great, cultivated gentleman, about whom nasty legends and caricatures completely distorted reality.

In the middle of all these people, the Italians, Albanians, Romanovs and us, formed a little royal colony. The Romanovs had formerly lived in Rome, guests of the Savoy family, and had left Italy with them in 1946. Prince Roman Petrovich, the father of my cousin Nicolas Romanovich, had moved to Alexandria with his family. His grandmother, the Grand Duchess Militza, was one of my Italian grandmother's sisters; we thus have a great-grandfather in common, King Nikola of Montenegro. Apparently, she and her sister Anastasia were the ones who introduced Rasputin to the court. My mother was very fond of this part of her family. It was with them that she had spent her youth in Italy. What's more, it is to this relation that I owe my Slav blood, and Mama was very proud of it.

Other families also came to this end of the world. The Greek royal family passed through Alexandria when the Germans arrived in Athens, before going on to South Africa. Queen Frederica and their children left first. Another sovereign, King Zog of Albania, had moved there with Queen Geraldine, an absolutely exquisite woman. He, too, was an interesting character: the head of a clan who became minister of the interior, and then prime minister, he was finally proclaimed king in 1928. With the invasion of Italian troops in 1939, they had to leave the country. When the two of them would come to have tea at our house, and because they knew we were living from hand to mouth, the king would leave such a large tip for our two Bulgarian servants that it would cover their monthly salaries. After the death of Zog, in Cannes, the queen came to live in Madrid with her son Leka, who became a friend. Their situation was no longer so buoyant, Zog having spent heavily on his political activities.

My Hesse first cousins, children of Princess Mafalda, had also come to live close to their grandmother. The story of their parents is tragic. In the 1930s, their father Philip, like many Germans, was seduced by the Nazi system. After the assassination attempt of July 20, 1944, followed by the arrest of Mussolini, he was sent by Himmler to the camp at Sachsenhausen, reserved for political prisoners. My Aunt Mafalda, who had just come back from Bulgaria, where she had attended the funeral of my father, received a letter faked by the Gestapo, in which her husband instructed her to come back at once to Germany with the children. She had a bad feeling and left the three of them at the Vatican, entrusted to the secretary of state, Monsignor Montini, the future Paul VI. The oldest, Moritz, had stayed in Germany to do his military service.[5] As a devoted wife, my aunt went back to Germany and was arrested and then interned at Buchenwald, using the name they had forced her to take: Frau Weber. She lost an arm in an American bombing, before dying on May 5, 1945, two days before the liberation of the camp by the Allies. All this without ever knowing that her husband had not written the letter. As for him, he knew nothing of the fate of his wife and children. And my grandparents knew nothing of this drama until the end of the war. When he was freed in 1948, my Uncle Philip came to stay in Egypt. He was pale and thin. I got to know him well; he was a man with an extraordinary historical and artistic knowledge. Afterward, whenever I was in Rome, I was happy to stay with him in their magnificent Villa Polissena, a wedding present from my grandparents to their daughter.

My grandfather, King Victor Emmanuel, was vehemently precise and meticulous. He was the only son of Queen Margherita, who was also a Savoy. Very cultivated, he had put together a beautiful, complete collection of Italian coins, of more than 126,000 pieces that he had cataloged himself. When he left, he bequeathed it to the Italian state. It is today exhibited in the National Roman Museum.

He was demanding toward everyone. One evening, during a dinner at the Villa Savoia, my Uncle Umberto, the crown prince, arrived a few

---

5. At fifteen, he had been assigned to the anti-aircraft defense force. His helmet was too big for him and fell down over his eyes, he told me later. Pathetic: the youngest recruits among German youth sacrificed to the insanity of an inept war.

minutes late. He was severely reprimanded by his father in front of the other guests. A little while later, my mother, who was there on a visit, appeared and sat down at the table. Grandmamma Elena couldn't help but say to her husband, "But really, Giovanna is even later, and you said nothing!" The king turned toward her and said dryly, "But Giovanna is a queen!" This is an example of one side of his personality.

Legend has it that Hitler gave him the nickname "Feathered Monkey" because of his small stature and the fact that marshals of Italy wore dress uniforms with a white feather decorating their helmets. Hitler blamed him for not admiring Mussolini sufficiently. In 1936, during a military parade honoring Chancellor Hitler, the latter realized that royal protocol demanded that only he and the sovereign be seated, while *Il Duce* had to remain standing with the other dignitaries. Despite all the calumny, I know that, in a passive fashion, my grandfather managed to resist some of Mussolini's worst extremes. Once more, I find that situations must be judged in context, and one must be careful about making hasty judgments, nourished on untruths. I also think that there is nothing he could have done to prevent fascism from coming to power.

Another family anecdote concerns my Calvi uncle, who, when things started going badly for the Germans, proved his exemplary courage and showed that he knew how to live up to his responsibilities. After the American landing in Sicily, the Germans began to tighten their grip and to be attacked by the Resistance. As the military governor of Rome, my uncle had to hold his ground against the leaders of the German forces, who demanded that he list one hundred well-known Romans to be shot in reprisal. As an answer, my uncle held out the sheet of paper he had been given, on which he had written a single name: his, followed by all of his titles. He was arrested and subsequently liberated by the Allies in June 1944.

After embarking at Naples in 1944, my grandfather would never see the peninsula again. He died a year after our arrival in Alexandria, on December 28, 1947. After his first heart attack, my mother went to his bedside. "Giovanna, I know I'm dying," he said. "One thing weighs on my mind . . . I want you to know that by having Mussolini arrested in my house, the Villa Savoia, I did not live up to my sense of hospitality."

This event had affected him so much that it came up as he examined his conscience on his deathbed. Curiously, it was I, long after, who revealed the confession that my mother had confided to me. No one else had ever talked about it. In Alexandria, my grandfather had kept a little court around him: an aide-de-camp, Count Torella, and no more than four or five employees. When he died, King Farouk organized a spectacular state funeral. The streets of Alexandria were dotted with soldiers in white and wearing the red *tarboosh*, framing the passage of the Royal Guard that followed the gun carriage bearing Grandpapa's coffin draped with the Italian royal standard, which had been the flag of Italy since its unification—a grandiose ceremony, engraved in the memories of many.

My mother was very discreet and reserved, especially for everything concerning the family. All that was personal was a taboo subject for her. I inherited this trait from her. Once we were adults, my sister and I laughed often at her penchant for secrets. In my turn, I have sometimes been accused of being secretive, but in fact I am discreet, which is quite different. I prefer to be master of my silence rather than victim of my words.

Since 1951, I have been back to Alexandria only once, for a weekend organized by King Hussein of Jordan to celebrate the fortieth anniversary of our class graduation. It was highly amusing to get back together with all of the boys—who were no longer boys. The two days were dedicated to sport events, excursions and dinner parties for us and our respective spouses. We named President Mubarak an honorary member of the Old Victorian Association, since he accommodated a large number of the guests at Ras El-Tin Palace. At the time, I thought that he had reached the height of his power. He had even said a few words in Russian in an aside, since he had trained in Moscow as an officer in the air force. I saw the old sections of the town and our school, of course, which is now called Nasser, meaning "victory" in Arabic. There is even a little mosque on what used to be a soccer field. I noted how religion was taking up more and more room in Egyptian public space. I saw our house on Salt Street, as well as the one on the corner of Marshal Allenby. Number 6 is still standing. When I went to present my respects to the patriarch of Alexandria—a Greek who cut a fine figure, and a cultivated man who governed the destinies of the Orthodox world for all of Africa—I told him that I had lived in Alexandria: "My son," he said, "when you were here, we were two hundred thousand Christians out of six hundred thousand inhabitants; we are now no more than fifteen thousand out of four million."

I went to pray on the tomb of my Italian grandfather in the Catholic Saint Catherine's Church in Bakos, one of the sections of Alexandria. I was filled with great sadness and nostalgia; I felt the injustice of him still being exiled even after death. His place should be in the Pantheon in Rome, or, if need be, in the Savoy family vault in Superga, the beautiful abbey built above Turin in the eighteenth century by the architect Juvarra. My grandmother Elena is buried in the Saint Lazare cemetery in Montpellier, where she was in the care of her doctor, Professor Lamarque, until her death in 1952. We went to see her several times in France when she began to make extended stays there. One or two summers she had rented the Château de la Croë, on Cap d'Antibes, a sumptuous villa that had also been inhabited by the Windsors. As for Uncle Umberto, he is buried at the Monastery of Haute-Combes, on the shore of Lake Annecy, in France, where the dukes of Savoy are buried. Like the others, he is not buried in Italy.

I find this type of politicization and resentment toward historical personalities despicable. It is saddening to see that pettiness and ingratitude can still be seen among the leaders of certain European countries.

CHAPTER SEVEN

Youth in Madrid

WE REMAINED IN ALEXANDRIA UNTIL 1951, WHEN I WAS FOURTEEN. My mother wanted her children to live and pursue their education in Europe, and thus we could not envisage staying in Egypt any longer. She began again to look for a place for us to move. It was not easy. My mother dreamed of Florence, where some of her cousins lived, including the duchess of Aosta and Queen Helen of Romania. But Italy didn't want me, for diplomatic difficulties might have spoiled its good relations with the People's Republic of Bulgaria. Having heard that Queen Giovanna was planning on moving, the Spanish ambassador in Cairo came to see her to ask whether she had ever considered Spain as a country of exile. We accepted this unexpected offer. Spain was for us a welcoming country, and a European country above all, closer to our roots.

To be truthful, we were already starting to feel the beginnings of a certain malaise in Egypt: demonstrations were being repressed, the political climate clearly becoming more rigid and the monarchy starting to be questioned. Nationalism began to fill the air. The time of an open, cosmopolitan Alexandria would little by little die out, in an irremediable manner, and all this would be true for the rest of Egypt as well. Nasser's revolution came after our departure, lightening the weight of our regrets about leaving. I am very happy to have known Alexandria as it existed then. I was able to get to know my Italian grandparents, to learn English and even a little Arabic, to be immersed in a far different world from that I had known in Bulgaria, and also to have learned to fish. Above all, I discovered a part of the world that would become very important through the future actions of my classmates, the future leaders of their countries, to whom I would remain attached for the rest of my life. The Near East would become for me a revivifying resource, a place of human passion, friendships, and dawn visits to the archeological sites of antiquity. I would come back often to Libya, Kuwait, and above all Jordan, thanks to close ties of friendship with the Hashemite royal family.

*

The American liner for Barcelona took several days to cross the Mediterranean; it was called *Atlantic*, an amusing detail. Once again, I contemplated the horizon of the sea thinking of the new life that awaited us. Our mother had told us that we would be discovering a new country. We were not unhappy. Those days must be seen through the eyes of the young people that my sister and I were then. We were in that time of life when everything seems possible. The trials that we had gone through had made us close. We were mischievous, playful—and we knew that we could count on one another. We had been raised with the same sense of duty, thanks to the iron hand of my mother, who was—as always—serene at the idea of our new living arrangements. I never really saw her upset: she was always solid as a rock.

When we disembarked in Barcelona on July 20, 1951, our presence caused something of a sensation. Numerous journalists awaited us, and the governor of Catalonia was there to greet us. He had arranged for us to visit the Benedictine monastery at Montserrat. I remember the spectacular view of the mountains of Catalonia, as well as a bit of Barcelona. In those years, Spain was still very much closed in on itself. The country had made enormous progress since its dreadfully destructive civil war.

It was the month of July, and the heat was terrible. The following day, we arrived in the Spanish capital by a night train. We very much felt that this was our final destination—quite different from Egypt, which was only an extended stopover. Before setting up our household in Madrid itself, we stayed for two months at the Felipe II, a chic hotel that had been recommended to us in the small town of El Escorial, an ancient and former royal city located about thirty miles north of Madrid. The famous monastery of San Lorenzo de El Escorial was built by Philip II to commemorate the Spanish victory over the French at Saint-Quentin in 1557 and above all to raise a sepulture to his parents, Isabella of Portugal and Charles V. Their ashes had been transferred from the monastery at Yuste, where the emperor had withdrawn after his abdication. The building consists of a gigantic monastery in the shape of a grill—object symbolizing the martyrdom of Saint Lawrence—a basilica, a royal residence, an extensive library, and a pantheon where the kings of Spain rest. It is one of the most beautiful monuments in Europe. At the time, El Escorial was still considered a spot for residents of Madrid to spend the summer, as it is situated at a relatively cooler altitude. We spent the whole summer until September there, waiting for our mother to find a house for us to live in. The season was in full swing, and my sister and I went out a lot. We were intrigued that so much went on out-of-doors, the Spanish being very attached to going out at night, especially in summer, when the *paseos* filled with people. We loved joining in with the crowd. I attended my first bullfight on the day of the Feast of Saint Lawrence in August. It was quite a show, I must say, a curiosity for a "tourist" like myself, even if as yet I understood nothing about it. I saw only the brutal confrontation between man and animal. Later, I would learn to appreciate the differences in the breeds of bulls, the breeders, the gestures of the bullfighters and the elegance of their handling of the bulls. At a certain moment, the bloody side is forgotten, so that you see only the beauty of the two main characters facing off in the arena.

While we were discovering this new world and its new language, my mother went off each day by car to Madrid to visit houses. The poor thing was terribly courageous: I think she must have visited nearly one hundred of them to find the one that is still our family home, the famous "Coburg's Lair."

She was helped in her search by a charming couple living at the hotel, José-Fernando and Josefina de Calderón, both of them from Madrid families of long standing. This was the beginning of an extended and close friendship between our two families. Since then, Fina has become a personality in the world of letters, in French and in Spanish, and has won several literary prizes. They regularly visited my mother in Portugal afterward. The intelligence of this woman and her liveliness were infectious.

I particularly remember their house on the banks of the Tagus in Toledo where they organized a large lunch to celebrate my turning twenty-eight, the tenth anniversary of my reaching my majority. I have never forgotten that day, nor all of the goodness they constantly showered on us, for which I am very grateful.

To buy a house, we had at our disposal a sum allocated by the queen of Italy, a budget that had imperatively to be respected. The villa on which my mother set her heart dated from 1927 and had belonged to the architect who had designed the Madrid subway, Carlos Mendoza. And it was, in fact, in a section called *Metropolitano*. It is amusing, because the mayor who signed the housing permit was Count Vallellano, future minister of public works under Franco. I knew him well, since the ministers of the *Generalissimo* were important figures, keeping their jobs for a long time because he did not change them willingly.

The house was habitable, but we had to redo it a bit. The Malchevs had come with us from Egypt, as had one of the Petrov sisters. However, our two servants had stayed behind; both of them married in Alexandria, one to a Greek woman and the other to an Armenian woman.

Our faithful cook Misho, who had begun his career as a cook's helper in the kitchens of the palace at Vrana in my father's time, had, of course, made the trip. As in Sofia, there was the same ritual every morning: he submitted a menu plan to my mother. The dishes were French but written in Cyrillic. In the evening, when we had people for dinner, he kept watch over the table as if we were still in the palace, proud of maintaining the beautiful customs. He stayed with us fifty-five years, and his presence constituted an important link between my children and Bulgaria, since he taught them about cooking while mostly speaking to them in Bulgarian. Kubrat and Kalina saw him as their adored uncle—a great gentleman who died in their arms.

A Bulgarian businessman, formerly consul to Berlin and then a representative of Volkswagen in Spain, Mr. Dimanov, helped my mother with the moving procedures. In Madrid, we had also come across the widow and daughter of the last minister of foreign affairs from the time of my father, Parvane Draganov, who had been shot with my uncle in 1945. Before that, he had been the head of our legation in Spain and had been able to leave his family there. The presence of this handful of people was important for us, making us feel less alone.

At the beginning, we had nothing with which to furnish this large villa: we put our mattresses directly on the floor. We camped in this way for a good year, acquiring furniture in colonial style that we discovered in the neighborhood. I believe that today our house is one of the few that still remains from the period; we were on the outskirts of the city, between wasteland and countryside. I considered it our true home, the place where an enormous number of my memories are to be found and where I spent my adolescence. While we might still dream of Bulgaria—Mama continued to talk about it to us every day—it was unrealistic to believe that we might return there. The Soviet empire appeared to be a wall so solid that we could not imagine that one day it would break up so easily.

During these years, I was a witness to the fantastic development of Spain. In the early 1950s, it was still possible to see the scars of the civil war just about everywhere, although the fighting had already been over for more than ten years. Not far from our house, for example, most of the houses had bullet holes in them. The front line known as "University Residence" passed quite near us. This was where the last desperate fighting took place in the Battle of Madrid, one of the last in this fratricidal war. At the time, I noticed the extreme simplicity of the way people dressed. Coming from booming, lavish, colorful Alexandria, it was a shock. In the street, we came across people wearing *alpargatas* (espadrilles with soles cut out of old tires).

It was only in 1953 and the first defense agreements with the United States that signs of development and well-being appeared. Contrary to the other countries in Europe, and for political reasons, Spain had not benefited from the Marshall Plan up until then. The country was poor. In December 1959, President Eisenhower's visit was covered by the international press, an event that revealed the support of the Americans for the government of General Franco. This was something of a turning point for the regime. I remember we were allowed out of high school for two hours to watch the cavalcade go by on *la Castellana*. At the same time, there was also an extraordinary film, *¡Bienvenido, Mister Marshall!*, directed by Luis Berlanga, where the visit was a subject for derision, turned into a tragi-comedy. Let us not forget that we were in the middle of the Cold War and that the construction of American air bases—of strategic importance for the defense of Europe—supplied a large number of jobs. The oil pipeline linking the naval airbase of Rota on the Atlantic to those of Torrejón in Madrid, and Zaragoza was proof of it. These military installations still exist, but they have become Spanish in the meantime, and are integrated into the NATO network. The general feeling at the time was that Spain was returning to the bosom of the West, coming out of the isolation in which it had found itself since the end of its civil war. Sometimes, too, the merits of Franco's actions are forgotten: first, that of having frustrated the plans of the Comintern in 1939, and second, preventing the Germans from taking control of the Straits of Gibraltar, which would have compromised the Allied landings in North Africa. Above all, this new openness was the sign of the Spanish economic miracle, which would continue its progression at a steady rhythm of almost 7 percent growth per year.

At the time, the vision that I had of Spain was the one that I had been taught at Victoria College, a series of clichés inherited from the age-old rivalry between the two naval powers constituted by Spain and England since the days of the Invincible Armada. For me, Sir Francis Drake was a national hero and the Spanish dreadful pirates to be deeply mistrusted. Thus, when I arrived, I was full of prejudices and wondered what kind of a sinister country we had landed in. Of course, reality showed me quite another version, and I very quickly came to passionately love the country and the Spanish people. It is from this time that I draw my conviction that history should be taught at an age when maturity allows one to step away from the preconceived notions that we drag with us for the rest of our lives. It is grave indeed to indoctrinate children by the light of nationalistic sentiments.

Until the death of Franco in 1975, the Spanish economy never ceased to expand. Little by little, the country became more open. In the course of my later professional life as the representative in Spain of foreign corporations seeking to establish themselves there, I would come to be interested in it. And I am not even including the extraordinary leap forward resulting from its move into democracy, opening the way to the common market and thus to Europe.

But to get back to my story: In October 1951, the three of us were received at El Pardo Palace by the head of state. I can still picture the members of the Moorish Guard—mostly Northern Moroccans—impressive in their uniforms with their halberds. Franco received us with great pomp, both to demonstrate his monarchist feelings and to insist on the fact that he was receiving a king who was a victim of Communism. Let it not be forgotten that Franco had earned his promotion as Alphonse XIII's youngest general through merit, and the latter had decorated him numerous times after the Rif campaign. The monarchic tradition was deeply rooted in the officer corps of the Spanish army. Franco impressed me right away, for the figure I saw facing me was not at all the one that had been described to me. I discovered someone completely different—affable, modest, far from the cliché of the Latin dictator. The expression in his eyes was of an astonishing vivacity, enhanced by a high-pitched (yet quiet) voice. I will take this opportunity to say that we accepted Spanish hospitality with gratitude, but it did not imply that we were "maintained" by the regime, as some people have supposed, with me being Franco's so-called "guest of honor"! We were political refugees in Spain, and simply for that, I am grateful to him.

The question of continuing my studies came up as soon as the summer ended. My mother would have like me to continue learning English, but Madrid had no English school, with the exception of the British Institute and it did not offer a complete curriculum. As I did not speak Spanish well yet, it was decided that the French *lycée* was the only alternative. It had a complete program of classes—and I stayed from the eighth to the twelfth grade.

My sister would take courses in economics at the University of Madrid. She traveled around Europe much more than me. A beautiful young woman, she was invited to various family celebrations in Germany, Portugal and the Netherlands. I think her vocation would have led her to study fine arts, a family talent she had inherited, but my mother did not approve of this choice because of the nude portraits she would have had to do. She thus worked for the Red Cross as an anesthetic nurse and, at age twenty-four, married Prince Karl of Leiningen, whose father was a naval officer who died as a Soviet prisoner, and whose mother was Maria Kirillovna of Russia. The couple emigrated to Canada to build their new life. After her departure, I remained alone with my mother. Everyone says that I was a devoted son: more than anything, I became an only, very protected son. What undoubtedly helped me in the way I was brought up was that my mother had a very great influence over me and very persuasive principles.

Before being enrolled in school, I already spoke French well: it was the language in which my parents spoke to each other, but above all the one spoken by my friends and used when we played hooky in Egypt. In Madrid, my sister and I had of course learned Spanish—which seemed easy to me—by ourselves. I immediately realized that to integrate into society, it was preferable to speak the language. Also, while the grand families of Madrid tended to be able to speak French, I noticed that the Portuguese were better at English, having historical ties with Great Britain—not to mention port, a sweet wine seriously appreciated on the other side of the Channel.

The French system was very different from what I had known up to that point. Students were taken much more seriously, and much earlier, which did not thrill me at the beginning. Another discovery—this one pleasant—classes were coeducational. At Victoria College, it was boys only, and we eagerly watched the girls leave Sacred Heart or the British Girls School located nearby. In Madrid, everyone was mixed together in the same classes. I remember especially the warm and eccentric Maya Picasso, as well as the daughters of the ambassador of Haiti, two brilliant students called France and Marseille. I met many interesting people, the children of Moroccan and Algerian exiles, and friends whose parents had moved for business reasons and then stayed. All in all, a quite cosmopolitan atmosphere, looked upon, however, with distrust by the Spanish authorities—rightly—as fostering secularism and leftism. The *lycée* had a very good reputation for its quality, but not from the point of view of its ideas. The intellectual ideology favored then in Spain was under the influence of religion, and I was struck by this. This certainly was a change from the multicultural, multireligious society of Egypt, where basically everyone did as he wished. One day we discovered that one of the teaching assistants—extremely popular, what's more—was a Spanish police inspector undoubtedly to monitor what we said there. We laughed a lot about it.

Our teachers instilled in us the image of a libertarian France and taught us to think by ourselves. To them I owe my open-mindedness. In the 1950s, most Spanish schools were assumed to be under the influence of the Catholic Church—it remains to be seen whether this was true and, if so, to what extent. But at the *lycée*, catechism classes were optional.

I learned and read a lot during these formative years. My way of thinking was structured by contact with our teachers, and with the benefit of hindsight, I can say that the years were very productive. It was at the *lycée* that I became a liberal. We studied and discussed a great number of subjects with no-holds-barred. Philosophy was an essential discovery for me; the manner in which it was taught particularly fascinated me. Our teacher, Mr. Grasset, had no compunction—he said what he wanted to say. I remember that one day he scolded me for having misspelled *Das Kapital*, of which he had made us read excerpts—this would have been rather subversive had it not been that we were reading it for his class.[1] And I can still hear the voice of M. Bertelangereau, our history teacher—"You, there, with the fabulous titles, are you listening to what I'm saying?" as I dreamily contemplated my pretty neighbor. The entire class burst out laughing. I really liked him and maintained a correspondence with him and then with his family, right up to now.

My friends from that time, and especially the girls, eagerly and passionately discussed politics. All talked about subjects in the news and the debates of the moment, backing up their opinions with arguments studded with fascinating quotes. When we married, my wife and I agreed that our children would be educated in this system. When, years afterward, I

---

1. I then read *Capital* by Marx, and while I recognize that certain sociological aspects are interesting, I've always thought that his preaching could be dangerous and goes well beyond the simple framework of a political theory. In general, I read much of the Communist press during all those years of exile so as to keep informed of what was going on behind the Iron Curtain.

went to the United States to study, I realized how much these few years of *lycée* had put me ahead of others. During my first year at university, some material that we covered—including history and international relations—I had already learned in my next-to-last year at the *lycée*. This is how the system is superior, even if it has a tendency to cram your head with idea after idea: you arrive at your final exams with many different concepts. However, it must be recognized that specializations are much more serious in the United States.

Madrid has never been a city shut in on itself—life there is always bubbling. Near us was the Puerta de Hierro Club, where young people from Madrid society liked to meet. However, I only went there occasionally. Of course, we kept up relations with the prominent Spanish families, either by affinity or at my mother's request. However, only a handful of young people from that social background attended my school. Tradition had them attend their own institutions, like the Rosales School or the one run by the Jesuits. It was the same for holidays: while we went once or twice in the summer to San Sebastian—where everyone at the time was going—we often went abroad with our mother, either to Portugal to stay with the Count of Paris, who moved there in 1955, or to my Uncle Umberto's, or to Switzerland for a change. I had also met my French family at the wedding of my cousin Henry of Orléans, the present Count of Paris. Also, I attended the wedding at Estoril of my first cousin Maria Pia of Savoy, the oldest daughter of King Umberto. She married Alexander of Yugoslavia. In the Portugal of those years, this marriage was a real fairy tale: more than three thousand Italians arrived by boat to attend it. Then we would also go to Italy once or twice a year, to the Savoyard fiefdom in the Piedmont.

In Spain, my mother met the Duke of Alba—his was the highest-ranking title in Spain—the one who had been ambassador to London during the war, at a delicate period for bilateral relations between Spain and the United Kingdom. During my schooling years, new students would arrive every year in the fall, or sometimes in the middle of the year, and were immediately adopted. There were thirty-six to forty of us per class. I also remember the son of a family of perfumers from Grasse, Yves de Chiris, who had a magnificent property near Seville where I was sometimes invited. They were lovers of bullfighting and the wide-open spaces. I have a particularly extraordinary memory of a visit during Holy Week. Several of my Spanish friends from the *lycée* went on to have political careers in the Spanish left, which resulted in me keeping up friendships in all walks of life—and this turned out to be useful during my term as prime minister. I also ran across some of them in Strasbourg: Miguel Angel Martinez, for example, who served for a long time as the Socialist vice president of the European Parliament, a man of admirable integrity. I also shared classes with Gregorio Peces-Barba, one of the fathers of the Spanish Constitution of 1978, a distinguished law professor and great friend. One day he invited me to lunch at the Cortes when he was presiding over the chamber. He had invited all the alumni from his year, and I can still see the astonishment of certain members from liberal and right-wing parties when they saw me in such company, not knowing that it was an alumni reunion: "What in the world is Simeon doing in the middle of all those socialists?" The qualities of humanness, intelligence and generosity have always seemed to me values to be placed above political convictions. I have never worn blinkers when it comes to friendship.

The *lycée* was then still housed in its original setting, a decrepit building covered with graffiti. My children, by contrast, studied in the superb establishment that today welcomes several thousand students. It is now the turn of my grandchildren to keep up the tradition.[2] I was awarded my *baccalauréat* in 1957, even winning a book by Bossuet as a prize. For the oral exam in philosophy, one of my examiners—upon learning that I was Bulgarian—revealed to me that he belonged to the Universal White Brotherhood, an esoteric Christian movement based on the teachings of Peter Deunov. Son of an Orthodox pope, Deunov was a sort of spiritual master who taught in Bulgaria in the period between the two wars. It was even said that he had gone through an initiation in Tibet! My father

---

2. General de Gaulle's minister, André Bettencourt, came for the inauguration since André Malraux refused to set foot in Francoist Spain.

was suspected of having been under his influence. I have always wondered whether the good grade I got for that oral exam was thanks to that connection. What a small world!

*

The first big family reunion goes back to those *lycée* years and consisted of a memorable cruise organized in 1954. This was Queen Frederica's idea to give a boost to Greece, still affected by its civil war, which had lasted until 1948. I would meet for the first time a vast number of my relatives. Because of the circumstances of my life, I knew only the closest among them, and we had made a plan to all get together after the Second World War. Queen Frederica asked the well-known ship owner, M. P. Nomikos, if he would kindly lend her a cruise ship, the *Agamemnon*. The combination of members of the royal families getting together and the magic places of ancient Greece made a great success of this epic journey. It was also a media event, focused as much on jump-starting tourism as on a large family reunion. Many reigning monarchs attended, such as Queen Juliana of the Netherlands, Grand Duchess Charlotte of Luxembourg, King Olaf of Norway, and the princes of Denmark, Sweden and Belgium, but also non-reigning monarchs such as the king and queen of Italy and those of Romania, Michael and Anne, as well as those of Spain, of Baden, of Bavaria, of Württemberg, of Schleswig-Holstein (whom we did not know), and of Hanover, including the parents of Queen Frederica—Catholics, Protestants, Orthodox and many others. Marie Bonaparte—well known for her work in psychoanalysis—was also present, despite being eighty years old, with her husband, Prince George of Greece. And the Count of Paris with several of his children, as well as my cousin Michael of Greece, were there, too. All of Europe of earlier times was represented in this gathering of imposing surnames.

This get-together was obviously meant to be relaxed, with a minimum of protocol. Many of these relatives were meeting again after a number of years of separation, while the young generation was getting acquainted. There was some talk of this being organized to arrange weddings, but I think that was exaggerated: only one marriage resulted.

The cruise began at Naples, our point of boarding. During the day, we visited archeological sites, monuments and marvelous sites, and walked the beaches. For meals, Queen Frederica found a clever system so that all the generations would mix: we had a hat where the names of all the participants were placed; in the morning, the men drew for the names of the ladies who would sit next to them, and in the evening the ladies did the same. It was quite amusing. We traveled to Corfu, where we visited the family home of George I of Greece, a villa called *Mon Repos*, and then on to Olympia, Delphi, Rhodes, Delos, Santorini, with the trip ending in Athens. There was a lunch at Tatoi, the residence of the royal family in the hills above the city. There was a second cruise in 1956, but its itinerary had to be curtailed because of the untimely Suez Canal crisis.

In 1955, to celebrate my turning eighteen years old, we organized a ceremony to mark my constitutional coming of age. We explicitly did this to underline that we were recognizing each of the stages in the dynastic tradition—that I had not abdicated and had no intention of doing so. In an improvised pavilion in our garden, a little altar was set up under the icon of Saint Boris, and we had the only Orthodox priest there in Madrid—a Russian—come to sing the *Te Deum*. My mother also wanted the portrait of my father to occupy a prominent place. Franco delegated three ministers to represent him, those for justice, foreign affairs and defense. My uncle, King Umberto, made the trip from Cascais to underline his support, as well as a good one hundred or so Bulgarians, coming from all over Europe and the United States. For the occasion, I was awarded the Grand Cross of the Order of Charles III—the highest civilian distinction given in Spain—by the head of state to mark his support for the cause of a free Bulgaria.

Our social life allowed me to mix with Spanish and foreign diplomats, members of the military, and intellectuals. I can say that I was also trained in the art of hosting, supervised by my mother and dear Misho during the dinners we organized at home. At the beginning, my mother usually invited people for 8:30 in the evening, but that was not done in

Madrid, since Spanish dinners at the time usually began at ten at night.[3] "We're coming for tea at your mother's," my friends would tease.

Gradually, after I turned eighteen, I would choose the people I saw and worked with. With them, I created a newsletter for Bulgarians in exile, so as to keep spirits up about our cause, and spread information concerning the life of emigrants. For me, this was a moment of emancipation. I was the sole link between many of these exiles. Little by little, I took charge of our enormous correspondence, then of the accounts for the household. These responsibilities made me mature faster. I met with many people because we were a political center. Ten years after the celebration of my coming of age, in 1965, we organized a similar event to remind people that I had never abdicated.

But to get back to my eighteenth birthday: the uprising in Budapest made me want to make a statement. I was deeply distressed by the images we had seen during those dark days. Russian repression represented a serious threat for us, and I felt that it was my duty to advise my fellow countrymen in Bulgaria to remain prudent. As young as I was, my impression was that the insurrection could not succeed since the power of the Soviet Union seemed unlimited.

During the 1950s, occupied countries each had a time slot on Spanish National Radio to broadcast information in their own language. These were programs responsible for encouraging opinions different from those distilled from Soviet propaganda; for us, this was clearly a space for freedom, and it was using this channel that I counted on broadcasting my speech. A Spanish ambassador whom I saw often and had become a friend, the marquis of Prat de Nantouillet—half French, as it happened—took me aside: "Listen, you are a refugee here, and courtesy demands that you ask prior permission from the head of state." I thus wrote a few words to Franco and went to deliver the letter in person to the door of his residence, El Pardo. The next day, a Saturday, at 8:30, an aide-de-camp presented himself at our house, telling me that even though Franco had gone hunting, he had sent me a letter. This was November 2, 1956. Franco's missive was four pages long, written

---

3. Fortunately, it has now become nine o'clock.

in longhand, and its central idea was that anything I could say from the outside might "awaken sensitivities that would divide any patriots who might rise up. . . . It is preferable to remain mute than to stammer, as we say in Spain. This is my loyal advice at this hour when we begin to see some hope for your Nation on the horizon." He had probably written this very early, and God knows he had other fish to fry than to answer a nineteen-year-old kid. I have never forgotten it, first as a political lesson but also as a consideration toward the king of Bulgarians. The letter is in my archives, like other important correspondence from those years. Franco always used these kinds of subtleties; they say it is a character trait of the people of Galicia, the classic joke being that if you meet one on the stairs, you never know whether he's going up or coming down. In addition, Franco's patience was proverbial. He never reacted to events immediately, taking the time to let others approach him. I think that this trait helped him to maneuver in many complex situations, and it is perhaps also one of the secrets of his longevity as head of state. He took the time to see things long term, risking the irritation of his adversaries, no matter what side they were on.

After that, I saw him several times at hunting parties or official events. Once I came of age, he decided that I should attend the annual Victory Parade, commemorating the end of the Civil War on April 1, 1939, and taking place on *la Castellana*, the large avenue that goes through the center of Madrid. My small loge was located facing his. Once the parade was over, Franco would host members of the military at the Royal Palace, standing next to the throne. This was to signify that Spain remained a monarchy. Right up to the last day of his life, he never took himself for its historic successor. Spain remained a kingdom, demonstrating Franco's political wisdom. Had he imposed his government alone, everything would have collapsed after his death, since basically the Spanish Falange had no ideological affinity with the monarchical concept and toned down neither its irony nor its criticisms about the Bourbons, whom they blamed for having dragged the country into civil war. Their followers were something like right-wing republicans.

During the last political meeting I had with him, in the early 1960s, I wanted to sound Franco out about the possibility of forming a Bulgarian government in exile, like those that had been formed for other occupied countries more or less all over Europe. The tendency of those years in exile circles was to set up parallel institutions defending democracy and legitimacy: no one recognized the people's republics in place. Above all, we wanted to demonstrate that an alternative to the regimes imposed by the Soviet Union existed. More than anything, we were fighting not to be forgotten. He thus received me in an office filled with bundles of papers and documents. After five minutes of polite chitchat, he launched into a thirty-minute tirade explaining to me in great detail his ideas on the system of vertical unions that he had established in Spain. And, at the end, he said to me, "I hope that one day, God willing, you will be able to apply this model in your liberated country." Knowing that audiences lasted no more than forty-five minutes, I understood that the meeting, though cordial, was at an end. He had very giftedly kicked the ball out of play. Or, rather, his silence (to a question I hadn't been able to ask) was his answer!

Afterward, I found out that the moment was particularly poorly chosen, since in 1961 Spain needed the support of an Eastern country in the Committee of Twenty-Four, in charge of applying the Declaration on Decolonization. Franco naturally had Gibraltar in mind, since it remained one of his great international political goals. It just so happened that the People's Republic of Bulgaria had supported the Spanish claim. Rather than being disappointed, I took our interview as a lesson in political cunning. Inwardly, I said to myself, "Bravo to the artist!" Above all, I realized the importance of backstage diplomacy.

In November 1975, Franco died. We went through a week when we knew nothing of the real state of his health. I attended the funeral in the monumental basilica carved into a granite hill, the *Valle de los Caídos*, impressively located not far from El Escorial in a spot he had chosen at the end of the war to render homage to its victims. This funerary tribute—unique in the world—had been put together at the cost of huge human efforts to gather together in the same spot all the soldiers who had perished during the civil war from both sides. The day itself was astonishing and taught me a lesson about the fragility of power.

The marriage of King Boris III to Princess Giovanna of Savoy, daughter of King Victor Emmanuel III of Italy, in Assisi in 1930. King Ferdinand I is in the foreground.

The royal palace in the center of Sofia.

The royal couple in 1938 with Maria Luisa and Simeon.

Princess Clémentine of Orléans, daughter of Louis Philippe, in Sofia in 1889.

In the gardens of Vrana Palace during the war.

Wearing the cadet uniform in Sofia (1943).

A detachment of the Royal Guard on an excursion around Borovets.

Prince Kyril and Princess Eudoxia in Bulgaria.

Burial of King Boris at the Rila Monastery, August 28, 1943.

The diplomatic passport given to the royal family when they left Bulgaria in September 1946 was only valid for three months.

Starting in 1943, as head of state, King Simeon appeared on Bulgarian banknotes as well as on postage stamps.

Coming-of-age ceremony of the young King Simeon II in Madrid, on June 16, 1955, in the presence of King Umberto of Italy.

Brother and sister in the 1950s in Madrid.

The wedding of Princess Maria Luisa in Cannes, in 1957.

With Princess Sophia of Greece and King Michael of Romania, in Athens.

Wedding, exiting the chapel of Vevey, in January 1962.

With the princess of Monaco for the wedding of King Constantine in Athens in 1964.

A visit to Jerusalem, to the Orthodox Patriarchate, in 1964.

With Generalissimo Chiang Kai-shek in Taipei in 1969.

With his family in the house in Madrid.

With Juan Carlos for a hunt at the home of George Alexiadès in Spain.

Meeting with John Paul II after the handing over of the Holy Shroud in Turin, in 1984.

With Maurice Druon in Morocco.

King Hassan II and King Juan Carlos at the house in Madrid during his last official visit in 1987.

With King Hassan at the golf course of Marrakesh in 1991.

The whole family in the garden of the house in Madrid.

The Spanish royal couple visiting Sofia before the return of King Simeon in 1993.

King Simeon's triumphant return to Bulgaria after fifty years of exile in May 1996.

Balloons released into
the sky over Sofia.

Queen Giovanna in Estoril, Portugal.

On the day of the swearing-in ceremony in Parliament in 2001, in the presence of the Ortho-dox patriarch of the Bulgarian Church.

With President Jacques Chirac in Paris, during an official visit.

Another very moving experience during the 1996 return journey by train to Pleven.
© ANTOINE GYORI / SYGMA / CORBIS

"This 'unique' life would not have been like this without Margarita's patience, which has remained the same throughout all these years." —Simeon II
CRÉATION STUDIO FLAMMARION

The Basilica of Santa Cruz was bursting at the seams with thousands of people. The entire esplanade was covered with an enormous crowd, including units of the different military forces, the universities, Falangist organizations and the whole of the diplomatic corps. The Spanish have a very keen sense of setting the stage for death. A true show. Among other things, I remember the strange presence of Imelda Marcos in the middle of this areopagus; she was an exotic beauty, heavily made-up, rather tall and with a certain charm; she had eyes that never moved, even when she laughed, which many people found quite alarming. The impression she gave me was that of a woman greedy for power. On that frigid day, she hardly went unnoticed, for she was followed around by an aide-de-camp holding a parasol in delicate lace over her to protect her from a sun that was nowhere to be seen.

At the end of the ceremony, while I remained a bit to pray, I was able to observe those in the front rows surge together, as if a single man, behind the new head of state, King Juan Carlos. In the ranks of the government, only a single man remained, in uniform, seated, his features sagging and his back bent over. Large tears ran down his face; he was missing his master and friend. This was the minister of labor, José Antonio Girón, a historically loyal member of the Falange. Upon leaving, I stopped by him to say a few words of comfort. Later, I mentioned it to the king, thinking of the crowd of senior officials that had swarmed around him in order to be seen at his side. *Sic transit gloria mundi* . . . The page had already been turned.

We all felt the coming of the end of an era. Since 1969, it had been clear that my cousin Juan Carlos would succeed Franco as head of state, so carefully the public opinion and the young prince had been prepared for the transition. Franco had created the title of Prince of Spain for him. However, he had made no statements concerning the name of his heir, leaving free rein to all kinds of speculation, from Alphonso, Duke of Cádiz, who had married Franco's granddaughter Carmen, to the Carlists, and especially Juan Carlos's father, Don Juan, Count of Barcelona, but with whom the *Generalissimo* did not really get along. This period of uncertainty had lasted ten years. As for Juan Carlos, he had come back to

Spain to prepare his admission into the military academies. For his 1962 marriage in Athens to Princess Sophia of Greece and Denmark, Franco had given an important sign to show his favor, sending a war ship with his naval minister aboard to represent him. Franco opted for what was basically a return to legitimacy, but with the younger face of my cousin.

In April 1969, the first military parade took place with Juan Carlos at its head, appearing next to the head of state, a sort of official designation. It was feared that Falange sympathizers would boo and that disappointed partisans of Don Juan would express their unhappiness. Franco was very fond of the young prince, his successor at last. This choice was not an easy one to accept for my uncle Don Juan, himself the son of Alphonse XIII. In exile at Estoril, so as to stay as close as possible to Spain, he had successfully built an image of himself as a dedicated democrat, in the tradition of the liberalism of Alphonse XII and thus able to incarnate a true alternative. I first got to know him in 1954 during the trip through Greece when, after eyeing me, he said, "So, you're the one who's lucky enough to live in Spain?" Don Juan, Count of Barcelona, was perceived as a very valuable alternative, even by enemies of the monarchy. A man with very great presence, he was open, big-hearted and overflowing with extraordinary *joie de vivre*, the contrast with Franco being almost inevitable. It was only well after his son had mounted the throne that he officially renounced his rights. In 1977, at a very emotional ceremony at Zarzuela, the residence of the sovereigns in Madrid, Don Juan pronounced a few very clear words, "Restorations of monarchies do not take place as they should, but only as they can," before speaking the words renouncing his dynastic rights. Finally, standing at attention in front of his son, he proclaimed, "*¡Majestad, por España, todo por España, viva España, viva el Rey!*" Without being there but having only watched on television, and despite all the years that have passed, I still have tears in my eyes when I think of this event. Some of my children who were old enough still remember it as well.

Being close to both father and son, and given the complexity of their reciprocal situations, I had at their request shuttled back and forth to Portugal to convey certain family messages. This task was painful for me, but I did my best. I believe that Juan Carlos could do no other than to accept the role reserved for him by General Franco if there was to be a return to a monarchy, while still envisaging a system guaranteeing the unity of Spain. When Juan Carlos was proclaimed king in the grand Church of Saint Jerome, behind the Prado Museum, I did not go, not wanting to be bad luck as an "ex," like a bird of bad omen. At the death of his father in 1993, the king had his remains placed at El Escorial. His tombstone is engraved with "Juan III," not just Count of Barcelona. This was a moving ceremony, one that gave me the impression that I was seeing all the pomp and glory of the Spain of Philip II.

CHAPTER EIGHT

Apprenticed to Life

ONCE I EARNED MY *BACCALAURÉAT*, I SPENT AN ENTIRE YEAR TAKING courses in law and political science at the University of Madrid. But my coming of age had brought its share of family responsibilities, a situation that was not obvious for a boy of my age. When I turned twenty, I was not so sure that I wanted to rush into what would be the never-ending whirlwind of adult life. I soon had to become involved with Bulgarians in exile and to take over—at her request—my mother's complex affairs. Although I was not alone in dealing with those obligations, I felt it was better for me to continue with my studies for a time. My mother was of the opinion that a young man must fulfill the obligation of doing military service. I jumped on that opportunity and pushed away my professional working life for two years—even if, in fact, it had already started long before, with the death of my father. We began searching for a practical solution, asking for advice from those around us, and following up the leads at our disposal. We thought of Sandhurst and Saint-Cyr, where I thought I could get in, but I didn't want to give the impression of preferring one over the other, since that would have, alas, been interpreted in a political manner. For the same reason, I did not follow up on the idea of enrolling at the prestigious military school at Zaragoza, since I did not want to be seen as too "Spanish." This is when a letter arrived from an American friend of my parents, who had been posted to Sofia during the war and was a former governor of Pennsylvania, suggesting Valley Forge Military Academy and College, located not far from Philadelphia. I remembered the man very well, as he had been widely talked about when he got in a fight with some German officers in a cabaret in Sofia, resulting in his being transferred to be the American representative in Ankara—in fact, a promotion.

To be eligible for the Academy of West Point, the most prestigious military academy in the United States, a foreigner must be directly nominated by the president. But I did not know General Eisenhower, and so I needed to find an alternative. I thus arrived in New York, and then in Philadelphia, in August 1958, after crossing the Atlantic aboard a four-engine TWA Constellation—one of the jewels of Lockheed—with a stopover in the Azores.

I immediately liked Valley Forge, quickly adopting the academy rhythm and the rules and regulations that were quite new for me. Above all, I was happy to socialize with young people my age and to make new friends. I discovered a whole new atmosphere, and only the lieutenant general, head of the school, knew who I was. As my passport was Italian, in the name of Rylski, no one tried to find out anything more. And thank God, in America, titles have no importance. Only an employee of the establishment, a Bulgarian, called a "DP,"[1] recognized me, and I had to make him swear to say nothing.

In June 1959, I received my diploma, having obtained the rank of second lieutenant in the Army Reserves. In fact, the two years of courses were fantastic. This was a classic American college, added with very strict discipline and classes in military organization, tactics and sports. The spectacular parades in which we participated on holidays required a great deal of work. I remember that our company marched through the streets of Philadelphia. Another time, we were sent to a charity tea held at the house of the entrepreneur John Kelly—father of Princess Grace, whom I met up with some years later in Monaco under my other identity. I was also able to take a course in law, a subject that already interested me greatly and which I would need in future. One of my professors, a Freemason, was a passionate teacher of his ideas on the notion of justice. In class, we could say whatever came into our minds, but it went without saying that we were not to touch the basic principles of the Constitution,

---

1. *Displaced person*, as refugees from Eastern Bloc countries (among others) were called.

one of the oldest written documents of its kind still in force. I understood that the American system was that of freedom within a framework, especially in the context of the Cold War years with their exacerbated patriotism. No one dared touch the person of the president, regarded almost as sacred, like a royal family. Half a century later, I can see that opinions have profoundly changed in this regard, the Watergate scandal having been the trigger for the collapse in the status of the president. Today, political campaigns seem to me more and more controversial, and no one is spared anything in this media-obsessed society.

One really needs to realize what America represented at the time to a young man of my age. Like most people of my generation who had known the trials of war, I found it a fascinating world. Seen from Madrid, from still traumatized postwar Europe, the United States seemed an El Dorado. This may sound silly, but the cult of individual happiness and the "success story" of Americans greatly pleased me, as did their positive attitude. This was what we needed. Also, the first time I saw the buffets laden with food on display in the restaurants where we ate with friends on weekends, I could hardly believe my eyes. I didn't know that such abundance was possible. Americans truly lived at a level of comfort that was entirely different from that to which we were accustomed.

I regretted that I could not stay longer, as some of my friends did, taking advantage of that time to discover the interior of the country and crossing the continent from East to West, by car, hitchhiking, or traveling by Greyhound bus. This sort of breath of freedom would have done me good, especially at age twenty. Unfortunately, I didn't have the time to follow their lead, as I had to get back to Madrid. I think that I really missed those couple of months—afterward—because since then my life has never really slowed down. I would never stop dreaming of Route 66 and its infinite horizons. I have never had the pleasure of feeling carefree, and it's a shame.

During my stay, I was, however, able to take advantage of rare vacation time to leave the Academy, which allowed me to better understand the American mentality at the time. I want to highlight an anecdote that impressed me deeply even if it happened at the school where I was able to see the other side of the (sometimes perhaps too shiny) coin. At the end-of-year ball, we were allowed to dance with the wives of officers. I asked the wife of one of my instructors, a member of the Mohawk tribe, to join me on the dance floor. She was a Navajo herself. A week later, at the end of a course, my instructor took me aside to thank me for my consideration. It was then that I understood that it must not have happened often, and I believed that I had seen evidence of a form of racism that shocked me. What an odd country, I thought! A country that is so open and tolerant in terms of its democratic lifestyle and so rigid with issues of race and even religion. Without wanting to generalize—an important consideration for me—I have often been wary of moral lessons coming from the other side of the Atlantic. I said to myself that each one of us has a worldview and that the one defended by Europe was nothing to be ashamed of. Also, there was not a single black among us, neither in the cadet corps nor among our instructors. But a lot of water has flowed under the bridge since then. When I returned to the United States for the fiftieth anniversary of my graduating class, the band leader was Thai in origin, several students were African American, and young women had enrolled as cadets.

I have kept some friends from this period, but fewer than from Egypt because I didn't stay as long. For the European that I am, America is another world, one where it is more difficult to become close to people with a mentality that is fundamentally different despite identical appearances.

I was able to go to Philadelphia, Washington and New York several times. The people I would socialize with were elegant and rather wealthy, with a whiff of old Europe. But their way of thinking was so different that I was an alien for them. Only a few rare individuals had any idea of my country of origin or of the history of my family. If America is isolated, it is not only by geography but also by the fact that this great country built itself cut off from the rest of the world. I remember a couple I knew where the wife was French: *He married a French girl* . . . the rumor went, with voices full of awe and some degree of insinuation about the nature of her morals—loose, of course. The Bulgarians I met in America were very proud of having become citizens of this nation after the trials of the statelessness that had led them there. They expressed a real desire to integrate, and above all great joy and—this was astonishing—a sort of self-conviction that they had always been "Americans." The *melting pot* we kept hearing about had become a reality for them. Yet the ethnic jokes and segregation in the Southern states shocked me. It is for this reason that I felt so European—*Europeanist*, perhaps—and happy finally to have a return ticket in my pocket. The DPs whom I hung out with at school had no choice: they had landed in America with a one-way ticket and could not return to their respective countries. Indeed, had they any wish to do so? Where would they go?

As for me, I knew that duty required me to return to Europe: to Spain first, and then wherever I needed to go to help my refugee compatriots who continued to come out from behind the Iron Curtain. The question of Bulgaria was never very far from my thoughts, even if I tried to take some advantage of this parenthesis of calm. At a dinner at the Spanish Embassy in Washington, where I had gone for the occasion, I met a number of American personalities, among them Allen Dulles, head of the CIA, and the secretary of state for foreign affairs, John Foster Dulles—I remember that one of the guests dared to say to my face that we were an underdeveloped country! I saw red, allowing myself to respond, "Sir, if you have Bulgaria in mind, we might be underdeveloped in your view but certainly not under-cultured!" Of course, I was thinking of the average level of American general knowledge, and I think everyone understood that. I was ready for a candid discussion with this person, had he wanted one. I have always had been appalled by the sense of superiority of big countries. No one has an innate right to speak to us in such a paternalistic tone: we have our history, our identity, our poets, our writers, our scientists and our painful experiences as well. I have noticed this attitude in my life with certain representatives of great powers who give us the impression that we are still children in short pants. When we entered the European Union in 2007, I certainly felt the idea of a hierarchy with the founding countries, but never condescension. We were piloted—yes, sometimes as if we were being tutored—but in serious discussions we were on equal footing. The Europeans behaved very well.

It makes me think of Zhou Enlai, one of the founders of the Chinese Communist Party, who was asked one day what he thought of the French Revolution: "It's still a little early to say." That's an answer I respect.

When we went to New York, my friends and I were watched over by the Military Police and we had to behave. There were whole streets in Manhattan where we were not allowed to go—Third Avenue, for instance, off limits because of its bad reputation.

These forays were the setting for delightful anecdotes. I had the opportunity of spending an evening with the future queen of Spain and her brother Constantine, crown prince of Greece, who was traveling in the United States at the invitation of the secretary of defense, Robert McNamara. Outfitted in my best dress uniform, I accompanied them to the Waldorf Astoria for dinner. Imagine my surprise to find that the waiters were dressed practically identically, so the impression I was trying to make on young Sophia was ruined. The next day, at the request of Queen Frederica, I attended a musical on Broadway. As we left, I saw photographers rush toward Rainier and Grace of Monaco, who were in the same section of the orchestra that we were!

During the same period, I went to see Maria Luisa (already living in Toronto) for Thanksgiving. We thus cooked our first turkey together. Another time, it was my mother who made the trip from Europe to visit me in the United States. She was very proud to see her son in uniform, and we have some beautiful pictures of our time together. We wrote often, for there was only one telephone line at the Academy, and to use it, you had to stand in line. In the years that followed, my mother continued to go to Canada regularly, especially as her grandchildren began to grow up. I know she suffered, for she did not like the New World and said so straight out. It was another universe for her. But she pursued her trips without complaining, at least once a year until she turned eighty. My sister told me over the telephone that she counted the days until her return to Portugal. Family was sacred for my mother. She adored telling stories and talking about Bulgaria to her grandchildren. I admired her will to continue to travel when the country was not really her cup of tea—she who was so sensitive to the formal side of things and to the etiquette of her background.

In the course of those two years, meetings with Bulgarian communities went on in the United States, and even in Canada, where my sister served as a relay, organizing meetings for me. In 1959 in New York, for example, I was invited to celebrate the New Year with six hundred fellow countrymen. I was touched to be so warmly welcomed so far from our country. All of them had eventful personal histories that they wanted to share with me. My own memories came back to me as I listened to theirs. We understood each other. In the line of people who wanted to shake hands with me, I saw two families with Asian features speaking perfect Bulgarian. They told me they were Kalmyks, from the ethnic groups that had been so mistreated by Stalin. Some of them had been able to reach Bulgaria during my father's time. I found it astonishing to be meeting these Buddhist descendants of Genghis Khan in a grand hotel in New York. That, too, is America: the entire world meets there. I think there is not a people on earth that doesn't have a representative there. A sort of Noah's Ark of humanity.

Bulgaria had known two distinct emigration movements: a first wave in 1923 after the rightist repression, which can be explained by the economic difficulties of the years between the two wars, and then another after 1944, a flight from the Communists. These two flows were quite separate since they were politically antagonistic, one basically against royalty and the other leaning toward monarchy through anti-Communism. But it was not so clear-cut: many emigrants from the 1923 wave—who were not favorable to us, a priori—made a distinction between my father and his prime minister, Alexander Tsankov. I must also point out that Bulgarians, unlike the Greeks or the Armenians, never organized themselves abroad. Each time I was able to do so, I tried to smooth over the tensions without ever trying to dominate, while trying not to give the impression of giving a preference to one group or another. In Paris, for example, there was a small core group of antimonarchist republicans. Well, over time, we reconciled. I challenged no one and met with everyone.

In Canada, as I have already said, my sister helped me a great deal to meet our compatriots who were spread out everywhere and to try to patch things up between scattered coteries, whenever possible. I was struck that our fellow citizens could not seem to unify: our chronic individualism prevented us from founding broad movements. Unlike the Poles, Greeks, and Italians, especially in North America, where united communities were already established, we had no lobbies. I was devoted to my mission, and I wanted to see with my own eyes what people thought. Often, there were priests who helped me, and we attended numerous religious services. Well afterward, I returned to the United States several times to continue these encounters. For example, in Portland in the 1990s, my wife and I sponsored a meeting that brought together more than a hundred Bulgarian children adopted by American families. Most of them were of Romany origin, and it was touching to see how happy people were to welcome them. Some parents asked me for books of texts to teach them the history of Bulgaria.

*

In 1959, I came back to Madrid with a beautiful American car as part of my baggage, a Chevrolet convertible with large tail fins. I went to pick it up at the Port of Algeciras. I can still see the astonishment with which this beauty was greeted as it was hoisted up out of the ship by crane—containers didn't exist at the time. There is no doubt whatsoever that it helped me charm my future wife! What a time that was . . . I had to sell it later, alas, as I didn't have room for it. But I did have it long enough to make a few trips, particularly to Portugal to see my cousins from France, especially the girls, whom I found attractive and fun.

Naturally, we flirted, as one did, and I was charmed by Anne, the present duchess of Calabria. At the last moment, her father, my uncle, the Count of Paris, suggested that the question of religion was important and that our children would need to be raised as Catholics. Because I was an Orthodox king, this was not acceptable to me. Uncle Henry had a very marked influence on his eleven children, and it seemed to me impossible to go against his will.

During the summer of 1960, I took to the road to go to Sweden, joined by a friend who was older than me. We went unnoticed in the Europe of the time, where there were still few fast-speed highways. We liked taking smaller roads, staying in country hotels to admire the charm of the small towns where we made stops. In a certain way, I was getting to make the great road trip that had tempted me in America and that I still hadn't gotten out of my mind. I remember an anecdote that says a lot about Swedish civic mindedness: a policewoman stopped me to have me pick up a cigarette butt that I had thrown out of the car window. I did so immediately, very embarrassed to have been caught doing such a thing.

With my Bernadotte cousins, I spent a few days at the Solliden Palace located on the island of Öland, in the southern part of the country. My mother was perhaps hoping that I would meet one of the girl cousins whose mother was a Saxe-Coburg, with an eye to a future marriage. All four of them were lively and spirited. I was especially taken with Désirée, a given name that has remained in the family as a souvenir of her ancestor Désirée Clary. She said, "Simeon, I'm very fond of you, but one day I want to marry a Swede!" And that is precisely what she did with Count Silfverschiöld. During this trip, I had the good fortune to attend with my cousins in Stockholm the premiere of the famous film *A King in New York*, in which Charlie Chaplin plays a deposed king to whom a thousand ridiculous incidents occur. I must admit that this comedy saved me from many pitfalls and taught me while I was still young that my independence would come through hard work.

The idea of being a parasite had always frightened me, as had that of using my title or social position in return for favors. I never wanted to be one of those little kings looked at with an air of pity. For all that, I made it my identity, without renouncing it. Nor did I ever create a court in exile. I have a sense of the ridiculous that is particularly strong—my Orléans side, practical and pragmatic. I have sometimes felt a prisoner of this heritage. "My goal in life is to look like my cat thinks I am" is a quote sent to me one day by my sister, since I have a cat that I am very fond of. Replace *cat* with *people*, and you understand part of my life and my behavior. It has not always been easy. I have been caricatured as boring and distant, all because I've never created any scandal and my personality is not juicy enough for certain media. I have always tried not to judge individuals but to learn from them, to consider people for what they are, even during unpleasant conversations. I matured quickly and continued to learn.

On the return trip from Stockholm, my friend and I covered the three thousand kilometers separating us from Madrid in barely three days, relieving each other at the wheel. At the French border, some truck drivers asked the two "Americans" that we seemed to be—I had kept my

Pennsylvania license plates—to have a cup of coffee with them. They asked us what we were doing sleeping in the parking lot, like them, when we had such a beautiful car. On the road to Zaragoza, we gave a ride to two hitchhikers, American girls of Baltic origin. Forty years later, when I became prime minister, I got a letter from one of them who had recognized me on television!

*

Once back in Madrid, I was swamped by an avalanche of work. My mother determined the priorities in what was awaiting me and where she needed my help. "*Fai tu!*" she would say to me; it was time I took up my responsibilities—it was now time for me to take care of her. At barely age twenty-three and inexperienced, I was managing various files on on-going projects.

All of a sudden, I found myself up to my neck in all of this. Until my marriage in 1962, I barely saw the time pass in these first years of adulthood. We had already discussed these questions before, so I was not ignorant about the various subjects at hand. I had met our administrators and bank managers. My initiation took place progressively. The financial aspects did not put me off—yet another character trait inherited from my Orléans ancestors—I asked questions and carefully reviewed the spread sheets presented to me by our accountants.

I put an end to my studies. It is one of my great regrets that I did not continue at university. I'd have been tempted to study for a doctorate—in law or philosophy, but above all in theology, so as to explore the nature of the practical links between our daily life and the teachings of the Evangelists. Then again, what possible use could it be to me? I must say that, thanks to prominent Italian lawyers, led by the very distinguished Carlo d'Amelio, whom I met regularly during our Italian property claims, I certainly learned as much as any law degree student! I also fed on a diet of texts by the great thinkers like Tocqueville, who vaccinated me against embracing fanciful solutions.

Still, I envy people who have earned two or three PhD degrees and those who have a profound knowledge of a subject, like historians or archeologists. I believe I could have done much more, but my mother didn't encourage me, finding that I was already of an age when I should stop learning and start doing. For her, I was henceforth the man of the house.

Among the things I took care of, one in particular was important to us: the case to settle the estate of my grandfather, King Victor Emmanuel III of Italy, begun in 1948, and then that of my grandmother, Queen Elena, as of 1952. My mother and her younger sister, Maria Francesca of Savoy, had asked me to represent them in what became a series of never-ending court cases.

I rushed to meet public notaries in Rome and London so that they could explain the nature of the legal disputes to me. I took a certain pleasure in all of it. The experience helped me prepare for my future professional life and to become familiar with the business world. It provided me with a close look at history and its realities. But above all, I was very proud to be of service to my mother and to become relevant to her. She had absolute confidence in me. A last non-negotiable advantage: financially, our everyday fare improved as we won our legal cases in Italy.

At the fall of monarchy, the transfer of our private holdings to the state had already begun. This was spoliation in good and due form. Several branches of my mother's family were represented: that of my cousin Moritz of Hesse and that of my aunt, the Countess Calvi. I had a great deal of respect for Aunt Anda (as we called her in the family), a woman who had been very beautiful, with very Montenegrin looks and delicate, elongated features. She was a great hunter, skilled with a pistol, at ease in any situation—on horseback, in the bush—charming, yet as hard on herself as she was on others. She was very different from my mother, who also had a strong personality, but one that was expressed differently. We were all on our best behavior around her. White haired and over seventy, she caught two poachers who had broken into her house in Ostia and kept her gun pointed at them while she called the *carabinieri* with her free hand. We listened to her opinions and advice very carefully.

I was both flattered and frightened by the task entrusted to me. And this only got worse when I understood that the litigation was going to last longer than expected, until the early 1980s. I discovered all kinds of legal details and through them became acquainted with the history of my Italian ancestors. The palace administrators had meticulously detailed the differences between the various kinds of property. Nothing was left to chance. On each object was a mark: "C" for crown property, "D" for state property, and "PP" for private property. It was simple to understand and respect, but a decision had been made in the postwar political context, and, all of a sudden, the Italian royal family no longer had any belongings.

Eventually, the Italian courts ruled in our favor, which is in accordance with a country under the rule of law. Over forty-some years, we won eleven cases in all. We took up this legal battle to ensure the family's continuity. A small part of the property of King Victor Emmanuel III was abroad. I am thinking especially of a bank account that had been opened in London at Hambros Bank by his father, King Umberto I, who had purchased a life insurance policy, something that was not common at all at the time, particularly among royal families. My ancestor was assassinated in Monza in 1900, shot to death by an anarchist, and finally, it was thanks to the resulting indemnity that we could go on with our respective exiled lives. An amusing consequence: When Italy sided with Germany in the Second World War, the English got their hands on these assets, investing them in "Victory Bonds," with the intention of punishing the "enemy." In September 1943, Italy joined the Allies and the funds were restored. Unintentionally, this forced investment was beneficial to us, for the firms where we had invested in stock before the war had all gone bankrupt since. I advised my mother to keep the account open, since we were fifth-generation clients—something unusual.

As of the mid-1950s, the financial conditions of the family improved. Not that we were in need, but we had to be careful each time we bought something. As soon as she could, my mother made us share what she received from other sources, even after my wedding. I can say that a substantial portion of these sums was used to meet the needs of Bulgarian refugees who asked us for help and financial support. This was in the form of scholarships for students, help in medical emergencies, charitable works that we supported and myriad other needs that presented themselves over many years. This reminds me of an anecdote on the same subject: My mother knew that King Boris had opened a bank account in Switzerland, and we finally discovered it in a bank in Interlaken, where my father enjoyed staying. What a disappointment—there were only

12,000 Swiss francs each for my sister and me. This was the fruit of his savings from 1918 to 1943! When you think about the amounts revealed in cases of political corruption nowadays, I think there needs to be a bit of restraint in the criticism made after the fact, as on the question of the cost of monarchies, a trite old news story that is regularly trotted out. Polemics are never a good omen; I distrust snap judgments.

In Rome, we met to work right in the palace, in the offices of the *Amministrazione Eredi Savoia*, which took care of managing the family properties. Basically, I was happy about these trips, during which I met up with friends again, from the Alexandria period—people who had left Egypt after the arrival of Nasser to power—children of friends of my mother's and my Hesse cousins whom I liked very much. I took pleasure in perfecting my Italian, which I knew only phonetically. Words related to legal vocabulary soon had no secrets for me.

The mildness of the climate made these stays a great pleasure, even if they were exhausting because of the amount of work that awaited me each time. It is true that I wanted to study the files myself, a habit that I kept on having during my years as prime minister. But I was happy to leave Madrid and find myself somewhere else. Rome was an interesting mix, with a sort of light and friendly Mediterranean mix, even if Roman society had the reputation of being quite closed to outsiders. It was a city that I didn't know well, about which my mother had told me a lot and which remained virgin territory for me.

I remember having attended a magnificent Giacomo Puccini *Turandot* at the Scala in Milan, where the scenery had been done by my cousin Enrico d'Assia,[2] a remarkable painter. The opera was dedicated to his mother, my Aunt Mafalda of Savoy, a young girl at the time it was composed. The evening of the première, I met the famous painter Giorgio de Chirico whose work—right on the edges of Surrealism—I appreciated. There was also a Bulgarian sculptor whom I knew well, the darling of Rome at the time. Like me, Assen Peikov had left Bulgaria when the Communists took over and had married an Italian *marchesa*. He sported large rings on each thumb, had a huge mustache, and liked

---

2. He chose the Italian transcription of his name, Heinrich von Hesse, since he lived in Rome.

exercising his Asian charm—he had slightly slanting eyes. I was proud of knowing such a personality, someone who had done so well abroad. We delighted in seeing each other and liked sharing relaxed moments when we spoke Bulgarian to one another. He had done statues of well-known personalities, including Fellini, and another in particular of Leonardo da Vinci holding in his hand the famous model of the helical airscrew as an allegory. He gave me a small replica, which has never left my side.

Occasionally, my wife accompanied me on these quick trips, since she knew how time-consuming meetings with lawyers were. We took great pleasure in rediscovering Rome together. Margarita liked my cousin Enrico, who lived at the Villa Polissena, where he often hosted friends and relatives. These were, in a way, years of the *dolce vita*, and I was quite happy since, after all, I'm half Italian. I felt a part of my personality reveal itself—a more relaxed side, perhaps, even if that is a cliché on the nature of Italians. As in all countries, cultural differences exist, countless ways of living. But it is above all a rich life—tragic but also comic. If Italians give the impression of not taking themselves seriously, it is not true. I often went to the movies to see films by Fellini, Vittorio De Sica and Pasolini, whom I liked a lot. The reality in them blended with wonderful poetry. I periodically dropped in at the *Circolo della Caccia*, the "Hunting Club," one of the oldest clubs in town, of which I am an honorary member. Housed in the magnificent Borghese Palace, I met many members of the Italian aristocracy there, names linked to the history of Rome and of the country.

Among the properties restored to us was the Pollenzo Estate, in the Piedmont, a Middle Ages pastiche whose moat had been emptied to house the cages of wildcats. My grandmother Elena used the name Pollenzo as a pseudonym when she wanted to travel abroad. This was the first of the possessions that we were compelled to sell to satisfy the claims of the various heirs. I recently saw it again when on a short trip tracing this inheritance, and I must recognize that most of these dwellings are now extremely well maintained, often by local authorities or by the state. There was also the fortified castle of Sarre in the Aosta Valley, a hunting lodge for my grandparents, its walls covered with hunting trophies. The story of its acquisition is interesting: it was during an expedition in these mountains that Victor Emmanuel II, having glimpsed this fortress hemmed in by steep hills, ordered his steward to buy it. But the latter misunderstood his indications and bought the one facing it on the opposite hill! In Turin, the Palace of Racconigi, where my Aunt Mafalda was married, also had to be sold. And finally, the Villa Savoy property in Rome, whose grounds were larger than those of the Vatican, was also jointly held by the family and sold. My grandparents had lived there, and my mother grew up there. We had had to take responsibility for the royal palace, the Quirinal, which now belongs to the republic. After the war, King Farouk had generously rented the Villa Savoy as a residence for his ambassador in order to help us avoid confiscation alongside the rest of our properties by the Italian government. I already thought at the time that the right to property, as well as that of inheriting from one's parents, should be sacred in any democratic country under the rule of law. The economic aspect being only the consequence of a moral right. I was in a front row seat to witness this, since each of these properties had often been owned by the same family for several centuries and survived the vagaries of history through wise marriages and rigorous management. I didn't like the idea of our parting with this wonderful legacy. We all questioned the need, but we couldn't do otherwise. Reality forced us to do so, making us sad, if not bitter. I know that more than one signed reluctantly. There were already eighteen of us in my generation alone, and I don't see how we could have maintained this inheritance without having substantial revenues. The land included with these properties, where there was any, fell very short of providing enough income to cover the necessary expenditures.

King Umberto stepped down from these negotiations out of discretion. In fact, he was excluded from inheriting, the republic having attributed to itself his share of the estate. Without hesitation, my mother and my aunts made the decision that each would pay a fifth of their share to their brother so that he would not be penalized. Needless to say, this gesture was both very elegant and generous. Nowadays, such behavior would be extremely rare, but for the generation that preceded me it was a question of principle.

In his turn, my Uncle Umberto designated my cousin Moritz and me as executors of his will. At his death in 1983, we put our noses to the grindstone, and this went on until 1986. If I bring up this particular memory, it is because I was very fond of my mother's brother. He always impressed me, and even more so after his death, when I immersed myself in his interior world and his library. I realized that he was a man of profound spirituality, with an acute sense of duty and a political vision steeped in history.

He lived in Cascais in Portugal, in the superb Villa Italia whose construction was made possible by a generous group of Italian monarchists. But he set himself up as if in a monk's cell: his bedroom had a bed without a box spring, a bedside lamp and a night table on which there was a worn little Italian royal flag and a breviary. A lightbulb hung from the ceiling with no globe or shade. I discovered a personality that was totally different from the one I had regularly come across for decades. Nor was his destiny among the most enviable—subjected to the strictest paternal authority and having to live with the impossible dream of restoring the monarchy.

His last instructions were precise. He had planned everything down to the least detail. It was with interest and abnegation that I did the work, which for me was a way of thanking him for being the model that he was. The number of bequests was impressive; he wanted to forget no one, no institution—he even specified the number of masses to be said after his death. The succession was long and difficult, for some of the provisions made by my uncle were not legally formulated. Jewelry was divided on the principle of scrupulous equality among the children, with usufruct for Queen Marie-José. I must admit that my situation as the holder of full powers was not easy. I had the impression that I was meddling in matters that were not my business, and I was too close to the family to be impassive. Moritz and I had been informed of our appointment only two days before his death, which had dismayed us to the highest degree.

On the Montenegrin family side, there was no estate. My grandmother Elena had helped her nephew, Prince Michael, the heir of the male branch of the Montenegro family and father of my cousin Nicolas, who became an architect in Paris. After 1989, the latter became very involved in Montenegro issues, particularly cultural aspects. He became even more active after the independence of his country in 2006.

Today, even if we do not see each other much, we are good friends. He is an interesting man, attached to his roots, committed, cultivated and focused on art.

My mother valued her Montenegrin roots and was very fond of this branch of the family. Montenegro was the last country of former Yugoslavia to accede to independence. And yet it is the only country in the region never to have been under the Turks, even becoming an autonomous kingdom in 1910, much to the pride of its population. In 1990, an Italian warship brought back the remains of King Nicolas of Montenegro from San Remo, where he had been buried, to the historic royal capital, Cetinje. After a short exile, hopeless of returning and saddened by family sorrows, my great-grandfather died on the Côte d'Azur in 1921. His ties with France went way back, since he had been a student at the Lycée Louis-le-Grand in Paris. He had reigned until 1918, and it was he who proclaimed the sovereignty of the kingdom vis-à-vis the Ottomans and Austria-Hungary.

In 2003, I was able to visit Cetinje on an official visit when I was prime minister, when I saw the icon of Our Lady of Filermos, *Panaghia tes Phileremou*. The tombs are in a cemetery a hundred or so meters from a modest palace, the oldest members of the family—a dynasty of Orthodox princes-bishops. My mother, who had made an incognito visit to the country in the 1970s, had been moved by the solemnity of the funeral ceremonies in honor of her grandparents, which were broadcast on television, and I know that she was also thinking of the fate of her own husband.

CHAPTER NINE

A Time for Living

MY LIFE CHANGED WHEN I MET MY WIFE. AFTER OUR MARRIAGE IN JANuary 1962, my mother gave us the house in Madrid as a present and settled in Portugal, in a beautiful villa that my sister inherited after her death.

We were able to marry only after two long years of negotiations between the Catholic and Orthodox Churches. The question that was raised by the Vatican was which denomination our children would be. It was cumbersome and exhausting, but we succeeded after three audiences with Pope John XXIII, in addition to a mountain of correspondence and talks with Vatican officials, and as many in Spain with the metropolitan Archbishop Andrey, the representative of our Orthodox church in America and Australia. I had had it. The precedent of my parents did not help us much, since they had been married in Assisi according to Catholic ritual first and then in Sofia; yet my sister and I had been immediately baptized Orthodox. It was for this reason that the Vatican was skeptical of our promises. On my side, as king anointed by our church, I could not sign the "guarantees" demanded from me by Rome, in which I had to promise that our children would be raised Catholic. This was a condition *sine qua non*. My resolution was all the more unusual at a time when, as I have said, the weight of the Catholic Church counted heavily in Spanish society.[1] I thus patiently went to the

---

1. Another important fact also had to be taken into consideration: historically, there had not really been any contact between Spain and the Orthodox world except for a few Russian families who had fled the Soviet regime and whom we met up with on religious holidays in a little Orthodox chapel near the bullring (Plaza de Toros).

very end of the process. It was not conceivable for me that a question of religion should prevent our wedding.

One day, a lawyer who was a specialist in these questions gave me a solution that he had unearthed in an article on canonic law, an exception dating from 1938 and ruled in Japan that established jurisprudence in these types of mixed marriages. A Shintoist governor wanted to marry a Catholic but could not sign the same "guarantees" that were being asked from us—this was a period of fierce Japanese nationalism—and the bishop took it upon his own conscience to celebrate their wedding without this step. In the time that it took for the information to reach the Vatican, the wedding had been celebrated. It was thanks to this precedent that Rome was able to accept the idea of our marriage and agree that Margarita would not be excommunicated. Despite all the hurdles, she wanted to marry me! Subsequently, we jointly agreed on the denomination of our children. I did not want to impose anything. Our two oldest are Orthodox, in the spirit of the tradition of my country, while our three others are Catholic, because we thought their life in Spain would consequently be simpler.

A private service took place at our home in Madrid, celebrated by Father Albendea, confessor of King Baudouin and Queen Fabiola. Then we had a civil wedding in Switzerland at the Lausanne town hall, and finally an Orthodox ceremony took place in the Russian church in Vevey, Saint Barbara, co-celebrated by the Russian archbishop Antoine de Geneva and our metropolitan. What a way we had come! More than fifty years later, Margarita and I laugh over the fact that, if our marriage has lasted so long, it may be because to divorce from these three marriages would be too complicated!

I was immediately charmed by the beauty and independence of Margarita. Hers stood out from the mindset of young women of the period. I think that at heart she was something of a freethinker. Above all, we fell in love with one another. She was an orphan, so I didn't have to ask her father for her hand, but I did ask her older brother, José Luis. At the beginning of the Spanish Civil War, their parents had been shot, since, as wealthy "bourgeois," they were considered enemies of the working class. The Gómez-Acebo family were Madrid bankers who had been ennobled at the period. They were kidnapped from their villa about forty kilometers from Madrid. I believe that this common fate—our families having been victims of similar abuses of power—brought us closer together. But we barely spoke of it; everything was in nuance and half-spoken words. This similarity struck Bulgarians when they learned of my wife's past, the kind of tragedy that many of our fellow citizens could identify themselves with.

Margarita is a person who knows no resentment. After the Civil War, and despite all the evidence, she and her brother never sought to find or pursue the murderer of their grandmother, the same person who probably informed on their parents. I was shocked. She said, "That wouldn't bring them back." She has never been resentful. When I went back to Bulgaria with her, God knows she saw lots of these kinds of shady characters—believe it or not, she was able to remain admirably calm. Had she been more radical, her attitude would certainly have influenced my behavior vis-à-vis Bulgarian Communists.

As early as 1934 in Madrid, the acts of violence began. They increased in 1936 after the nationalist uprising of July 18. The "Reds" never made any bones about getting rid of people in their way. The tragedy of civil war is that rise in violence that everyone knows so well. The horrors of the Paracuellos del Jarama massacres, and those of numerous members of the religious community, largely contributed to the triggering of that fratricidal conflict. In Madrid, suspects were loaded into trucks and taken outside the city to be shot: this was called "taking a walk."[2] The general secretary of the Communist Party, Santiago Carrillo, who was at the time the young political superintendent for public order, was able afterward to come back to Spain and be elected to the Cortes, thanks to the agreement of the young king, Juan Carlos, and his prime minister, Adolfo Suárez. One of the first decisions made by this tandem was to legalize the Spanish Communist Party, whose historical leaders were in exile. A part of the army was outraged, but for the situation to be normalized and the party demythologized, this was a necessary step. This was the price to be paid for the future of democracy.

---

2. *"Llevar de paseo."*

It was only many years after our engagement, which had caused quite a stir, that we received some scraps of information about the fate of my in-laws. One of their former cell mates at the Villalba prison asked to see us. He had been a doctor and after the war became the director of public health in San Sebastian. When we met with him, he told us, "I was in the same place where your parents were detained and I understood that your father had been killed after there was a note from your mother one day in my morning ration of bread asking how he was." According to him, my father-in-law had been shot a few days after his arrest, in November 1936, and my mother-in-law in December. Imagine for a moment what a drama it was for these young parents to have to leave behind them a son of four and a two-and-a-half-year-old daughter!

In Madrid, Margarita had many friends—she has always been very sociable—and we went out in a group for dinner in various small restaurants in the old part of the city. She had studied in Belgium, at Sacré-Cœur de Jette in Brussels, according to the wishes of her uncle and guardian, since her brother married quite young. She had enough funds to travel rather freely afterward. For example, she spent two months in Japan—this had impressed me—having traveled to far-off Asia by boat, stopping to visit Ceylon and Vietnam on the way.

Both of us were products of complicated childhoods, and this circumstance made us close. I must say that the fact that she had no parents made it easier for us to see one another, especially in the Spain of that time when conventions were quite strict. She lived in a very elegant apartment that had been decorated by a Frenchman: I can still recall the more or less Brazilian scenes painted on the walls. I courted her and I admired her, even if it was said that she already had someone. It was only after my return from the United States that I began to see her more frequently, often through mutual friends. A few days after my return, I called her to tell her that I had bought a Chevrolet convertible.

Margarita's character is very open, surely because of her extensive travel and her natural curiosity. Once married, she immediately loved our visits to Portugal to see my mother—often traveling aboard the Lusitania Express train—as well as our trips to Italy, Germany, and the Scandinavian countries, and easily integrated into our large European family.

Not being a "blueblood," I might have dreaded that she would be overly scrutinized, but that never happened. She was accepted as she was. Even today, I guess that Margarita is more popular than me among certain branches of our families.

My generation was the first not to be forced into so-called equal marriages—that is to say, between members of royal families. It was certainly not in my plans to have an "arranged" marriage, having seen that many hadn't worked out.

I wanted us to be married in the magnificent Russian church in Geneva, but we had to fall back on Vevey, since the authorities of the canton feared that the ceremony might be politicized and thus bitterly criticized by Communist Bulgaria. A number of my Catholic cousins did not come, out of fear that the marriage would be condemned by the Vatican, not knowing that we had obtained the necessary authorizations. On the Italian side, my mother did not judge it necessary to bring up the question with her brother, King Umberto, though they had dined together several days before! My uncle was terribly sorry and afterward had gifts sent to us. Only my first cousin Pier Francesco Calvi came, making the trip from the Piedmont to Lausanne with his wife, who was seven months pregnant. At the time, a juicy rumor went around in the Italian press that I had abandoned Margarita for a very pretty Italian girl shown in a photo: she was none other than my cousin's wife, Marisa Allasio!

At the church on that January 21, 1962, King Farouk was present, faithfully wearing his dark glasses and dignified as a statue; my cousin, Prince Michael of Greece, representing King Paul; and my witness, Dimitri Romanov, my Hesse cousins, and friends from Madrid. General Franco's envoy, Spain's ambassador to Berne, the Marquis de Lojendio, brought us a small gold box with a ruby clasp from him.

Returning from our honeymoon in the Bahamas, we had to go by way of Switzerland to retrieve our car in Lausanne, and I thought we could pay a courtesy visit to the Villa Vieille-Fontaine, where the widow of Alphonse XIII, Queen Victoria Eugenie, lived, to introduce Margarita to her. She was the granddaughter of Queen Victoria, and it was at her home that Juan Carlos and Sophia celebrated their engagement.

In 1968, a year before her death, she was able to come back to Spain for the first time since 1931 so that she could attend the baptism of her great-grandson, Prince Felipe, at La Zarzuela Palace. The Spanish government exceptionally authorized her visit, as well as that of the Count of Barcelona, who triggered enthusiasm for the monarchy in the streets of Madrid. That day, at the lunch at the sumptuous palace belonging to the duchess of Alba, where she was staying, she said something that touched me a great deal: "This morning, I was thinking of you, of whether one day you might also return to your country like me."

In Madrid, upon our return, we saw the princely couple, Juan Carlos and Sophia. The two of them were married not long after us in Athens. The four of us are the same age, and we enjoyed going out together: they would come to our house by a lake for weekends, we were invited to the same shooting events, and we would see them in Majorca, where later on my children went to spend time with their cousins. They loved seeing Juan Carlos, who, for them, was the prince who was going to become king. As for the future queen, I have always admired Sophia, a woman of duty and devotion, in an "occupation" in which one cannot do well without a profound sense of humanity. Our attachment has grown stronger over the years.

I will never forget the night that was so significant for the contemporary history of Spain, that of the coup d'état on February 23, 1981. My wife and I were then in Switzerland when, at four o'clock in the morning, the king managed to call me by telephone and said, "I'll tell you later what happened, but make sure your children go to school tomorrow as if nothing had happened. I've already told my sisters to do the same thing." It was rather surprising that he should think of this kind of detail when the entire country was wondering how the attempt at a *putsch* was going to turn out. After all, the Spanish are a hot-blooded people! I was unable to get through to home because of the overloaded phone lines, but the king had a call put through to wake them up: "Everybody off to school!" What a disappointment! They thought they were going to have a day of vacation.

Juan Carlos and I have known each other since the famous cruise organized on the Aegean Sea by Queen Frederica. I saw him grow up, mature, and always face the most delicate circumstances with the same willpower and good humor. He is thought of as a "Bourbon" sovereign, bon vivant and cheerful. This is perhaps true, but he is more than that. He is also someone whose character was formed on the back of the tense relationship that existed between his father—who was, after all, the logical successor—and Franco. Juan Carlos managed to have the Spanish people accept the transition process as it had been decided. Spain would not have been what it is today without his skillful actions. I am convinced of it.

The king has always been pro-democratic. In my opinion, he was able to maneuver in an exemplary fashion. Once, as he was working on a draft of the 1978 constitution, I saw him crossing out numerous paragraphs. He found that it gave him too much power compared to what his fellow citizens would accept and told me he did not want to be a "mini dictator," just as he decided not to restore the court of the former monarchy of Alphonse XIII. This decision was taken badly by part of the nobility, including certain very renowned Spaniards, heirs to prestigious functions and very old titles. Juan Carlos needed to make known to the people that his reign was an instauration and not a restauration. In the same spirit, if I may be so bold, Sophia took care not to be surrounded by ladies-in-waiting. Over time, the king has successfully convinced everyone—Republicans and Communists, Falange members and traditional supporters of Franco—of his legitimacy.

His master stroke remains his nomination of Adolfo Suárez as prime minister after the resignation of Carlos Arias Navarro, a loyal supporter of the *Generalissimo*. Every Spaniard remembers his deathly pale face on television when he announced the death of the ruler in 1975. Juan Carlos was able to confound predictions by choosing Suárez, using the enlightened advice of Don Torcuato Fernández Miranda, one of his law professors (whom I also knew). The young Suárez had been the director of national radio and television, secretary general of the National Movement—the Falange—and governor of the Province of Segovia. A product of the regime to date, he was the one who really dismantled it. The king and Adolfo Suárez found each other at the right time. I remember well the announcement of his appointment: I was in Madrid and listening to the news. The news fell like a thunderbolt; the left was outraged: "But how can it be? He's the secretary of the party!" In Paris, Munich, and elsewhere, exiles began to screech. However, in order to last, the challenging of the system had to come from the inside. The first elections also confirmed this point of view, resulting in victories for Suárez's party, the UCD. I had met him several times before his nomination, and afterward at La Zarzuela when he would go to see the king, and I found him resourceful and charming. He always emphasized dialogue, which I agree with completely. At the end of his career, the king gave him the Order of the Golden Fleece.[3] Suárez died of Alzheimer's disease in 2014.

After the victory of the Socialists in 1982, the king also got along well with Prime Minister Felipe González, contrary to what one might have thought. González was pragmatic, quick and very intelligent. Both of them wanted what was good for Spain and for it to work well, rather than seeking to impose their respective credos. Each of them accepted the prerogatives of the other and, paradoxically, Spanish Socialists were the ones who demonstrated the least reluctancy vis-à-vis the monarchy.

The Spanish population was won over by the charm that is so characteristic of Juan Carlos, along with his spontaneous character. His use of colloquial language to address those around him—this used to be a privilege of the sovereign, and he brought it back—as well as the way he speaks respectfully and yet from the heart, make him an extraordinary leader. I have learned a lot from him. I still remember how, with panache and drollness, he stood up to the Basque members of parliament in Bilbao who were screaming, "Get out, get out, get out," *Fuera, Fuera, Fuera* . . . He did not move and was not put off: "I can't hear you, I can't hear you, louder, louder!" This is his natural instinct; he has a feel for the crowd and for events.

Many people in Bulgaria were waiting for me to be able to re-create the Juan Carlos experience. But this was not possible after half a century of staunch propaganda; public opinion was far from being prepared

---

3. The name of this historical order was inspired by the Greek myth of the Golden Fleece. Founded in 1430 by Philip the Good, Duke of Burgundy, it still exists, but in two forms: the Austrian order—limited to 46—and the Spanish order, granted by the sovereign since 1770.

for a return of the monarchy. Let us not forget that the Spanish re-instauration had long been nurtured by General Franco. Personalities like Suárez allowed for a gentle transition from an authoritarian system to a parliamentary monarchy.

Forty years later, we saw a completely normal succession between father and son. While provisions had not been made for abdication in the Constitution of 1978, it was approved by the Cortes with a very large majority and the king was able to hand over to Felipe VI. As a close friend and cousin, I felt the need to be present that day, June 18, 2014. The act of abdication was very moving, taking place in the Column Room of the Royal Palace—on the same table where, in 1985, the king had signed Spain's membership of the European Union—in the presence of the members of the royal family and the most senior authorities of Spain. As Juan Carlos had once said to me that "we began together," I came expressly from Sofia—without being able to be there the next day for the proclamation of the new sovereign, since I needed to get back. Despite the fact that constitutionally all was normal, I was greatly moved and embraced him as he came out of the room. I could picture several decades of shared history in front of me. I thought of the journey since I had met the young prince, full of drive and whose political future was far from being obvious. On my way back, I asked myself whether the act had been one of abnegation and lucidity or one accomplished with a certain relief.

*

I soon had to undertake responsibility for running my household and find the means to insure my financial independence. Having married an "heiress," according to the media, I absolutely did not want anyone to think that I was living off my wife. People are so quick to be rash in their judgments. At military school, one of our instructors always came back to the same lesson in strategy: "Never underestimate your enemy." Little by little, I entered what is called the business world—even if I don't care for the expression, which sometimes is perceived negatively.

My responsibilities in family inheritance and court cases had trained me to deal with both legal and financial issues, where I could apply my judgment and sense of the practical.

I enjoy reading biographies for inspiration, including those of industry leaders, and I must say that I challenge the myth of the *self-made man*. I find it too narrow minded when considering how a number of external factors must come together, including the work of others, luck, and the opportunities offered by the market.

I accepted no favors; I did not want anyone to say that I had taken advantage of my charm or even my title. I wanted to make a future for myself that would be of my own making. I was lucky in that I met with some of the heavyweights of the Spanish economy and the major names in European industry, and I traveled a lot. I quickly became the go-between for several companies looking to expand, either in Spain or internationally. I had always wanted to work in a team, practicing teamwork and not simply creating a "business" around myself. I don't have a big enough ego for that. I liked working in groups and meetings where we discussed strategy, development and new markets. If I got results, it was in part due to the people I knew and my ability to cultivate them, my capacity for hard work and my perseverance, to say nothing of the contributions of Luck and Fate! Meeting influential people is not everything; you need to know how to be of relevance to them and cultivate relationships for decades. That's where the experience of life tells you how it is not about diplomas, but rather about human nature. And I spoke eight languages, which came as an advantage.

My impression was that it was the most interesting thing I could possibly do, and do well. I'm not sure that I would do it again today, though. The rules of the business world seem to have changed. I used the rules of my background—listening skills and diplomacy—and they worked. I shouldered the role of director, a dedicated one, not the kind who collects his director's fees once a year and is not really interested in the business or its employees. I saw my function as that of an advisor whose goal was to contribute to the development of the business as a whole. Directors have experience, and despite my young age, history had already provided me with good doses of it. I wanted to be useful.

At the time, a friend's answer to my question of how many employees he had struck me in a way that has stayed with me: "Three thousand families depend on me." The market economy must at all costs take into account human beings; if it does not, we are creating monsters.

One of the projects in which I got involved early on was *Eurobuilding*, a five-star hotel built in Madrid with a group of friends. This building was the first of this kind in Spain in the 1960s, and it was an adventure. The project was daring, since we asked each participant to come with ideas on an ideal hotel, without necessarily being experienced in the field. We wanted to invest our money while being careful about the slightest expenditures; we couldn't afford any mistakes. I brought my ideas as well as my international experience. Years of work turned into decades.

This experience was important for me. I wanted to "slave away" as people around me said. The meaning of the word *work* during those growth years was action, and for me the best incarnation of that was in business. Spain was taking off economically. I was not at all of a mind to be decorative or privileged. You need some humility in life; otherwise you get nowhere.

One of the board members of our hotel, Narciso Amorós, was also a member of the board at Thomson Grand Public, and one day he proposed the chairmanship of the Spanish subsidiary of this great firm to me. I held that office for thirteen years. I would point out that this was not the military branch, for I never wanted to have anything to do with arms and their trade. Much later, in my capacity as prime minister, when this kind of sensitive question had to be dealt with, I took all the necessary precautions to have witnesses in order to ensure the transparency of the process, to avoid any suspicion on decisions taken. Given my code of ethics, I fought against bribes and "sweeteners," which earned me considerable hostility.

This is how I began to have my own income and no longer depend on inheritance. At the time, Thomson was a large business in the full expansion that accompanied the economic opening up of Spain, a country where everyone wanted to invest. We had a factory in Vic, Catalonia, in a joint venture with the Japan's JVC, another in Cuenca to assemble televisions, one in Madrid. A good number of "white and brown" products—as we called household appliances—were then made in Spain, with the rest of Europe as their selling destination. Our domestic market was in full growth: our numbers were those of Asia today.

We all met in Paris twice a year to give our reports. Otherwise, our French executives came to see us in Madrid. It was a fascinating world. I also began to see a return on my efforts in the equity stock of our hotel business and my income as director of the boards of Thomson and of the Spanish dairy products group Pascual. At the same time, I was managing the family properties, and I believe I did not make too many mistakes in the years of crises. There were pyramid investment (or Ponzi) schemes, like the type of setup created by Bernard Madoff, which had already cleaned out several large fortunes. At the time, I was approached to make a significant investment, but I backed out at the last moment. My instinct worked well since, three years later, the capital of the firm was written off in full. My distrustful personality perhaps preserved me from serious financial disasters. All the more so in that it was not my personal money, but that of my mother, my sister and, indirectly, all of our children. If someone proposed returns that were over that of a normal bank, I got the feeling I should be suspicious. Above all, I understood that it was no longer possible to live off a private income in our times, let alone put all one's eggs in the same basket.

My wife and I have always refused to make unnecessary expenditures, and even less those that are extravagant, driving the same car for years—perhaps also because we hated showing off. Even today at Vrana, I have no servants and I cook myself when I have to. I am given no subsidy or retirement pension from the state, and I ask nothing from anyone, so much so that I was—and still am—incapable of asking for money, even for worthy and charitable causes. I prefer to put my hand in my pocket and donate, quietly, for this is how my mother taught me to think of charity. In hindsight, I realize that I spent a lot of money helping refugees who turned to me in Madrid—and I continued to do so after 1989, but now in Bulgaria—which I could have used to help my own children instead. They can acknowledge the extent to which we did not spoil them, and I very much regret it. Did I do the right thing?

Since my coming of age, I have never stopped helping my compatriots out. This was done with the assistance of my office staff, who helped me in organizing the settlement of many Bulgarians and the all the international correspondence: with royal families, politicians, diplomats, businessmen, historians, journalist, and especially with regards to issues related to Bulgarians in exile. In foreign countries, we organized visits to our "colonies," as we call the expatriate community, since the first request of refugees coming from behind the Iron Curtain was to ask the police to contact me. Some of them had no passports to prove their identities, but by researching and cross-checking we were able to have them accepted.

In Madrid, there was no Bulgarian Embassy until 1974. De facto, my Madrid address became the point of reference. Given the circumstances, I knew that I was spied on by the People's Republic, and much later this suspicion was confirmed when I had access to my political file in the archives of the Ministry of Justice. I was able to confirm the extent to which I was of interest to them. On the one hand, the smallest details of my daily life were reported, and, on the other, the reports were duly amplified to levels of quasi-conspiracy, probably in an attempt to impress their bosses.

During the years of exile, refugees would not hear of the least contact with official Bulgarian authorities: I was the one that they came to see to help them with their paperwork. The question of papers was critical. I was delighted to help them as much as I could, but what a task! For this, I always spent long hours at the office, as a sort of exceptional consulate, in addition to my more standard professional activities.

My wife could testify to the time that this required. I think that it was very hard on her, for she also saw the money go out just as quickly as it came in. It's basically a peculiar life, rather thankless, but I have no regrets. I took life as it came, for that was my duty.

In 1958, we launched a newspaper for exiles, the *Bulletin*. The staff was made up of a small team of Bulgarian journalists, two of whom worked for the Spanish national radio.[4] The idea was to maintain contact between all of us, with all of our compatriots who no longer had access to a press published in their language. I took charge of this monthly,

---

4. At the headquarters of Radio Free Europe in Paris and Munich, a meeting place for emigrants from occupied countries, refugees provided me with information. I would go there to update them on what the news was in our countries.

because I didn't want to be dependent on anyone, or to be suspected of being politically biased. Several thousand copies were printed, and we sent them as far as the United States and Australia.

The refugee camps that I have mentioned before were at that time in Austria, Germany (near Nuremberg), Italy—Rome, Trieste and Naples—as well as Greece. I wanted to visit them as often as possible. These exiled communities were not wealthy. For me, it was natural to act in this way. Refugees were arriving one-by-one and young people formed the majority, as they were the ones who had enough physical strength to live through an escape from the country. Border guards had the right to shoot them. I know of a certain number who were killed. North of Rome was Fraschette camp and near Naples that of Latina, which I visited. They were surrounded by barbed wire. Bulgarian Franciscan fathers helped me. I particularly remember the energy of Father Gagov, and that of several families based in Rome who worked in a completely selfless manner for the good of their exiled fellow countrymen. All of them were very frightened for the members of their families remaining in Bulgaria. They were able to see for themselves that the West was not as bad as propaganda had presented it to them. In the face of the uncertainties surrounding them, I gave them moral support by describing the life that they would be able to lead going forward. The future was open for these young people. I asked them where they were from and about their family histories, and they would tell me about their escape and their sufferings. The Berlin Wall is always spoken of, but in fact there was a wall all around the whole Soviet world, and those who came over it risked a great deal. Courage was needed—or despair—to thread their way through the meanderings and mines of the forbidden zones, patrolled by armed soldiers who had the right over life or death. No escape was legal. If you had to leave the country as an athlete, artist, or something else, assurances were made before your departure: it was implicit that families would be penalized for those who did not want to return.

The International Committee of the Red Cross also helped enormously, particularly at the time of the massive exodus of Turkish minority members from Bulgaria in 1984, including Cornelio Sommaruga, president of the ICRC, whom I went to see for an emergency meeting in

Geneva to heighten awareness of this drama. Due to a policy of forced "Bulgarization" launched by the Communist government, some three hundred thousand Bulgarian Muslims were forced to leave the country for Turkey over a few days. This expulsion was called "the great journey."

In the aforementioned camps, American, Canadian and Australian delegations periodically came through to interview candidates for immigration. I noted that the only nation at the time that accepted those who had been refused by the others—and sometimes left to languish in the camps—was Sweden. It accepted them, paying them a salary for six months and providing compulsory language lessons. I will never forget this generosity, and I was able to formally express my gratitude before the Swedish parliament during my official visit as prime minister.

Throughout the years, I went to Greece to inspect other refugee camps, some of which were in place until the 1980s. They were run by the United Nations, by the unit that is nowadays called UNHCR.[5] Bulgarian refugees were mixed with those arriving from Yugoslavia and even Albania, but these were much fewer as a result of the ferociousness of Enver Hoxha's regime. One of these camps was located on the island of Lavrion, another one on Makronisos, the latter meant for refugees whose identity had not been established. Having visited both, I can say that the conditions were more than spartan. Given that this was taking place during the Cold War, the security agencies of these countries were afraid that Soviet agents would infiltrate the camps, and a particular scrutiny was made to clearly confirm the origins of each individual. Time and again I was asked to identify people whose families I might have known, so as to provide a reference, even if the great majority of those who risked escaping were from border areas. While we exchanged letters with the various administrations, these poor people were left to count the months in their makeshift shelters. At different periods, I was able to employ a few of them, yet always with the risk that they might be informers for the regime.

In 1965, we created a sort of council whose role was to support me in my political activities. Having received the agreement of around one

---

5. United Nations High Commissioner for Refugees.

hundred key persons—Bulgarian and foreign—it was called the "Council of the One Hundred," and each member had a specific area of competence. There were writers, historians, politicians, artists and diplomats with whom I corresponded and whom I met with whenever I could, in Spain or during my trips. I realize now how very useful they were to me, often reassuring me in the decisions I made. The organization lasted the time it was needed, or a good fifteen years. Among others, I remember the famous Spanish journalist Luis Maria Anson and the historian Sir Steven Runciman, who had written a history of the First Bulgarian Kingdom and who, as a diplomat posted to Sofia before the war, had known my father. My mother, who usually was rather reserved about English politics, greatly appreciated him.

Chapter Ten

The Orients

As of 1975, I began to travel regularly to Morocco thanks to the friendship that was beginning between King Hassan II and myself. My first contact with the country went back to April 1963, when Margarita and I participated in a car rally organized by the much-regretted Alfonso de Hohenlohe, who ten years before had founded the legendary Marbella Club Hotel, on the Finca Santa Margarita estate. It soon became a meeting place for celebrities from all over the world, and the beginning of what the Italian writer Alberto Moravia was the first to call the "Jet-Set." At the time, I owned a Jaguar E-Type that I had bought in England, at Coventry, where the brand's famous factory was located. Departing from Marbella, we made an extensive tour of Morocco with some thirty or so teams, all driving sports cars. We spent two marvelous weeks there, a real introduction to the country. I remember the truly subtle beauty of the landscapes, the Straits of Gibraltar, the desert on the other side of the Atlas, the mountain passes with their twisty roads. We had to stop near wells so that we could cool the engines; we switched from stops in simple villages to those in great imperial cities like Marrakesh, Meknes and Fez. The idea behind was to promote Morocco, which was far from being the popular destination for tourism that we know today. It was a revelation to both of us, so much so that we went back many times afterward with our children.

At the time, I did not know King Hassan, whose personality would have such an impact on the fate of our family. In 1955, I had met his first cousin and brother-in-law, Prince Moulay Ali, at the wedding of Henry of Orléans with Elisabeth of Württemberg at the Château d'Anet. I saw him again at the rally, as well as Prince Moulay Abdallah, brother of the king. Much later, in Madrid, during a visit of the latter for a hunting trip, he conveyed an invitation from Hassan II to come to see him in Rabat. I was very curious about this meeting because I had heard a lot about him. In 1956, his father, Mohammed V, had come to Madrid for a spectacular visit that had left its mark on everyone. I was a student at the French *lycée* then and very intrigued by the occasion. I had always kept up with the politics of his country, finding fascinating the fact that the Alaouite dynasty had endured since the seventeenth century, despite the presence of colonial powers.

A few weeks after the invitation, I arrived in Rabat. Dr. Moulay Ahmed Laraki, then minister of foreign affairs, accompanied me to introduce me to his sovereign. I had already met him since he had been Morocco's ambassador to Spain. Together, we entered the Grand Mechouar, where I reviewed a detachment of the Royal Guard. The royal palace is located right at the center of Rabat, protected by high walls. A considerable number of people live and work there, a compound made of courtyards, pavilions, offices, reception rooms, living rooms and gardens. When the king passed, the custom was for the guards to call out, "*Allah l'amrak ya sidi,*" which means "May God give you everything you could wish for, Sire." Preceded by a kaid (tribal chief) in traditional costume, I went upstairs where the members of the North Guard opened before us a succession of doors leading to an office. There, the kaid knocked twice: "I bring you an illustrious guest." The door opened, and, in a fragrance of sandalwood, the silhouette of King Hassan moved toward me. The ceremonial was impressive.

The king first received me with his minister of foreign affairs; then we met in a tête-à-tête by the desk that had been his father's. We spoke at length together; his French was impeccable. I felt an immediate warmth, a true kindness on his side. He was eight years older than me. In the course of the dinner to which Margarita and I had been invited, he gave each of us a gift: I received a jewel-encrusted dagger and my wife a very pretty box in leather, worked in Moroccan style. She was delighted with her gift, but imagine her surprise when the king asked her to open it and she discovered a gold evening bag inside! She couldn't get over it—she who had been brought up in such an austere fashion. We still laugh about this incident.

During the conversation, he said something that struck me: "When you came into the office, I had the impression that I already knew you." I answered, "Why, Sidi?" He said, "Because, from my window, I watched how you walked in front of the guard. I am basically quite shy, and I usually do this when I don't know the person I am meeting, so that I have an idea of what he might be like."

I never forgot this remark, and in Madrid, in my turn, I began to adopt this way of observing what the body's movements could reveal to me about a person. I could thus prepare better the meeting that was about to take place. One small detail can tell a lot. Later, he organized a memorable tour of Morocco for us with our young children. I remember this first period very well, for it came after the Green March in November 1975 to the Spanish Sahara. The country was still in an uproar. The event had made all the international news headlines. By means of this peaceful, yet crowded, march, Hassan II had gambled on a throw of the dice to annex the southern territories that were under Spanish rule. The claim for Western Sahara went back to the independence of Morocco in 1956, a territory that the country considered historically its own.

In March 1985, for his first visit to the Sahara, the king asked me to join him. I landed at Tan-Tan on the coast, at the edge of the desert. From there, I joined the royal procession as it entered the town very slowly, so thick and joyful were the crowds of people, waving their Moroccan flags. He made his entry on horseback, and we walked slightly behind him. This was the first time that the king had come to Laayoune since the withdrawal of the Spanish troops and the change in administration. For the occasion, as a foreigner and exceptionally—as I had not taken part in it—I was awarded the Green March medal, along with the French writer Maurice Druon. Hassan and he got along very well, sharing a passion for literature and history. The scene reminded me of one of those Oriental chronicles where the sultan is received with magnificence anywhere in his kingdom: the entry of Saladin in Jerusalem after the city had been reconquered as part of the Crusades must have looked like what I saw. I felt that I was witnessing a historic moment, and I was grateful to him. The next day, the king took us along the wall of embankments that had been built against the attacks of the "Polisario Front" and asked us to wear uniforms. This was because, according to the Geneva Convention, anyone dressed in military uniform who fell into enemy hands would receive better treatment. A tailor took our measurements, and that is how I found myself clothed in the battledress of the Royal Moroccan Gendarmerie. After breakfast, on the terrace of the only acceptable hotel in town—formerly a Spanish *parador*—Druon arrived, sleeves rolled up, shirt open to his waist: "Sire, I don't look too much like a firebrand, do I?" He was delighted with the impact he made.

The troops on duty came to greet the sovereign with cries of joy and cheers: "Thank you, boys, but better get back to your positions, for if ever there was an attack, who would defend us?" The war against the Polisario had been going on for years, having followed the enduring battles with their neighbor, Algeria. Coincidentally, my son-in-law Kitín Muñoz, the son of a Spanish officer, was born in this isolated spot whose terrain reminded me of the film *The Desert of the Tartars*.

I met with King Hassan four or five times a year subsequently, either on business or on family holidays. In the latter case, we would stay in one of the guest villas, where we would find pastries and magnificent fruit and perfumes of all kinds waiting. It was his habit to host in this manner. His hospitality knew no limits. As I was raised during World War II, I once felt compelled to tell him that such abundance was not necessary. "Simeon," he said, "have you noticed that after meals there is a van that stops by all the villas? Nothing is lost; everything is redistributed among the employees in order of hierarchy, and believe me, there is not a crumb lost. I am very conscious of the world in which we live."

He nicknamed Margarita "Isabella the Catholic," as he found her very strict with our children. I always called him Sidi, and he asked my mother, whom he met soon after, to call him "Hassan." She answered, "In that case, call me Giovanna." As he couldn't quite allow himself to do that, the king replied, "I'll call you Mama II, as you are the mother of my youngest brother." My mother was delighted; she was very fond of him.

His charm was enormous. Whether in a suit or in a djellaba, he had a presence, an authority and gravitas that was felt across the board.

Our children saw each other regularly; they grew up together in a certain way. As soon as we had vacation time and were able to do so, we went to Morocco. All of them spoke French and Spanish. For my son Kyril's fifteenth birthday, the king gave him fifteen gold coins, Napoleons that he promptly turned over to me, wide eyed in fear of losing them. In July 1979, my sons made a dream trip to the United States with the two princes, including the present King Mohammed VI, and his friends from the Royal College, traveling from Fez to Orlando, California, and then to New York, and chaperoned by Ambassador Abdeslam Jaidi, who was close to the sovereign and whom the children liked very much. I remember that at the last moment, the king delayed the trip by twenty-four hours because he had been informed that a Russian satellite was to enter the atmosphere and disintegrate.

I once had a car accident near Marrakesh on the way to ski with the children, and, having learned that I was injured, King Hassan came to see me shortly afterward, with Edgar Faure, who was there on an official visit: "As you see, Sire, an old Republican like me, attending the sickbed of an ailing king." An unexpected remark that made us laugh heartily. As the years went on, I felt closer and closer to the Moroccan royal family. We both adopted a fraternal relationship. I felt that he wanted to give me a sort of protection, a link that I still do not know quite how to define despite the time that has passed since his death.

How many coincidences would have been needed for us to have met in a normal life? Who would have believed it? Would he have come through Sofia one day? He, the Prince of Believers, and me, an Orthodox king, overthrown by a coup d'état.

During one of my trips, the king proposed that I should become a member of the board of COSUMAR, an important Franco-Moroccan consortium dealing in sugar,[1] Morocco being a heavy consumer of this product. The chairman was Prince Moulay Ali: "You speak Spanish, you

---

1. In 1929, the Casablanca sugar refinery site was founded by the Société Nouvelle des Raffineries de Sucre de Saint-Louis of Marseille.

can help us negotiate with Cuba and Fidel Castro," he said laughingly to me. This never happened. Later, after I had proven myself over the years, Hassan announced to me that he wanted me to go on the board of ONA (Omnium Nord-Africain), Morocco's largest private industrial and financial group, in which the royal family was also a shareholder. I stayed there about twenty years, and I saw the industrial group turn into a vast holding group diversified over several economic areas. French and Spanish banks had holdings in it. I was very flattered by this position, which put me at the boardroom table with some of the most well-known names in corporate world.

Malicious gossip had it that Hassan was the sole owner of ONA—which was, of course, false—and that the royal family monopolized all the profits—even more false. I can assure readers that, while I was there, all the family members together owned 13.2 percent of the shares. With two other directors, I represented their stake at the heart of the group. Above all, this was a fantastic consortium that employed thousands of families in Morocco. Thinking about it now, I can say that few countries in North Africa were so lucky.

On this board, I met more than one worthy co-member, including Antoine Riboud (chairman of Danone), the CEOs of Paribas and BNP, and other leaders who ran subsidiaries in mining, oil refining, tourism, hotels, food processing and banking. There was also Vincent Bolloré, whose family was involved in packaging, transport and tobacco. One of my colleagues, who also represented the interests of the royal family, was Driss Jettou. He later became prime minister, same as I did. He told me, "Who could have said when we sat on that board together that one day both of us would be the executive heads of our respective countries?" I answered, "Dear Driss, the probability was infinitely greater on your side than on mine!"

Morocco was a passion for me. During a visit as prime minister, the crown prince, Moulay Rachid, brother of Mohammed VI, said to me at the airport, "Your Majesty, I can't say 'welcome to Morocco' to you because here you are at home." King Hassan and I were close friends. I saw him as a sort of world character, nurtured on great knowledge. His library, where he received me several times, was home to a rich collection. He was very religious, and in my opinion that is what allowed him to overcome the challenges and pain in his life. This was a field where we understood one another well. He read the Koran every day. It was during his exile in Madagascar before the return of his father Mohammed V that he also found the time—at his young age—to read the Bible and the Torah. He spoke to me about it with a certain pride, all the while evoking their forced departure from Morocco, underlining the undeserved humiliation of his family. The journey to Madagascar had begun in a DC-3 that was not even equipped with seats. I wonder whether this beginning in life didn't toughen him and make him mature more quickly. But he also knew how to be magnanimous. For instance, he had put men he trusted—former French gendarmes, preferably Corsican—as stewards in his palaces. They were the ones who had guarded him during an exile that was more like an arrest. This gesture showed that he did not bear a grudge and, above all, that he knew how to appreciate the qualities of people for what they were. I knew some of them—discreet and efficient men—whose loyalty to him knew no limits.

During our political conversations, if he had to be harsh vis-à-vis certain individuals, he was careful not to let his judgment carry over to the whole of a country, a religion or a community. He was much too subtle to simplify or take shortcuts. He took great care in choosing his words. Hassan II is for me someone who was mistreated by legends and myths, and it is for this reason that I allow myself to refute them. It seems to me that there is too much bias in the way he is spoken of abroad. He was feared by many, dreaded for his wit, his culture, his erudition, and his jokes—as well as his political cunning in its most noble sense, that of defending the interests of his country, of his "beloved" people as he used to address them in his speeches. These qualities made him intimidating. My fate and that of my family touched him. I was sensitive to his charm. His wide smile showed the face of a man like any other behind the mask of the sovereign. He cast a spell over his world easily when he wanted to, even his enemies. This was an exercise in wizardry that I admired and that fascinated me. No one could remain insensitive to it. I know, for example, that President François Mitterrand succumbed to it. The king spoke of Mitterrand as a politician who had a vision of the future: "It was impossible to ignore him as a personality," he said.

I was able to see another side of his personality once I accompanied him to the inauguration of a dam in the north of the country, in the region of Tafilalt, where there had been terrible flooding in 1965. I was seated in the back seat of his car with the minister of justice, Mr. Reda Guedira, while he was in the front seat so that he could stand up to greet people as we went through the villages. In a small town, the car slowed down, Hassan II stood up, and a woman in a djellaba ran out of the crowd and threw herself in front of the car. With my Balkan mentality, I thought the worst—an assassination attempt. I pulled on the king's jacket to get him to sit down, when in fact the woman only wanted to give him a letter. He took it, opened it and passed it along to his justice minister as if nothing had happened, saying, "Simeon, I think you're slightly nervous." I had before me at that moment one of those characters only found in age-old legends. I asked him whether he was afraid of an attempt on his life. "Our only protection comes from On High, and even armored cars can do nothing," he said. "Not only that, they're much too expensive." The letter from the woman asked for a pardon for her husband. "Make a note of that," he said to his minister, "so that for the next religious holidays, this man is pardoned. I think that in seven years he's had the time to reflect on his crime and repent."

On the dam, a large tent had been set up, as well as a little area screened by canvas where the king would go to pray: "Simeon, take off your shoes and join me, for we are of the same Book." He was very serious about it. For him, the revelations of religions were all on the same level. He liked to quote this *surah* from the Koran: "Do not engage in controversies with people of the Book, except in the most honest manner, unless these are bad men. Say rather: we believe in the Books that were sent to us, as well as Those that were sent to you. Our God and Yours is one. We must give ourselves over to His will."

In this spirit of ecumenism, I remember that when he received Pope John Paul II in Casablanca—this was already by itself a first for a Muslim country—he gave him an engraved chalice mentioning the "two faces of a same Book." King Hassan proposed crossing the town with the pope in a shared convertible. But Vatican protocol does not authorize a head of state to accompany the sovereign pontiff in the same vehicle. Far from being offended, the king, with diplomacy and to guarantee a large crowd, found a solution: two cars traveling in the same direction, side-by-side. Hassan II was received in Rome, and it was Cardinal Agostino Casaroli, who was then secretary of state, who went to fetch him at the airport: "For the private audience with His Holiness tomorrow," he asked, "how many people should we expect, Sire?" This detail had not been provided and was the only information lacking. "Your Eminence, we will be forty" was the answer. That number had never before been seen at a private audience. "Your Eminence, has a Muslim sovereign ever visited the Holy Father before?" To qualify his question, he explained to the cardinal that, as he was used to giving the trip to Mecca to his servants, he wanted to do the same thing for the Christians in his entourage: the Spanish house-keepers, his French employees, and several people in the court. The day of the audience, all the ladies wore magnificent lace mantillas. The Vatican was, of course, touched by this attention, and the pope gave a rosary to each person and blessed all of them in good humor.

When he had the time, King Hassan would get in touch and I would join him in Rabat, where we would take up our conversation where we had left it the time before. There was always some ONA question under discussion. During long games of golf, I was also able to observe his way of conducting business. He tried to play every day, as much a way for him to get outside as it was to have audiences with his ministers where he compelled them to get away from their offices. They walked with him, and it was good for everyone. For those who were summoned, it was a signal honor. His trusted servant, Marjane, was given the task of signaling to one or the other of the ministers, senior civil servants, or members of the military, to approach the king. This was a way of more easily ruling on political issues, having a file explained, addressing palace affairs, appoint-ments, and all sorts of other details that were more efficiently taken care of away from everyday protocol: "You know," he once said to me, "it's eas-ier for me to say no walking next to someone surrounded by the beauties of nature, than to be stuck in my office looking at the person opposite me." I did not play golf, but I took the opportunity to speak with the people who mattered in the kingdom, among them several of the king's senior advisors, including some who had the quasi-medieval privilege of having his seal. Several of them became friends. I am thinking of André Azoulay, who was very well considered in the United States, especially in New York by the Jewish diaspora and elsewhere, where he was in charge of "a whole lot of jobs," as the king told me. A wise, friendly, and cultivated man, with whom I had a spontaneous relationship.

There were several times in the year where we would go to Morocco at the invitation of the king: for the Celebration of Allegiance and Loyalty on March 3, date of his accession to the throne—but I generally went to this event alone—or for his birthday on July 9, when we would go as a family for a huge outdoor reception. After a spectacular arrival on horseback, the speeches on March 3 were often political. He was a great speaker, not in the melodious voice of the grandstand, but in a captivating way that drew attention. He spoke generously and always managed to slip in a personal and spiritual touch. I would stand with the diplomats, the ministers and those who joined on official visits. He once told us after the death of one of his friends, who was a French professor of medicine, "He now is in the world of truth, far from our illusions and trivialities, he has but gone before us." We also used to join them in the new year celebrations. Each time we would go to a different destination, whether Rabat, Casablanca, Fez, or Marrakesh, which the king liked for the mildness of its climate. There were foreign guests, including princes of the Gulf and Arab states, his doctors, reputed businessmen and entrepreneurs, actors and occasionally celebrities such as Demis Roussos, originally from Alexandria, or Mireille Matthieu.

The king's tastes were eclectic, and he had friends of all sorts of backgrounds. For his New Year's parties, there was a buffet followed by a musical show. The men were separated from the women, and only the king could go back and forth between the two parties. He kept an eye on the arrival of the food, had a word to say to every guest, and didn't miss a detail. The ladies of the "court," like Margarita, were dressed in stunningly refined and embroidered caftans and had their heads bare. One New Year's Day, I went golfing with him; we saw a group all dressed in dark suits approaching. I thought they were lucky citizens chosen to present their good wishes: "Not at all, those are my doctors! We Muslims don't have confessors, so I confide in them." Among them were university bigwigs, many of them eminent specialists in their areas.

At the beginning of my visits, I had noted that some of those around him kissed his hand, while others kissed it on both sides in a sort of double hand-kissing: "If they turn my hand over, it means that I am the one who 'gives food' to them; in other words, that they work for me." I've noticed that the present king and his brother, Prince Moulay Rachid, always try to pull back their hands before they are kissed, but people remain very attached to this sign of respect.

*

Hassan's manners, his thoughts, his political finesse, his art of manipulating his opponents, his generosity as well as his openness, also made an impression on me. He was artful in handling international relations and did so exquisitely. With his children, he was very demanding, really training them rigorously to the extent that he personally taught his daughters how to correctly iron the collars of his shirts, miming the necessary gestures in the middle of the conversation. "They'll need to know how to do everything when they're married!" he said. He wanted his children to know how to use their hands and to not be happy just being served. His ability for managing such contrasts always puzzled me. I also discovered that he liked to cook, a kind of relaxation therapy, and he enjoyed supervising the menus served to his guests at official dinners.

He confused those who didn't like him; they would approach him on the defensive, and Hassan II would then know immediately how to turn the situation around. He told Barbara Walters, a journalist who reproached him for having sheltered the exiled shah of Iran in Morocco, "But Madam, if Fidel Castro asked me for asylum, I would gladly grant it to him because for me, a sense of hospitality toward someone in distress rates above everything else!"[2]

---

2. At the beginning of his exile, after Egypt, Reza Shah Pahlavi made a three-week stopover in Morocco from January 22 to March 30, 1979. King Hassan II resisted pressure from Iran and student demonstrations in Casablanca. In the face of the security questions involved, the shah decided of his own free will to leave so as to avoid creating any further trouble for his host.

I attended meetings with heads of state—what entertainment! One day he received an American delegation that needed his agreement for the use of a military air base—Ben Guerir—that had become important for NATO. He asked me to meet them before receiving them himself. They included senators who were in charge of defense questions and the head of the CIA for Western Europe—people who were rather conscious of their own importance. The king did not want to see them immediately. He was the one who decided when the meetings would take place, and especially at what time. He wanted to control timings, a political tactic to be in a strong position. At the end of the meeting, there remained only the two of us: "You let them cool their heels long enough; I got what I wanted." Everything was calculated.

Another time, in a meeting with President Jimmy Carter, understanding that the latter wanted to charm him by asking what his country needed, the king answered, "The only thing that I ask you is to give instructions to your ambassador to say that the king of Morocco *is a great guy!*" Carter was surprised by the answer, since he had been waiting for a shopping list of tanks, planes, and so forth. Let us not forget that these episodes took place in the middle of the Cold War.

In 1982, a large conference on Jerusalem took place in Fez. In the meeting room of the royal palace, his attention to detail meant that he verified in person that the interpreters' cabins were correctly wired to the microphones in the galleries. He called this room the "marshal's baton," its decoration showing brilliantly the splendor and quality of Moroccan craftsmanship: "Built to the greatest glory of our Lord," says a frieze around the room written in classical calligraphy. "Hassan II, Son of Mohammed," followed by the names of the thirty-three sovereigns of the Alaouite dynasty from its origin. He showed me a special button he had had installed at his side: "It's my panic button, so that if we bicker too much between ourselves, I can cut the sound to the cabins so that what we say goes no further!" Numerous heads of state came from the Near and Middle East—among them King Fahd of Arabia, whom I knew, and above all Yasser Arafat. In the course of the meeting, there were some clashes; I particularly remember an exchange with the Syrian minister of foreign affairs, who had said out loud just before the break,

"Come on, let's go eat; I'm hungry." And without raising his voice, King Hassan answered, "Your Excellency, my plane is ready to take you back to Damascus for your lunch."

We called Yasser Arafat "Abu Ammar." I had already met him, but dressed in regular clothes to pass incognito. Without his keffiyeh and tinted glasses, he was difficult to recognize. I also saw him at the inauguration of a chair at the University of Fez, where there were Palestinian students. I asked for news of his wife, Suha, complimenting her, and he answered with a smile, "I know why you are inquiring about her: she's Orthodox like you!" I know that he was keen to attend every year the Christmas mass in Bethlehem, seated in the front row of the grand basilica that went back to Justinian times. He came with all of his ministers in order to make the point that there were Palestinian Christians.

Arafat's eyes were particularly lively, with a darting quality, stressing that he was a man with a purpose: the liberation of Jerusalem. He was, of course, controversial when you think of the first "political" actions that made his reputation in the international arena. For some, he was nothing but a terrorist, but for others he was the incarnation of a cause, one that was close to my heart, for as an exile myself I understood the nature of his struggle. It is hard to be constrained to leave one's home with no hope of returning one day. I know something about it. And I wonder, up to this day and given recent events in the conflict, what the reaction of the international community would be if another country dared to use such disproportionate reprisal measures?

Back to Morocco: I was able to be present at other important moments, sometimes complicated meetings, such as that in 1982 with Algerian President Chadli Bendjedid, who had succeeded Houari Boumédiène. It was during the month of Ramadan; I was in Rabat, supposed to celebrate the end of fasting with an *iftar* dinner at the home of the king's sister, Princess Lalla Aicha. She had been ambassador to the Court of Saint James (the name given to London in diplomatic circles) and to Rome and was a woman of great intelligence, the spitting image of her father Mohammed V. Just before leaving, I received a telephone call asking me to excuse myself from attending the dinner, to pack some clothes (as we would be spending the night elsewhere), and to be ready in a half an hour. The king came to pick me up at the wheel of his car. There were only the two of us, followed by a car with security agents. He was silent and then said, "I'm am taking you to be a witness to a historic meeting because you are my brother. We are going to Oujda." I was speechless and intrigued, knowing about the bad relations between Morocco and Algeria. "I have a meeting with Chadli," he said. Political tensions were high, especially on the subject of Western Sahara. It must not be forgotten that the two armies had fought there in the 1960s and—just to make things even more difficult—Muammar Gaddafi's Libya supported the Polisario Front. In olden times, it was the tradition of the desert tribes to recognize the Cherifian sultan as their natural sovereign. The political borders born of colonization had not necessarily modified this behavior.

In the middle of the night, we sped along an empty road. His meeting was set for the next morning in Algeria. I remained in Oujda, in the governor's residence. After a few hours, he came back, picked me up again in his car, and said "*Bismillah*" before starting the engine in silence. As I knew him well, when I saw his sulky expression, I said nothing. "I found we have one point in common," he said suddenly. "Chadli and I have the same tailor!" That was it. I had a laughing fit, as this remark was typical of his personality, that of finding a something in common with any counterparty on which to build. It turned out that the meeting was useful in bringing both countries closer.

Sometimes I wondered why he wanted me by his side in such events. After so many years of friendship and discretion on my side, I think my presence was comforting to him and helped him feel at ease. Perhaps I was someone he could trust as a peer, not as a subordinate. I never hesitated to tell him what I really thought, and he appreciated that. I had also come to understand that the fact that I was related to all the royal families of Europe intrigued him. Was I a sort of bridgehead with the continent that he found so fascinating and interesting?

With Spain, it was easy for me to pass on messages that required confidentiality. I was friends with both sovereigns, a guest in each of the two countries. I admit that this was rather unique, and if I could prove useful, so much better. I would go to La Zarzuela Palace to report to King

Juan Carlos what had been said to me in Rabat, just as Prime Minister Felipe González (who got on very well with King Hassan) did, and this was not always the case with other government heads.

*

I was also able to witness the nature of the relationship between Hassan II and Hussein of Jordan, with whom I had been a close friend since attending the same school in Alexandria.[3] It was fascinating to see them together. The two of them were fond of each other, despite their very different personalities, with the Hashemite sovereign having more of a British education. Instead, Hassan was basically the portrait of the cultivated "honest man" in the eighteenth-century sense and a French speaker; Hussein tended to be a man of action and was English speaking. The one was more in nuances, the other more direct. In short, they did not always understand each other completely. They represented, each in his own manner, faces of a different culture that were as far apart as the geographical location of their two countries: the two sides of the Arab world, put simply.

At the end of the famous Fez summit, there was a "diplomatic" incident between the two sovereigns that is a good illustration of their different approaches. Unable to accompany King Hussein to the airport himself, Hassan II had his oldest son do so. The former took this decision visibly badly, considering that he had been slighted. In the plane, he found a copious Moroccan lunch, composed of tajines sent by the palace: he immediately had them taken off the plane and left on the runway. I was present when the young prince reported the incident to his father!

Curiously, and despite his dynamism, the Jordanian sovereign never wanted to play the role of leader in the Arab world; he left that to others. Another amusing anecdote concerning him goes back to the famous

---

3. King Hussein awarded me the Supreme Order of the Renaissance, the highest distinction of Jordan. In exchange, I awarded him the Order of Saint Cyril and Methodius, created by King Ferdinand in honor of our Independence. It was reserved for sovereigns and certain heads of state and, in some extremely exceptional cases, for Bulgarian citizens of merit. During my exile, I awarded a few to some heads of state, but since my return to Bulgaria, I have suspended the practice. I will leave to my descendants the prerogative of awarding, if they so judge, the Order of Saint Alexander, but not that of Cyril and Methodius, which remains a privilege attached solely to the sovereign.

night of February 1981 and the attempted coup d'état in Madrid, when he telephoned Juan Carlos to put a unit of special forces at his disposal to support the king's loyal troops. He was this type of character.

Hussein was an energetic, hands-on king who would drive his motorcycle along the desert roads of Jordan. Through the 1960s and 1970s, we visited him several times in Aqaba, on the coast of the Red Sea, where he would stay in rudimentary English military hangars with his still very young children. We took advantage of the turquoise waters of the coast and enjoyed boating and diving—he was very sporty. Once we even tried to water-ski, harnessed to camels that ran along the banks of the water. This did not last long, but we enjoyed ourselves greatly. He liked challenges, such as the acts of bravado he performed in planes that he piloted himself. Hashemites adore military-inspired courage.

At the beginning of Black September, in 1970, we happened to be together in Amman, and we found ourselves stuck in the city. Attacks had taken place in the preceding weeks. From La Bahia, the royal palace reserved for guests where my wife and I were lodged, we had heard the first noises of combat announcing a stormy period for Jordan and for regional equilibrium. Just before dinner, after several explosions, I realized that these were not fireworks but the sound of mortars. A few seconds later, an aide-de-camp knocked on our door to tell us to follow him immediately. We were not yet dressed for dinner; we were told that the staff would pack our luggage. In semi-darkness, we sped forward, hearing the dry snaps of gunfire. At the royal compound, a group of outbuildings of the palace, situated outside Amman, dinner was waiting for us—a buffet dinner in the Jordanian manner. King Hussein was still not present. Toward midnight, the door opened and in he came, in field uniform: "I am sorry for the delay, but we had a few problems tonight." We stayed two more days because no planes were flying. In the mornings, the king and his headquarters staff would study operations against the *fedayins* of the Palestinian Liberation Organization, which had created a true state-within-a-state. The Royal Guard, formerly the Arab Legion of General Glubb Pacha, protected us. The king asked me to join his uncle, Cherif Nasser, to inspect the troops, in a jeep with a heavy machine gun mounted on it. In the middle of the applause and the shots into the air, carried away by his enthusiasm, the prince began to shoot a few rounds skyward. Back at the palace and hearing all the racket, Margarita thought the final assault had come and we had all died.

Once the airport was secure, a small dual-engine plane was sent from the palace at Aqaba because international flights were blocked. It was a terrible week with thousands of deaths. The general in charge of the city used the artillery in the very streets of Amman.

Aside from his warrior side, Hussein was a very warm, charming man who hosted his guests with care and great generosity. We would go together to visit the Roman ruins at Jerash, which he carefully preserved. We also visited Petra, surrounded by horsemen in superb *keffiyehs* and impressively armed. In the course of our conversations, we talked about the history of the Ottoman Empire, the role of his ancestors in the Arabian Peninsula, the equilibrium of the Near East and American policy, and, of course, of our shared memories of our Egyptian childhood. He still had graduates of Victoria College in his entourage. Our link to Ottoman history made us close, for both Bulgaria and Jordan had suffered Turkish domination. My relationship with him was more than cordial, one of friendship from childhood. He was a little older than me but had been put into my class since he didn't yet speak English. An always polite and obliging boy, he was known by the name of Hussein Talal, from his father's given name.

When Hussein was sixteen, his grandfather, King Abdullah I, was assassinated before his eyes in front of the Al-Aqsa Mosque in Jerusalem, where he was attending Friday prayers. He told me about being hit himself, saved by the bullet ricocheting off a decoration he was wearing on his chest.

He was at ease in his relationship with his subjects and they reciprocated that feeling—especially the Bedouins, who venerated him. When the territorial waters between Jordan and Israel were opened, he was welcomed in the waters of Eilat by an ovation. He was popular on both sides of the border. When I went to Israel for the first time, I was given the opportunity of bringing back a message for the king confided to me by the minister of foreign affairs, Abba Eban.

I am delighted to have been able to follow the development of King Abdullah II since his birth and to observe how his father prepared him for his difficult role, despite the vicissitudes of his life. He also welcomed me when I was prime minister of Bulgaria, and it was as if I were seeing his father again in him. Another great friend is Prince Hassan of Jordan, brother of Hussein and regent during many long and difficult years, for whom I have very sincere admiration. An all-around man of matchless culture and sensitivity, who more than once has adopted courageous intellectual positions to defend inter-religious dialogue, including the defense of Eastern Christians. It is really very regrettable that due to the adverse circumstances, he was not able to become secretary general of the United Nations, especially in this part of the world where there is a deficit of men with integrity and charisma.

In the region, I discovered Syria for the first time in 1964,[4] having gone to visit the remains of the Stylite basilica, where Saint Simeon preached in the fourth century. The base of its column remains, situated on a knoll that dominates the vast rocky plain in the surroundings of Aleppo. I went to admire the land of my holy patron, and I was not disappointed by its majesty and austerity. I remember having begun to read the marvelous book by Jacques Lacarrière, *Les Hommes ivres de Dieu*, evoking the madness of those monks living at the tops of their columns. I asked our guide a question in Arabic, but as I have an Egyptian accent, he quickly suspected me of being a spy. That very evening, I had a visit from agents of the Second Office at my hotel. Of course, we visited Damascus, where, at the Great Mosque of Umayyad, I was surprised to see that a small chapel had been built around the relic of the skull of Saint John the Baptist. This was the proof that there were places of worship Christians shared with Islam. We went by Hama as well, where I was impressed by the size of the wooden waterwheels that had been carrying water for centuries—then saddened that the city was partially razed a few years later, in 1982. I can't imagine what state these places so rich in history are in now, after so many years of civil war.

I also visited Lebanon a few times, staying in Beirut, where I met Bulgarians as well as Armenians. The last time there was on an official visit where I was hosted by the much-regretted Rafic Hariri. I am heart-

---

4. There is a legend that my mother and I supposedly fled to Syria in 1944, when in fact I did not leave Bulgaria until September 1946.

sick as I follow the news of the Near East, having such strong personal relationships in the countries concerned. The memories of cosmopolitan Alexandria and the occasional encounters with my beloved classmates—who became lifelong friends—have opened my mind to vastly different societies while allowed me to witness the end of the old world.

I now realize that many of my trips enabled me to return to the Mediterranean, a part of the world where I feel at home, with a history that fascinates me and goes back to our roots in ancient Greece, Rome, and Constantinople with the Ottoman Turks, who kept the idea of an Oriental empire alive into the beginning of the twentieth century. My pet subject—that of a Union of Black Sea countries—comes to me perhaps from the influence of the Mediterranean Basin on cultural and economic grounds. I will never forget the first time I read Fernand Braudel's *The Mediterranean*, and above all the masterly biography *Frederick II* by the historian Ernst Kantorowicz, who introduced me to Sicily and the south of Italy. I have always been fascinated by the Lecce Palace, which is so strange in appearance.

*

In 1999, at the time of the death of Hassan II, I still remember the grief-stricken faces of all those close to him. It was Friday, July 23, or 9 Rabie II 1420 in the Era of Hijra. I was in tears. Even if we knew he was ill, no one expected such a premature end. Moroccan friends came to present their condolences to me as if we belonged to the same family, which greatly touched me. I didn't know how to react. He was for me such a great friend, a man whom I could really trust. Friendship is a rare thing in life, especially when it is given with generosity.

The next day, Margarita and I flew to Rabat with our five children to be at the side of the family and to comfort them to the best of our abilities. A period of national mourning of forty days was declared. Crown Prince Sidi Mohammed, features drawn and his face afflicted with grief, appeared on national television and recited verses from the Koran before appealing to his people to be "calm and patient." The streets were truly sad. Flags were at half-mast. In Islam, burial takes place very quickly, normally before the next sunset, but it was pushed back to the following

Sunday, to give time for numerous foreign delegations to arrive in Rabat. I was given the privilege of entering the mausoleum where his father, Mohammed V, also rests. In the streets of the city, there was an immense crowd, tumultuous and downcast. Everyone wanted to get close to the catafalque, covered in the colors of Morocco and quotations from the Koran. In the front rows, I recognized many well-known faces, heads of state from the world over, kings and presidents from Africa and Asia, all carried away in this daunting crush of people. Even an Israeli delegation had come. I can still see the face of French president Jacques Chirac, tall and elegant, head above the crowd, like Bill Clinton. The event was broadcast live by more than twenty-four television channels.

By a sad turn of fate, King Hussein had died a few months earlier, in February. I had lost these two brothers in just a few months. It has always stuck in my throat that I never knew what they'd have said, or thought, on the subject of my balloting victory and my role as prime minister of the Republic of Bulgaria.

CHAPTER ELEVEN

Travels

IN THE COURSE OF THESE YEARS, IN PARALLEL WITH BUSINESS TRIPS, I began to travel to maintain my high-level international contacts. Given my status as an exile, and particularly in view of the hostility between two blocs—the free world and the Communist world—these trips contributed greatly to my intellectual genesis. It was difficult at the time to isolate oneself from a geopolitical reality that entirely occupied media space. I resented that there were many countries forbidden to me. Basically, my world—like old maps—had entire chunks left blank with *terra incognita* marked on them. The only exception was a brief incursion in the summer of 1975 into the Soviet Union, when, out of curiosity, I accepted the invitation of a Greek friend to join him with my mother and wife for a musical cruise on the Baltic Sea. We were to make a stopover in Saint Petersburg (then Leningrad), and I was hoping that our Rylski alias would not be spotted—we still had our Italian passports with that surname—and that we could melt into the crowd of passengers. It was a beautiful experience: I visited the Hermitage and soaked up a little of the atmosphere of the lovely city I had heard so much about from my Romanov cousins. As we got off the boat, we were required to leave our passports at the sentry box at customs, where the person in charge gave us a receipt valid for the day. Everyone had to remain with the group. In the course of a museum visit, I asked to see the famous collection of Fabergé objects that had belonged to the imperial family. The guide told us that "the trinkets that ruined the state are not on display." I imprudently answered back, "There are plenty of other ways to ruin an economy."

Then, in a portrait gallery exhibiting Russian generals in ceremonial uniforms, I read the names of some of them directly from the Russian, which attracted the attention of some people near us. I couldn't help myself: the guide told us any old thing and refused to be corrected, confusing the Duke of Wellington with General Kutuzov—nonsense, even if both of them fought Napoleon's armies.

The next day, I thought it wiser to stay on the boat while my mother and Margarita visited the Cathedral of Saint Isaac—it had been transformed for a time into the Museum of Atheism. A few months later, in Madrid, a German friend, who visited the Soviet Union often to provide BMW motorcycles to the Russian public services, asked me, "Simeon, have you ever been to Leningrad?" I began by denying it, since I had never told anyone about that visit. He said that he had a message for me from Shchelokov, minister of the interior, who had told him that he regretted that I had limited my visit to Leningrad and that I could have continued to Moscow. There was a great deal of irony in this comment. In fact, during our stopover, the political police had been at leisure to photograph and study our passports. Retroactively, I broke out in a cold sweat when I realized that the KGB was so efficient that the information had traveled far up among the authorities of the regime. I couldn't help but parallel this situation with all the restraints that my fellow countrymen were enduring at the same time in their daily lives in Bulgaria.

In 1964, and despite the opacity of the system, the fall of Khrushchev was met with great hope. Above all, the fact that such a senior person could be in disgrace showed that there was movement inside that hermetic world, contrary to what we saw from abroad. However, the arrival in power of Leonid Brezhnev augured nothing good at all and plunged the Soviet Union anew into a long period of sleep. Thanks to good relations with the intelligence services of several Western countries, I was able to obtain reliable information to better follow the evolution of the infighting between clans and better understand what was happening by ricochet in Bulgaria.

Basically, beyond the political dogma, I discovered that their rivalries were profoundly human, the kind that exist in any society. Thus, despite appearances, there were tensions in the Communist regime, whether in the rivalries at the heart of the army or among ethnic groups. For example, after the fall of Stalin and Beria, Georgians became outcasts, as did Jews after the dismissal of Lazar Kaganovich, another former close associate. In Bulgaria, the guidelines decided by the Kremlin had instant repercussions, and, as a master in these sort of mysteries, Todor Zhivkov—in charge of the Sofia regime—managed to foil numerous plots against him and adapt to what was coming from Moscow.

In the same political climate, I went to Asia in 1969. While in Taiwan, I had the opportunity to meet Generalissimo Chiang Kai-shek,[1] who had returned to the international scene during the Korean War after having supported American intervention in Maoist China. I had contacted his government through the ambassador of Republic of China (Taiwan) in Madrid. The idea was for me to visit a country fully engaged in the fight against Communism. During this time, dear Margarita was waiting for me in Hong Kong, where we were to join a group of Spanish businessmen with whom we had already visited the Philippines and met President Marcos.

The very afternoon of my arrival, I was received by the elderly Chiang Kai-shek for a meeting at his palace. We wanted to talk about the situation of our respective countries. He spoke to me in Mandarin, and a Chinese naval officer who had studied at the War College in Madrid translated into Spanish for me. In the course of our exchange, thinking it would please him, I asked him whether he thought that the major incidents between Russians and Chinese that had just taken place on the Sino-Soviet frontier, near the Amur River, would not work in favor of his cause to "liberate the continent," to use the formula employed at the time.[2] There had been a dangerous escalation of violence between the two nuclear powers. Having taken time to think it over, as he often did in responding, he said, "Not at all, the Soviets are in any case imperialists." Cold shower. This was, first and foremost, the response of a Chinese man, someone who could take no pleasure in the misfortunes of his country. He was no doubt remembering the territories that had been taken from

---

1. Until death, his title was "President of the Republic of China," which enraged Mao.
2. The two powers had come to armed combat, causing dozens of victims on both sides, over the sovereignty of the island of Zhenbao, a border question that was only settled in 1991.

China at the end of the nineteenth century. In the 1920s, when he was a young officer, he went to Moscow on training courses several times in order to meet the leaders of the Comintern, the Third Communist International. This meant that he was well acquainted with their mentality and could read their intentions.

A few minutes before the end of the audience, an aide-de-camp announced, "Her Excellency, Madame." We stood up and his wife entered, dressed in a traditional Chinese outfit in dark red silk with black patterns. Having grown up in America, she spoke perfect English. Her older sister had been the wife of Sun Yat-sen, founder of the Chinese Republic in 1911. We spent a brief moment together, and I remember her very elegant silhouette and the dinner that followed. She died in New York in 2003, at almost 106 years old.

The National Palace Museum in Taipei had just been inaugurated and was fascinating, with a traditional Chinese façade backed up to a hill that had been hollowed out as a safety measure against bombing. It shelters the marvelous objects of Chinese art that were brought from Nanjing, in November 1948, or some ten thousand objects forming a part of the impressive collections of the Forbidden City. I was spellbound by the grace of these unusual objects in jade, bronze, and celadon—I myself have a small collection—that allowed me a closer approach to a culture that at the time was not popular at all. I had discovered China in the warm humidity of Taiwan while, at the very same time, the insanity of the Cultural Revolution had begun next door.

The day after this meeting, I had been invited to go to the island of Quemoy, which is located just across the Strait of Formosa, almost touching China. Two large garrisons face one another, in a situation comparable to what is still that of the two Koreas. I went there with the general in charge of the troops, aboard a rickety DC-3. The plane hedgehopped to avoid People's China's radar. It was scary; I felt that it could fall apart at any time. The Chinese pilot was an ex-Flying Tiger, the squadron based in China during the Sino-Japanese War. Highly experienced, he was an aviation ace, belonging to those pilots trained by the Americans under the command of General Joseph Stilwell, known as "Vinegar Joe." In an immense underground bunker, I addressed a group of several hundred officers who, when I entered, stood up as one man and warmly applauded me. They knew that I had been a victim of Communism too. We set adrift several balloons full of propaganda for the continent—a symbolic gesture—and then I got to observe that thanks to the masses of high-powered speakers on each side of the strait, the camps were able to enthusiastically insult one other. It was the eve of the Tet Festival, and on the return flight the officers brought back a particular kind of fish that can only be found in the islands. It smelled to high heaven! As the flight was just as bumpy, we all turned quite green. The poor general sitting next to me looked very ill indeed. He was wearing a high-necked uniform: "Very sick! Very sick!" he said to me.

When I was prime minister, I was put under pressure to recognize Taiwan. Although I was sympathetic to their cause, I did not give in, for despite their dynamism, the demographic weight of continental China will always be decisive. I don't yet see any possibility of the reunification of the two Chinas, since their mindsets are so different: in Taiwan, I had the impression that in a certain way "old" China had lost. Mrs. Hu Hi, the vice president of the Chinese government, brought a large delegation to Sofia, and naturally I received them with every possible consideration. She was very tiny, wore a Chanel suit, and spoke very good English. She took me by the waist to place me for the "family" photo, and for an Asian woman, that is proof of quite a personality. I had also received the Chinese minister in charge of European affairs, who happened to mention that they were in the process of building thirty-one nuclear power plants in the course of the conversation; I, meanwhile, was fighting like the devil for the construction of just a single new one.

One of my regrets is not to have been able to make the return visit to Beijing that might have consolidated our partnership during my time in office. Nevertheless, we were able to begin exchange programs that continue to grow even at present. The Chinese neglect not one single opportunity. For them, there are no small countries. As a return on their investments, I endeavored also to sing the praises of our region's tourist attractions, through a joint development project undertaken with our neighbors, which I call the "Golden Triangle": Istanbul-Sofia-Athens. I often tried to "sell" to my counterparties the idea of a tourist package that we could propose to the Chinese. But with all of our infighting in Bulgaria, we ended up forgetting what was really important. We are not yet capable of going beyond ourselves to think about the interests of our country! We have great shortcomings—not astonishing in view of our past—and I believe that the best way to make up for them is through education, the study of history, and opening up our country to the world.

After this visit, we went to Thailand to see the royal family, several of whom we already knew. The visit had no purpose other than friendship and discovery. I had met several family members at the marriage of King Constantine in Athens in 1964. Since then we had established ties with two of the princesses who often came to Europe to attend the marriages of our relatives. They were very up to date on European culture and kept abreast of everything going on in London, Paris and Madrid. When I first saw Bangkok, the city was still clustered around the lake, especially the palace buildings and the old quarters, so different from the megalopolis it has become since. King Rama IX spoke very good French, but our conversations were in English so that the queen could understand. The protocol was most spectacular: his subjects were forbidden to approach him standing up. I had been invited to attend a Thai boxing match, accompanied by one of the princes. We were seated in a sort of loge, and even in these circumstances, the military officers who approached went down on their knees to speak to him. As I was quite close, I, too, benefited indirectly from this attention: I was surprised, but each country has traditions that must be respected.

While speaking of trips that took place during those quite particular years of international tensions, I can hardly ignore a long visit to Angola and Mozambique at the invitation of the president of the Portuguese government, Dr. António de Oliveira Salazar. He spent his summers in Estoril, and that is where I met him. He did not travel and thought perhaps that we were linked together by anti-Communist solidarity. I was lucky enough to discover the two immense countries when they were still Portuguese provinces of great wealth and was welcomed as if on an official visit. According to a Japanese engineer whom I met in Luanda, Angola was "geologically scandalous," so infinite did its mineral resources seem. This afterward sharpened the appetites of many. Some of the country was already at war: the fight for independence had begun. When I returned to Lisbon, in his very refined French, Salazar said, "Your Majesty, now in exchange, you must answer my questions without holding back anything." This was how he informed himself about the efficiency of his administration, the quality of the men I had encountered, the governors, mayors, officers, directors of mines, and even about the advance of work on some projects. He paid great attention to my answers, and I saw that he was registering the smallest details. In the 1960s, the people expelled from Angola were called *retornados*; this group included almost one million people of Lusitanian origin who were forced to leave Angola, Mozambique, and Guinea-Bissau.

Among other remarkable personalities—the kind you meet only once in your life—I would like to mention the members of the imperial family of Iran.[3] Even if the shah came to Spain on an official visit with the Empress Soraya in 1957, I only met him for the first time in Iran at the very beginning of the 1970s. He knew many of my cousins and had made state visits to several monarchies and other European countries. His brother was already a friend of mine, Prince Abdorreza, an excellent hunter who often came to Spain. The charm of the shah was comparable to that which Iranians are reputed for. No one who has visited the country can avoid falling for it. I went to Tehran in 1972 with my wife. We wanted to explore the country, for we had heard so much about it, and at the time its development was absolutely amazing. We went as tourists, visiting the major attractions such as Shiraz, Isfahan, and Mashhad, one of the holy cities for Shi'a situated at the border of Turkmenistan. I was struck by the beauty of the monuments, the hospitality of the people, and the culture. I noted certain similarities with our language, especially in words dealing with food, transmitted to us by the lengthy period of Ottoman presence in our country. I had read the poetry of Ferdowsi in my youth and had dreamed about what the country might be like.

---

3. Historically, its first link with Bulgaria goes back to the time of Simeon the Great when a Persian ambassador came to see us and vice versa.

In Tehran, the shah invited us to visit him at Niavaran Palace, situated in the heights of the city in the Shemiran section and completed in 1968. Golestan Palace, in the middle of the city, where he had been the target of an assassination attempt shortly before, was more for official ceremonies.

I had noted that the shah had innovative ideas for the development of his country, especially in the area of education. He had also decided to modernize the economy but had upset religious authorities with his White Revolution.[4] In addition, he saw Iran as a military power to be reckoned with in the region. In the Indian Ocean, for example, he reflected on the naval role that Iran could play. I remember him telling me one day that the Diego Garcia military base might one day become Iranian with English and American support, an example of his vision in terms of foreign affairs. Afterward, we had several invitations, one to visit an estate on the Caspian Sea, another to Babolsar. My feeling was that the man dominated that part of the world at the time. Foreign powers admired and paid court to Iran. It was also perhaps because of their greed that the government was at risk of being destabilized, but no one had foreseen what would follow, nor the thousands of dead once the Islamic Republic had been put into place. The shah's physical presence instilled unanimous respect. The fact that he was the emperor of an important country meant that he was the subject of many requests. He stood very straight and maintained a certain distance from those around him, more as a defense mechanism because he was basically rather shy. Once I went to see him in the company of his brother, Abdorreza, and after several anterooms, the prince quite ostensibly handed over his pistol to a bodyguard just before reaching the door to the office. For a good part of our meeting, he remained standing, whereas the shah had signaled me to be seated like him.

In the midst of all this protocol, Empress Farah brought a dose of human warmth, thanks to her youth, as well as the fact that she was educated in Paris, like the other young women of her age whom she

---

4. Beginning in 1963, the shah launched a program of agrarian reform against the large land owners and religious authorities, for which he was never forgiven. In social terms, the Revolution gave rights to women, allowing expansion of the medical corps and development of education in rural areas.

came across in architectural school. Since their exile, I have constantly been in admiration of her behavior and have never heard her utter neither a word of bitterness nor one of vengeance against those who have made her family, her friends, and her country suffer so much. A great lady, unquestionably.

At the time of Zhivkov, the imperial couple made a state visit to Bulgaria. Later, they described the house where they had been lodged by the regime, which is the one—by happy coincidence—where I now live near Sofia. Very kindly, the "Shabanou"[5] had a postcard sent to me in the diplomatic pouch in which she praised the beauty of the country, and this gesture touched me greatly. I also learned that the authorities had used the very beautiful yellow porcelain tableware that dated from the time of my grandfather Ferdinand because the imperial couple had noticed our coat of arms. This was a service I remembered quite well from my childhood.

To come back to the context of the Cold War, as early as 1959, during a dinner at the Spanish embassy in Washington after my studies at the military academy, I had the feeling that the alternative to the Soviet presence would eventually be a *pax americana*. This was after the war in Korea and before the American engagement in Vietnam in preparation. As far as both the Mediterranean basin and the Middle East were concerned, it was clear that the Atlantic policy included the fall of monarchies, completing a process begun after World War I. It is also worth noting that the United States sometimes abandoned its allies depending on its priorities of the moment. The result of such a policy remains to be seen.

Another great royal character who fascinated me well before I met him was the emperor of Ethiopia, Haile Selassie. I was introduced to him by one of his grandsons, Counter-Admiral Iskander—Alexander— Desta, whom I had met in Belgium at the wedding of King Baudoin. He was the son of the famous Ras Desta, one of the great chiefs who had fought against Italy during the Abyssinian War, whose head had been displayed on a stake by Marshal Graziani. I was the grandson of the man who, because of the war in West Africa, had been proclaimed king

---

5. Name given to the shah's wife.

and emperor; despite this fact, the Ethiopian sovereign always greeted me with real affection. During my stays, I was pleased to see that the Italians were still present and active in the country, especially in Eritrea, where Italian was still spoken by a fair number of people. On one of our trips, the emperor received us not far from Addis Ababa, in Debre Zeit, in his villa, which was called "Fairfield," after the residence he had lived in during his exile in England. We spoke French together. His presence was striking for someone who was so small, with his upright posture making him seem taller. His penetrating look was a reflection of his sharp intelligence, as did his slender hands with their elegant gestures. His voice was unconsciously monotonous, giving the impression that he expressed himself in maxims. He chose his words carefully, and they were never anything but to the point. It seemed obvious to me that, more than anyone else, I had in front of me an incarnation of the past millennium. This was without taking into consideration the famous speech that he gave before the League of Nations in 1936, which earned him his place in the great annals of contemporary history. The present I chose for him was a large book I had inherited from my grandfather's library: the hagiography of a Coptic saint—a beautiful work, then, that I had brought for him. According to Ethiopian tradition, I had wrapped it in red velvet. As soon as he opened it, he held it to his chest and closed his eyes: "I am very grateful for this present, which is coming back to a place it never should have left. Especially from your hands, you, the grandson of Victor Emmanuel III." That was when I understood that this was an important ecclesiastical book, taken by Marshal Graziani and given to my grandfather. Thus, without having done it on purpose, I had repaired a historical injustice.

Another time, we went to Eritrea, then a province of Ethiopia giving it access to the sea. I accompanied him to a high mass in Asmara, on the Feast of the Archangel Michael. The emperor held an important place in the national church. I then went to the residence of the governor general, the much-regretted Ras Kassa, driven in a green Mercedes. There was a lion skin lying at my feet, and people continually bowed when the car passed, since it was known to belong to Haile Selassie. Not long before, near my hotel, I had noticed a car parked, Russian made and with diplomatic plates. The next day, I was to have a secret meeting with a Bulgarian, the director of a large firm dealing in fish who had let me know that he wanted to defect. He absolutely wanted to meet with me, and I was very apprehensive when he knocked at the door of my room. The unknown man signaled that I should not say anything and headed directly to the bathroom, where he turned on all the faucets. Sitting on the side of the tub, I felt like I was in a James Bond film: "I don't want to return to Bulgaria. I'm trapped. Help me, I beg of you!" Seeing the state he was in, I informed Ras Kassa, the governor of Eritrea, and then telephoned my contacts in Rome. Within twenty-four hours, we managed to send him toward Italy, from whence he emigrated to South America, where his sons had good careers. The Ethiopian secret services confirmed to me that the owner of the car was a Bulgarian diplomat, who had taken the room just under mine, probably to be able to listen more easily.

In the 1990s, I was able to see from my file that the Bulgarian Communist services were informed about everything about me. My family and I were followed for all those years, something confirmed by studying hundreds of pages of information collected by a team of surveillance agents. As the irony of fate would have it, I had to work with some of them in my years as prime minister.

Ethiopia is a country of incredible splendor with startling contrasts, both in the landscapes and in the beauty of the people and their natural elegance. I was also introduced to the abouna—that is to say, the patriarch of the church—who encouraged me to visit the holy places of his country, Aksum and the rock-hewn churches of Lalibela. The diplomats posted there called him the "Richelieu of Addis Ababa." Each of the places he recommended had first-rate historical treasures.

Another time, I went there with a Spanish friend, Nicolas Franco, to hunt near the border with Sudan. As I knew the emperor did not enjoy the sport, I didn't think I needed to signal my presence. This decision was not well taken. His grandson Iskander even came to greet me at the airport: "His Imperial Majesty is not happy at all that you didn't say you were coming, but we can go by way of the palace to see him before you leave for the south." I went. The building was low, ocher in color and surrounded by a beautiful garden. Hearing the clinking of chains,

I turned around and saw one of his lions walking behind us. They had their forepaws shackled so that they couldn't attack. In the throne room, I found the emperor standing up, ramrod stiff and in ceremonial dress, for he had his audiences. I approached and held out my hand to him: "Sir, what a pleasure it is to see you again!" He remained with both hands on his saber, staring at me before answering in a quiet voice, "I don't believe it since you didn't let me know of your presence in Ethiopia." That was that, and naturally he scheduled a time for me to see him on my return.

In hindsight, I find that he had a very acute sense of history. His questions were always very polished. My Italian side intrigued him since it was a reminder of the war between the two countries. As is well known, my uncle, the duke of Aosta, was named the viceroy of Ethiopia. Interned and a prisoner of the English, he died in Nairobi in 1941 because his tuberculosis was left untreated. And yet, leaving Addis, he had made sure that Haile Selassie's property was protected, and the latter was grateful to him. I also got to know the Crown Prince Asfa Wossen. The end of the imperial family was despicable—some shot, some poisoned (even the women), and the emperor strangled in the palace after the Derg military coup in 1976. Its leader was Sergeant Mengistu Haile Mariam, who had been trained by the Americans before turning to the Soviet Union for support. The more things change, the more they stay the same. Alas.

Having known both of these countries, Ethiopia and Iran, before their respective revolutions, I can say that revolution brought strictly nothing better for their peoples. Along the same line of thought, even though I hate generalizations, the same could be said of other uprisings that sparked all sorts of blind enthusiasm. How many people of value were murdered in vain in this way? Those elites who were dragged through the mud remind me of the tragic fate of my Uncle Kyril in Bulgaria and many other victims who had no blood on their hands but were sacrificed on the altar of ideology.

*

During a trip to Israel in 1972, once again the history of my country and the legacy of my father caught up with me. I had been invited to Tel Aviv for the bar mitzvah of the son of one of my friends, Nick Mor-

ley, who had made a fortune in real estate. His father, Yossif Mechou-
lam, had known my father, as they owned a hardware store across from
the palace that was called "Buy and Break." Once settled in the United
States, they had Americanized their name to Morley. During the
war, the family had left Bulgaria with the help of my mother, Queen
Giovanna. She got passports for Jewish families through the Italian
legation; the Spanish legation did the same thing. My Aunt Eudoxia,
who had remained in Bulgaria since the beginning of the war, also
helped in that regard by calling on a network of the friends she had
developed as an artist. I thus saw the family again in Madrid, when they
came to ask me for a favor: they wanted me to ask King Hussein of
Jordan to allow the remains of Nick's younger brother—who had died
in the first Israeli-Arab War—to be repatriated. They were able to give
me the identification number, and forty-eight hours later, the coffin was
crossing Allenby Bridge.

In gratitude, Nick Morley absolutely wanted us to be present at the
bar mitzvah of his only son, Melvin. My memory of it is indelible. Too
moved to be able to answer his son as tradition demands, he announced
to those gathered, "I would like my king to answer in my place." I had,
of course, prepared nothing, but I couldn't let him down. I thus began
to address the six hundred or so guests, and after the usual "Ladies and
gentlemen" in English, I spoke to them in Bulgarian: "My dear compatriots." I immediately felt an intense wave of joy go through the crowd of
guests. People stood up to applaud me; the Bulgarians had tears in their
eyes, because my presence reminded them of the courageous positions
taken by my father, positions that had protected them from persecution
and probably from death. Six months later, I received a letter from one
of these Bulgarians, who had become Israeli, telling me that he had been
present at the celebration, but as he was in the military, he did not have
the right to write letters abroad until the end of his service. He thanked
me for addressing them as "compatriots" and not as foreigners. In Alexandria, I had already understood that my father was a hero thanks to the
presence of the Jews we had come across in Egypt.

A few years later, this same Morley decided to dedicate a bust to
King Boris as part of a development project. I regretted that my mother

was not able to make the trip with us. In 1992, during a visit to Los Angeles, Rabbi Haim Meyer very proudly showed me that on the main computer of the Museum of the Holocaust, when you type "Bulgaria," not a single death appears.

In April 1941, my country signed a pact with Germany. In Sofia, the representative of the Third Reich was infuriated when he understood that they had been tricked by my father's government, putting the pact in place to avoid handing over our Jewish citizens. As we were allies, no action could be taken, and the complaints and pressure exerted from Berlin about our lack of cooperation had to remain on a diplomatic level.

Dr. Djerassi was our dentist at the palace, and my sister and I trembled at the thought of going to see him. It was through him that I discovered the word *Jewish*. I remember one day my father saying to my mother, "Menahem is dead." Mama was very sad, but I didn't understand what had happened. Later she explained to us that he had committed suicide. He had become frightened and shut himself in his garage with the engine of his car running. This was also my first contact with the idea of death. There were no ghettos in our country, and the Bulgarian people were never anti-Semitic. Jews served in the army and were not barred from any public administration responsibilities. The church immediately raised opposition to deportations. In Plovdiv, Metropolitan Kyril threatened to lie down on the railroad tracks to prevent trains from leaving. The subterfuge found by my father was to say that he needed all the Jews in order to support the war effort. "I need them," he said to the Germans. Families had been moved to the countryside, to avoid them being close to the capital, where there might be incidents with Nazi sympathizers. During the day, men worked on community service projects but went home at night. The role of civil society was also very important.

My father played for time by every possible means. He knew that the war was a serious mistake, a lost cause. But his role was systematically minimized for political reasons, as if the idea that a king could behave in a heroic fashion was unacceptable. The philosopher George Steiner, whom I knew well through our common friend George Embiricos, said something very flattering about his role.

My sadness was great when, in the 1990s, Israel backed away from giving him a distinction for being one of the "righteous"[6] because of a campaign initiated in Bulgaria to denigrate him. After the war, we didn't know what to think; it was only in the 1950s that the story resurfaced. Rumors coming from Israel confirmed that many families had been saved by my Uncle Kyril. There is still much left to write about this painful period. I do not understand the resentment expressed by certain Jews remaining in Bulgaria against my father and myself. For them, King Boris was a collaborator working for Nazi Germany, and if he had been compelled to make the decision to save the Jews, it was certainly not of his own initiative but because he was forced to do so by the people and the Communist Party. I find it completely unacceptable that a noisy minority could rewrite history in a spirit that is purely political. I can no longer stand this attempt to make history disappear. Lies will be erased all by themselves.

In 1992, I was at the Parliament in Strasbourg to commemorate the famous Dimitar Peshev, my father's former minister of justice, who had opposed deportation. I was fortunate to be seated next to Simone Weil as Bulgaria was celebrated for being one of the rare countries in Europe that had defended its Jews. I was very proud of being Bulgarian that day, as I was on the day when I received a letter of congratulations from the Simon Wiesenthal Center. I note that the usual crew of revisionists always waits until the main characters are no longer present to reframe history in a way that suits them. And these are labels stick like mud. I think that even a very small amount of integrity and human conscience would give my father his true role back. The orders were clear, and they came from the highest level of the state.

---

6. "Righteous among the Nations": a certificate of honor attributed in Jerusalem to those who during the Holocaust risked their lives to save Jews. Nearly 25,000 are commemorated at Yad Vashem.

CHAPTER TWELVE

My Political Battle

Ferto fereris (Forgive and you will be forgiven)

AFTER MY TRIUMPHAL RETURN IN MAY 1996, I CONTINUED TO FOLLOW the advice of my uncle Archduke Otto: I returned to Bulgaria several times to understand the atmosphere, get to know the country better, and see what could be done to contribute to a better political transition. The economic situation was very difficult for many of my fellow countrymen, with a high rate of unemployment. Coming out of a long totalitarian sleep, society could not help but be in turmoil. The gap was widening dramatically between those who had something and those who had less than nothing. With inflation, pension payments no longer represented much of anything. It was tough for people to accept as good democrats those who had oppressed them, let alone see the heirs of the Communist regime enriching themselves obscenely on the ruins of our economy.

I wanted people to get used to my presence. However, it was practically impossible for me to bring down the curtain so easily on almost forty years in Spain. I had to think of my children and my grandchildren, my business, my home and my contacts. With hindsight, I realize that if I did not want to sell my house in Madrid at the time, it was because I considered that my rights in Bulgaria were not sufficiently warranted. The troubles that we had afterward with our Bulgarian estates, alas, have confirmed this intuition. I did not want to risk losing everything for my children or putting a great part of my life in jeopardy with no assurances for the future. News stories in Bulgaria still show examples of the violation of these essential rights. I deeply regret it, and we must constantly focus our minds on integrity.

However, these first stays encouraged me to go back and to keep up on political issues. I was looking for a way to involve myself more conspicuously, even while maintaining my rather unusual status. I was able to meet more people all the time, from all walks of life, which was the best way to understand my country. In my own way, I was carrying out the same task that my father had undertaken when he assumed the throne after 1918 when he was still so young.

I received numerous requests for meetings from all sorts of citizens, often from unexpected backgrounds. These would include doctors, teachers, university professors, artists, athletes, diplomats—foreign and Bulgarian—officers, cultural associations, the first NGOs in Bulgaria, students and journalists asking for interviews I willingly gave, as well as a wide range of politicians. A liaison group was set up in Sofia to help me with scheduling and preparing for these meetings. I was far from being alone; had that been the case, I would have never been able to cope. These were people who had appeared during the changes taking place in 1989, doing everything they could to help me, and I am more than grateful to them. As of 1997, the polls established that one Bulgarian out of two was ready to vote for a political party supported by me. This broad-based approval provided me with moral support, even if I was not really conscious of it. I dedicated long hours to interviews; when I did not, it was for lack of time. I had already gone through similar marathons during my exile when I visited cities abroad where there were colonies of Bulgarians, but this time I was visiting my compatriots in our home country.

For Bulgarians, I was The King, not only a link to the past but also the possibility of a more promising future. People shared their lists of "grievances" with me with great simplicity. This allowed me to enter in depth into the difficulties of their everyday lives. I enjoyed this simple, unexpected contact. The objective for me was to better understand the mechanisms of present-day Bulgaria, its administration, but also mountains of administrative barriers and inconsistencies, and other surprises of every kind. I think that my fellow countrymen used me in some way as a confessor: in me they found an ear that was sensitive to their worries.

They expected me to be able to help them—only I didn't have the means. What I saw was very distressing, and I was worried by the task to come. During these exchanges, I never felt the target of any aggressiveness. People were happy to meet me and share their thoughts freely, something they were not used to with the preceding regime. My humility disarmed more than one. What a difference from the attitude of certain politicians today who think they can do as they like and never go anywhere without an army of bodyguards!

I note that the involvement in politics inevitably changes what people think of you. My popularity probably would have remained the same if I had done nothing. If I had limited myself to playing the role of a "king" without power, the one they wanted me to confine myself to, I am convinced that my level of recognition would be as high today as at that time.

Then I incarnated something new, a sort of "exoticism" after the years of Communism and the depression that followed. I was the darling of the media. During my first stays, I remember a dozen days when the meetings numbered one hundred. I never stopped. I overworked the little team that surrounded me, but no one complained. I was, however, able to have my whole family come once for Christmas so that we could spend the holiday period together. I had been waiting for this so long! They were all delighted to finally discover the country that my mother and I had talked about for so long, even bragging to them about the beauty of its winters.

As I mentioned earlier, I also received people involved in politics: ministers, elected officials, congressmen, and mayors. Few were indifferent to my presence. They were curious to sound out my intentions. I particularly remember a leftist candidate for the town hall of Sofia who was interested in seeing me at the hotel and gave me a book as a present. Afterward, Roumen Ovtcharov became influential in his own party and was appointed minister of economy in the government that succeeded me. I also met with the leaders of the two major trade unions to sound out their opinions and understand their concerns. I likewise met the representatives of each professional branch, starting with the one considered on the right, Podkrepa (Support), led by Dr. Konstantin Trenchev; then, the other side, the KNSB (Confederation of Independent Trade Unions in Bulgaria), the delegation said to be leftist, headed by Dr. Jeliazko Hristov. The latter wanted to emphasize his support for the king and at the end of the interview said to me, "Your Majesty, stand firm for the good of Bulgaria!" I was astonished at this statement: it certainly showed that the political divisions were not so watertight as one might have imagined. This was a warm encounter and caused quite a stir.

Later, when I had been elected, the two unions revealed themselves to be tough at each negotiation that we had. This is the way democracy works. The supporters of Podkrepa even went to the point of burning a picture of me in front of the government premises in the course of a demonstration.

I took the time to travel around the country, accepting the invitations I was made. It was a great pleasure, but also exhausting. In 1997, for example, in Veliko Tarnovo, I spoke on the occasion of the anniversary of our first constitution in the same hall where it had been proclaimed in 1879 after our liberation from the Ottoman Empire. While I had made no political statement, to a question from a Spanish journalist addressing the future of our dynasty, my answer had been clear: "The instauration of a monarchy in Bulgaria only makes sense if it unifies Bulgarians and if it is supported by a considerable majority. I hold out my hand to monarchists as I do to republicans, to the left as well as to the right."

In Sofia, I paid a courtesy visit to the president of the Republic, Petar Stoyanov, and to the prime minister, Stefan Sofiyanski, the former mayor of the city who had welcomed me when I returned in 1996. At the end of the interview, the president said, "Your Majesty has kept track of the events in our parliamentary republic and it is a pleasure to talk with you." This did not commit him to anything, of course, but showed that dialogue was possible. Both of us had made reference to what was happening on the political scene, especially about the international questions to which I was very sensitive, in view of my openness to these subjects and my numerous contacts abroad. Our discussions went back and forth, in normal relaxed conversations. The contrast between what I discovered there and what I had imagined from abroad seemed quite astonishing to me.

As I look back, I sometimes have trouble remembering the details of these trips. What I do know is that during those years of preparation I moved around a great deal. Near Pernik, west of Sofia, I even went down a coal mine, like my father had done in 1924, despite my claustrophobia. In the course of these trips, I was able to continue to witness the diversity of Bulgaria and its beauty, with its green landscapes, its odors, its colors, the variety of its customs and its folklores.

*

During this observation period, I was able to see that the idea of a republic was deeply rooted in mentalities. Unfortunately, this was also true of the horrors that had been said about my family, to which the Communists had affixed the tag "monarcho-fascist." I am convinced that proposing the restoration of the monarchy given this context would have been a serious mistake—despite my popularity and the luster still surrounding King Boris. The idea would certainly have awakened a divisive mindset, destabilizing the order of the Constitution that had just been adopted. If the population was convinced that a republic was more democratic and modern, and that it worked, what was the good of wasting the energy? Above all, my instinct told me that a move in that direction would have been interpreted by my opponents as personal ambition: a very sad end to decades of work and sacrifice.

To me, a restored monarchy would have been a better solution for the image of our country after the fall of the Wall. But I did not want to force things, and I felt that all of the conditions necessary had not come together. It would have been impossible to convince a large majority of the population without the support of a portion of the political establishment, and I wanted to avoid at all costs throwing myself into a process of dividing public opinion or dividing our nation. The polls, though often unreliable, continued to show weak support for a return of the monarchy, and this deterred me from pursuing this direction. I did not have the right to play around with the idea of restoring the Kingdom of Bulgaria, for which my family had fought so much. I did not want to keep false hopes alive, even if I had never renounced my exceedingly legitimate rights during my forced exile. Pragmatic above all, I had seen that there had been no other restorations in Eastern Europe since the fall of the wall and that the only instauration known took place in Spain, with my cousin Juan Carlos. The circumstances, as we know, were entirely different: Spain had remained implicitly a kingdom, and his being accepted—on the political level and by public opinion—had been prepared long in advance by General Franco. Obviously, I could not do the same thing and risk having it turn into a farce that would have necessarily ended badly, ruining in a single blow all my efforts to reconcile Bulgaria with its memories. Perhaps, too, and I admit it willingly, I am not a monarchist strong enough to make the principle absolute. But I still think that when the break with the past is not too great, a balanced, parliamentary monarchy is the best political system to guarantee both democracy and the unity of a country.

Indeed, I think that monarchy is an idea of the future. Restoration does not mean re-creation, for it offers historic depth in addition to long-term stability, as well as points of reference in a time when we are desperately lacking in them. The seven monarchies that are members of the European Union are completely legitimate in this regard,[1] and I doubt that their role as guarantors of democratic rights can be questioned. They give an extra sparkle to each one of these countries, along with pride and respect for the past, while offering a projection toward the future. I have great regard for the work accomplished by my reigning cousins in Europe and hope that their descendants will be able to continue to assume their very heavy responsibilities with serenity.

At the beginning of 2000, the idea that I wanted to be a candidate for the presidential election spread. The country was once again going through a period of political unrest. How could it have been otherwise? After the rejoicing, the slump had come. All the Eastern European countries had gone through the same difficulties, that of creating a political identity that would be in line with the needs of the country.

---

1. They are the United Kingdom and the Kingdoms of Spain, Belgium, Luxembourg, Denmark, Sweden and the Netherlands. The Kingdom of Norway is not part of the European Union, though attached to it by a number of treaties.

To be a presidential candidate, there were three conditions: one had to be born in Bulgaria, to be over forty, and—condition added especially for me in an attempt to make me ineligible—to have resided in the country for the five years preceding the election. I had not resided there for that amount of time in a continuous fashion. This was spoken of as the "Simeon amendment" and was a low blow. Cooked up against me by the establishment, it demonstrated a certain nervousness, perhaps even fear, of seeing me enter the political arena. The idea of being a king-president did not please me much, as it represented some sort of intellectual incompatibility for me. Those who encouraged me in that direction thought that the role of president suited me in terms of both my circumstances and my personality. But I thought it inconceivable to perform both roles without ambiguities. I sometimes wonder how this would have played out in people's minds: I would have been king for some of them and president of the Republic for others, thus creating a division. My opponents would certainly have taken advantage of it to accuse me of seeking the restoration of the monarchy. I did not want this result. I did not see my destiny materializing itself in this way, as the head of the Bulgarian Republic. Another candidate turned up.

Ten years later, as our presidential elections approached in a country sunk in a political impasse, the proposal of my candidacy was persistently brought to life again by a large number of influential people. I declined again, for in my opinion you have to know your limits and your physical strength.

*

In 2000, I was able to have a confidential meeting with then Prime Minister Ivan Kostov, who received me at one of his Boyana residences. In the course of our discussion, I suggested a tandem by teaming up his party and my movement, to earn us more impressive results. I thought that cooperation was possible on the same shared views of the development of Bulgaria, which was my primary political objective. My idea was to form a center-right coalition to ensure that the positives of what had been accomplished by the preceding government would continue, while introducing innovative endeavors: a less authoritative central power, independent of the people involved with dirty money. I favor coalition governments that force participants of different parties to get along. He got up to put another log on the fire and then turned toward me: "No, I need another whole term, and afterward we'll see." This is how he rejected my proposal. "In that case," I responded, "we'll see what happens at the voting booths." We won, and he never forgave me. His conservative party would make my life difficult in parliament during my term.

The decision to accept the thankless task of becoming prime minister was not made overnight. This office was not my goal. Given the overwhelming results in my favor, it was my duty to accept, but did I have the right to impose it on my family? On my wife in particular, who had already had to take on so much responsibility?

As the parliamentary elections of 2001 approached, events quickly followed one another. I could not remain deaf to the hope that I had awakened in the country. I did not want people to blame me once again for letting the train of history pass me by, nor did I want to ruin the work that had been accomplished by so many devoted supporters since my return five years earlier. The time had come. The balloting date was speedily approaching. I had to make a move, to disclose my intentions and present an exciting program offering to my fellow countrymen. The enthusiasm of my colleagues and of those who would become the executives of my movement encouraged me greatly. My wife supported my decision with its heavy consequences. She knew that it was not one that I had taken lightly. Since then, she unceasingly and wholeheartedly backed me with all her strength, holding up under the difficulties—my being far away and the upheaval to our family life. At my side, she suffered the harsh attacks that I endured. Her advice was with me constantly. I was far from being certain of succeeding.

On April 6, 2001, at noon, I invited the media and a few sympathizers to the gardens of my Vrana residence to announce my intention of creating a political movement with a view to running in the upcoming parliamentary elections: "My dear compatriots, this day marks a turning point in my life. For decades, I have dedicated myself to serving you. For decades, I have suffered like you from an unfulfilled destiny. But I never lost my faith in a free and strong Bulgaria." My opponents wanted to prevent me from being a candidate in the presidential election? Fine. I would choose the parliamentary route, that of popular vote.

On April 27, I was already credited with 35 percent of voting intentions. This was much more than those expressed in favor of the exiting, right-leaning coalition, in power since 1997—18 percent—and the socialist, ex-Communist opposition—16.7 percent—which was accused of having led the country to the edge of bankruptcy until 1996. This campaign was my response to their fear of my becoming president. In the end, I was indebted to them.

While I was not myself directly a parliamentary candidate, my name still had to be given to this political movement, not as a personality cult, God forbid, but so that voters could identify it easily. Thus was born the Simeon II National Movement (SIINM). This precaution—and I believed it to be a solid one—was not sufficient since two false competing lists illegally making use of my title or my name turned up, taking advantage of the enthusiasm for anything representing me. The objective was to divide my audience, and it worked since, by picking away 3 percent of the votes, this maneuver prevented us from obtaining an absolute majority. Also, though the status of "party" was required to present one's candidacy, I had refused to use this term, given my position as king. We were thus not allowed to sign up our "movement" as such. I appealed the decision before the High Court of Justice, using as evidence two small, already-existing organizations, including the Women's Party. Under pressure, the electoral commission attempted by every means possible to prevent me from seeing it through to the end. I found this effort pathetic.

The polls continued to be very favorable to us, while I as an individual had a 70 percent approval rating. Although exhausting, the campaign went well, in a very emotional, responsible climate. I felt indebted for all the enthusiasm I elicited throughout the country. In the course of a very warm spring, I held meetings in practically every large city, from Vidin on the Danube and Silistra in the northeast to the Romany neighborhood of Sofia where I was invited to a wedding. Each time, I brought together thousands of people. I don't recall having ever been booed.

I had committed myself to starting a movement to fight the corruption of those powers that had seized entire chunks of the economy and fight political clientelism. The vast majority of my fellow citizens still lived in poverty and with an unreliable supply of food—a paradox for a country that was essentially rural, known during the Soviet era for the quality of its wines, fruits and vegetables. It was said that Bulgaria was the "orchard and vegetable garden" of the Comecon, the ex-common market of socialist countries. Now Bulgaria was "the poorest country on the list of candidates for European membership," according to the World Bank. Exhausted after ten years of economic reforms, the population was ready to support and trust me. My idea was to pursue certain reforms undertaken by the preceding government, while carefully avoiding the excesses of unrestrained capitalism. It was also important to me that we respect budgetary orthodoxy, for I had it in my mind that we should pursue the path to Europe. I especially wanted to make Bulgaria more attractive to foreign investors, while at the same time carry out social policies to care for the most needed. People thought that they could count on my principles and Western know-how to improve their situation.

To make me commit to this battle, the influence of certain people was decisive. I am thinking of Stoyan Ganev, who, before my election, was minister of foreign affairs and would become for several months my first principal private secretary. While living in New York, he had contacted my sister several times, insisting that she needed to convince me to launch a political movement. The idea was then taken up inside the country. There were others. Alas, I cannot mention them all, but I know how much their energy and advice were helpful to me. It was not my intention to enter into politics, but the moment was so critical for the country that I couldn't back away. I did not think, however, that we would win the elections so easily.

In the course of a campaign speech on June 8, 2001, I used a formula that earned me many criticisms afterward, and which I very much want to explain: "In 800 days, your lives will be better." By this blunt statement, I wanted to signal new impetus. I was counting on a spurt of national energy to follow my election. My mother, who had always idealized all that concerned Bulgaria, beginning with the image of my father, had inculcated in me the idea that we Bulgarians were the hardest workers and the most honest people in the world. These stereotypes were, of course, far removed from reality—as is typical of any cliché—for after half a century a totalitarian system had annihilated all individual initiative. I had not realized to what extent.

The "800 days" formula had to be powerful to help relaunch economic activity. I had drawn it from an interesting economics essay that explained that when a firm was failing, one had to stand back for one year, take one year to put it back on its feet, and a few hundred days to begin to see the first results. In this approach, it was not my intention—of course—to consider Bulgaria a private company! I was harshly and stupidly criticized for it—perhaps because I came from the private sector myself and had never before had to work for the state.

Another example of well-orchestrated calumny: I was mocked when I dared say that we needed to change our operating system—"chip," in English—implying that we needed to radically change our mentalities. I was criticized for having used a term from the world of IT, which had not been understood. Ten years later, it became part of everyday language to refer to this need for change—proof that I was right.

On a lighter note, I was also accused of having been an unrepentant gambler at casinos, losing all my presumed fortune on rolls of the dice. In all my life, I have only set foot in three casinos. The first time was at age twenty in Monaco: I went in at ten in the morning with an aide-de-camp of Prince Rainier to see what the Casino de Paris looked like. Another time, in Nassau in the Bahamas, I was invited by the owner, who wanted to show me his renovations. And one last time, in the 1990s, came in a hotel in Marrakesh where we were invited for a cocktail party. Not once did I gamble since I loathe betting and playing for money! Perhaps people were trying to sully my reputation with these lies because Sofia had become—very much despite me—the gambling capital of the region? I feel that some of those places offer other, unspoken activities and that my enemies did nothing other than expressing their own fantasies aloud.

Later on, in the first weeks in office, I felt like I was hitting a wall, given how different the mechanisms to make things work were. Each time I proposed a new way of proceeding, a new idea or even a simple reorganization of service, the first reaction was systematic: "It's impossible!" I was struck by the lack of initiative at practically every rank of the administration. It was customary to receive orders and apply them, and to avoid assuming any responsibility. "We are all equal, but I am more equal than you," they said under Communism, and it left a profound malaise. The person endeavoring to improve himself attracts disapproval. However, hierarchy is respected because it is feared. As soon as there is a problem, you still hear the same thing: "That's a decision for the higher-ups!" without ever assuming any responsibility. For my part, I like delegating in an atmosphere of trust so that everyone does his best. I didn't think I had to control everything, nor did I want to. It is in my nature to respect the work of others once I have expressed my confidence in them. I did not carry out a witch hunt among the staff members of my predecessor, having kept those whose competence was recognized—and I was criticized for it.

To be truthful, I can now state that my staff and I attained a good number of our objectives in one thousand days. I still remember the exact words of the criticism formulated by the president of the time, Petar Stoyanov, who accused us of "deluding the country with illusions and pretty promises." This is just to describe the environment, not to judge or condemn; after all, these are the rules of the political game. The greatest achievement for me is to have been able to serve the republic as its prime minister. Modern history knows of but a single other analogous case, and that is King Sihanouk of Cambodia.

The evening of June 17, after all of the votes had been counted, the National Movement obtained 43 percent of the votes, giving us 119 seats out of the 240 in parliament in a single chamber. As I didn't have an absolute majority, I immediately announced that I wanted to form a coalition with political forces that shared our goals of "stable economic growth, of acceleration of our goal to join the European Union and NATO, and of freeing the country from corruption." It was for these reasons that I turned toward the Movement for Rights and Freedoms, the so-called party of the "Muslims" and supported by the Turkish-speaking minority of Bulgaria, and to another party, Women, led by Vesela Draganova, the one that had allowed us to pass the test of the electoral commission.

Looking back, I do not regret this coalition. We cooperated and worked well together, despite the ill intentions that we were always being charged with. As early as 1997, in an interview that I gave to the *New York Times*, I expressed my intent: "The problems of my country are hunger and cold. These are urgent necessities. This is not the moment for discussion, but for extending a hand. Perhaps afterward, we could discuss politics."

After learning of the results, we went with my team to the National Palace of Culture (NDK), a gigantic convention center built in 1981 in the heart of Sofia. A press conference had been scheduled for ten in the evening. Following a post-balloting custom in our country, each party had to make declarations in the presence of the media and a large audience. At that point, the results were already known and the atmosphere was electric. The hall was full, everyone in standing ovation. I thanked and warmly congratulated those who had participated in our victory—a victory for all. I held back my tears. I was truly conscious of living a moment of history. In the audience, I caught the eyes of each of my children, who had come specifically for the occasion. Afterward, we all went to Vrana for a late family supper.

The next day, June 18, I continued to meet with the media, including French and Spanish television channels, then around six o'clock in the evening, I went to Movement headquarters to celebrate our sweet victory. Some of my Habsburg cousins had come from Vienna and Budapest for this milestone. The following day, I went to the airport to welcome Queen Noor of Jordan, who came to be present as well. We received a tidal wave of congratulatory messages from the world over.

*

After this excellent score, I needed a long moment for reflection. Many of my compatriots had the impression—and still believe—that I entered politics only in the early years of 2000, but this is wrong, for I have been steeped in it since the age of reason. No one is really conscious of the work that preceded the creation of my political party! It required many sacrifices that I accepted throughout my years in Madrid, as I continued to read everything about Bulgaria at a time when there was no hope of return or of democracy.

After our victory, it was not like me to remain in the wings, acting like some sort of guru giving orders from afar. This would have been a betrayal of my electorate! I had unofficially begun consultations to form a government. At that particular moment, I had not yet decided to head it. It took several days for me to be convinced that I was capable of bearing such heavy responsibility. Entangled in my scruples and my education, I began by examining my conscience. I had never worked in public administration, and I didn't know whether I felt strong enough to do so. I had my doubts. However, I knew one of my assets: I was experienced in the area of politics.

The days went by, and I was subject to more and more pressure from my closest collaborators. They made me understand that I should under no circumstances designate someone else. I couldn't retreat; no one is irreplaceable.

It was on a beautiful spring day, as I took a short walk in the garden at Vrana with one of the young representatives of the Movement, Nikolay Vasilev, that I made my decision once and for all. His arguments finally convinced me.

Since the beginning of the campaign, Nikolay and I had gotten into the habit of not discussing confidential subjects except on the paths of the garden, continuing the good old habit of suspecting being spied on. Vasilev was one of those young people who had been convinced by what I said and had come back to Bulgaria to throw himself into the fight at my side. Contrary to what was insinuated by certain members of the press, Vasilev had come on his own initiative, and not at the request of my son Kyril, who was then working in the City in London. Like the others, he had quit a good job abroad to offer his services to the Republic, with a monthly salary of a few hundred euros. Each of these persons can easily refute the rumor that they were "recruited" directly by my son, as if he had "pulled strings" for them. These lies are dishonest, as are many others told during the campaign. I reject the maliciousness of this rumor, for it is as damaging to their honor as to their sense of patriotism. I discovered both how low politics can stoop and how credulous public opinion can be regarding rumors.

It was thus decided: the next day, I would announce to the media that I was going to form a government led by myself. I then went to submit this decision to President Stoyanov, who, as stipulated by the constitution, granted me the mandate. At the end of our meeting, I made a declaration to the press: "The task is extremely arduous and complicated, but with good will and the help of all, we will succeed. I think only of the well-being of our people, while hoping to do what we have promised to the voters. May God help us and show us the way for the good of the people."

I had seven days to form the government, which had to be submitted by July 24 to the parliament. In the years since 1996, I had met countless people and recognized the capabilities of many. With my assistants, we began to make a list filling the ministries available. I needed to consider my own political group and my coalition partners. It was necessary to maintain a certain balance, while discerning the qualities of each individual. In this regard, I gave the important Ministry of Agriculture to Mehmet Dikme, one of the executives of the Movement for Rights and Freedoms (MRF), Turkish-speaking fellow citizen and former mayor of Ardino, a small city in the southwest of the country. I can state that he was the best minister in this field since the beginning of our democracy: he knew his subject inside out. In the process of seeking membership to the European Union, he brought remarkable know-how. In 1991, the leader of the MRF, Ahmed Dogan, had been the first Bulgarian political leader to come to see me in Madrid. He had been jailed during the regrettable events of the 1980s for his opposition to the policy of forced assimilation of Turkish minorities in Bulgaria. It is also important for me to stress that MRF is not a "Turkish party," as it has often been referred to for the reasons I have mentioned, nor is it a "Muslim party," given that some of its leaders are Christian. Also, in the spirit of our constitution, as in that of Tarnovo, whose 135th anniversary we have just celebrated, all notions of ethnicity and religion in the creation of a political party are forbidden.

The government quickly took shape. I cannot mention everyone, but that period was amazing. We were successful in finding political coherence and consistency with each person's capabilities. Everyone was prepared to take on their new responsibilities for me. Out of seventeen ministers, I had named five women, and I especially want to point out that, out of the 119 representatives from my Movement, there were fifty-five women, something that had never been seen in Bulgaria before. Among the other ministers, some had held highly placed jobs in the administration, others in civil society, others still in the world of business, and some had come back from abroad, where they had been trained in different working methods. I think of some of them in particular: Milen Velchev, a brilliant young economist, whom I appointed as minister of finance; the lawyer Plamen Panayotov, minister of justice, who had helped us in the formation of our movement; Meglena Kuneva, a civil servant already in place from the former administration, naturally found her place in European affairs. After our entry into the Union, she was the first Bulgarian to be appointed commissioner for consumer protection and was very active before creating her own political party. I must also mention Solomon Passy, who, in his four years at the head of our foreign affairs, did remarkable work, thanks to his original personality. I had met with him when I returned in 1996, when he had invited me to speak to the Atlantic Club of Sofia, of which he was president and founder. In 2003, just as the invasion of Iraq was taking place and as Bulgaria, by rotation, was presiding at the Security Council at the UN, young Passy showed himself equal to the responsibilities I had entrusted him with. We spoke every evening to review the situation, for I was hoping right up to the last moment that a way would be found to avoid military intervention in Iraq, but, as a candidate for NATO, we had no choice but to follow the American policy.

On the eve of the launching of operations against Baghdad, I was in Sofia in a small Italian restaurant. By a special line, I received a call from the vice president of the United States, Dick Cheney, whose mission, along with President Bush, was to inform allies of the beginning of operations. The airplanes were to begin their grim missions that very night at midnight. His voice was precise, without emotion and without details. I had not yet met him. I simply responded, "Mister Vice President, I hope above all that, in God's name, you know what you are doing." We know what followed. As a member of the military coalition, we had to send a company of Bulgarian soldiers to Karbala, in southern Iraq. Several of our soldiers lost their lives, including six in a single operation. I went to the airport with their families in the middle of the night when their remains were flown back. It was cold and snowing on the runway. The next day, I awarded them posthumously the Order of Military Merit. The horror of seeing these young victims fall in battle so far from home was very present, but I was even more upset as deep down I did not approve of the war. This memory remains one of my worst nightmares.

My organizational chart included three vice prime ministers, each with his own ministry. One of their tasks was to relay my actions to their colleagues. Drive belts powering the transmission, so to speak. I also asked two members of the Socialist Party who had good records as mayors to join our team. One of them, Kostadin Paskalev, was shaken up by this approach. He said, "Prime Minister, I accept on condition that you do not force me to give up my membership card of the Socialist Party!" Obviously, I was not going to ask him to do such a thing, which was also none of my business. I had seen his abilities as a manager and nothing else. This was also the case with Dimitar Kalchev, whom I named minister and who did an excellent job in his role. Needless to say, these choices were not approved of by everyone in my own camp. Our political classes were not used to this kind of openness, and these two nominations were the first of their kind. For me, the administration of a country should follow the principle of meritocracy alone, not those of political prevalence, networks of influence or interests of parties. Unfortunately, this was not understood.

These, then, were the circumstances under which I was sworn in before Parliament and the whole of my government. I had set one condition *sine qua non*: the presence of our patriarch for the inauguration ceremony. Such a thing had never been seen! According to the statutes of the assembly, only ministers or representatives were allowed in the chamber. This situation generated a crisis! A vote had to be taken by show of hands for permission to be given for His Holiness to be present for the duration of the ceremony. I finally was sworn in with my hand on the Gospels in his presence. With all of the ministers, we repeated aloud the formula required by the Constitution. Since then, the patriarch has attended the services of my successors, as well as those of the new presidents of the Republic, but at the time, it was unheard of. In so doing, I wanted to invoke the divine protection that we all need so much. And for the first time in Europe, a republic was going to be governed by a king. A possible referendum on the return of the monarchy—the one I had often been accused of preparing—was obviously not on the agenda.

Chapter Thirteen

Being Prime Minister

THE MONTHS THAT FOLLOWED WERE VERY INTENSE. I SUDDENLY thought of my mother, telling myself that she would not have approved of my choice. Of course, I know that she had no illusions about a return of the monarchy and did not fan false hopes in me. But I can still hear her saying, "A king doesn't take sides in politics." This maternal taboo weighed on my conscience, making me suffer.

Before I accepted the premiership, I was accused of temporizing and of being weak—this was a burden. Once my decision was made, I wanted to fully understand every file personally. I was demanding with my deputies with respect to workload, discretion as well as punctuality and dress. In a spirit of innovation and because each of them had been good at their jobs, I had included in our team a Scottish aide recommended by Prince Charles to help me, Bill Drysdale, as well as a French civil servant, Thomas Eymond-Laritaz, who had been suggested to me by Prime Minister Jean-Pierre Raffarin when I met him on a visit to Paris. I had also spotted a very capable young private secretary named Radi Naydenov, who joined me during all my term in office and who then became our ambassador to Vienna and to Berlin.

I worked twelve hours a day at the offices of government headquarters, a monumental building in the Stalinist style. This was a rhythm that I imposed on myself. I would work four more hours at home, Saturdays and Sundays included. I continued thusly during those four years, as God is my witness. I had to learn, keep up with reports, cover political questions and prepare official visits related to our most important international meetings. When it came to the management of public affairs and public monies, I took the business at heart, all the more so as the bad faith of our opposition was obvious and difficult to deal with. I would arrive at the ministry at 8:20 every morning. Those were years of appalling loneliness.

I had deliberately asked my children not to come visit so as to avoid mean rumors. I did not want to be accused of nepotism or wanting to restore the monarchy. However, with all of their experience, each in their own field, they could have been more than useful to the country. Moreover, it was too late for them to settle in Bulgaria, their careers and those of their wives having begun elsewhere. I remain convinced that if they had been able to freely commit themselves to working for the country, as is the case for reigning royal families, we would have been able together to have contributed to making Bulgaria better known—and then some.

I now regret it; I should have never burdened myself with all my scruples. I was faced by a large number of people with all kinds of resentments who took advantage of the situation to take out their personal or ideological hatred on me and, by doing so, were able to increase their self-importance. It's odd how people change: so many people have betrayed me and then afterward gone back on it. I have a great deal of experience in this area, but I hold no grudges; it's just a statement of fact. I see it as a phenomenon that I try to explain to myself and accept.

To save money, I did not ask to live in the prime minister's official residence, a pleasant villa perched on a slope of Vitosha. I chose to stay at Vrana, in my home, and traveled from there every morning. I continued to pay all the household bills myself, except for the electricity used by my bodyguards, who had converted the basement for their own use. I had only a cat to keep me company, a present from my daughter. His name was Boubou, and he was a very affectionate creature whose presence, I must admit, was very soothing. Despite her family obligations in Madrid, my wife came to Sofia whenever she could, the wife of the prime minister having no particular status in our country. She didn't want to leave me alone, but I felt bad when she came since I was not very available, not to say invisible all day long, even without official visits abroad, summits, and bilateral meetings. When visits were not controlled by strict protocol, we received our official guests in our home, which I find much more personal than an anonymous restaurant. People enjoyed discovering the palace at Vrana and the mementos of my parents. My sense of hospitality made me personally choose the menus, and I took pleasure in offering our best Bulgarian wines to foreign ministers and diplomats. In an entirely different context, I remember King Hassan II having President Mitterrand for dinner at his estate near Soissons and sending him the menu and the list of wines in advance to make sure that they suited him.

As prime minister, I saw myself as a citizen-king, a worthy descendant of Louis Philippe. This meant that I would meet everyday life with a certain degree of philosophy, and without any particular pomp. Paradoxically, it was as prime minister that I had a law adopted in Bulgaria granting ex-presidents of the republic—as former heads of state—a pension and fringe benefits that had not existed before but that afterward no one wanted to apply to me! This is amusing since, according to history books, I am also a former head of state.

I have a certain stoical side when it comes to work. This is shyness perhaps, or doubt, that lingers from the dramas of my childhood. I quickly noted that my good manners were often interpreted as false and insincere, which was certainly not the case. Sometimes I was also misunderstood by my compatriots who find me distant. I always use the formal grammar form when addressing them—in truth, it's out of respect for the other person that I do so. I would feel uncomfortable being artificially overfamiliar; it's not in my nature. I would be playing a role, lying, and that might be interpreted as demagogy, which I find horrible. I admit that I am distrustful by nature, and often on the defensive. Basically, I have been influenced by a strict upbringing, what my sister and I refer to as "the clamp." I have always been guided by a sense of ethics and integrity so that I can look at myself in the mirror without blushing. I have always tried to base my decisions on a precedent or reference. My discretion has helped me juggle delicate situations and earn the confidence of my counterparties.

I think I am quite worthless as a politician since I instinctively avoid bragging about my actions. I know this is not in keeping with current dynamics, where communication has become key. During my whole term of office, only one person was in charge of advising me on my relations with the media, Tsvetelina Ouzounova. I often preferred to say nothing, favoring "facts" and letting posterity take care of "broadcasting." This proved to be a serious mistake. I realize that in this era of social networks, I should have acted differently so as to explain myself better to my fellow citizens. I am still paying the price.

I allowed myself to sleep no more than five and a half hours a night, despite my great fatigue. Some nights, I was so worried about my responsibilities that I would remain sleepless. Then I would reread my notes and try to find solutions. Sometimes I had a new idea, sometimes not. I would then fall asleep at dawn for an hour or two. Today, I don't regret the enormous sacrifice, but I don't miss power: it was never my ambition.

At the end of my term in office, in 2005, I was especially relieved to not having to answer questions in parliament during stormy sessions, mostly on Fridays. The tension was nerve-racking for me, as I was under fire from three directions: criticism of the government per se, spitefulness from a portion of the right because of my victory, and the hostility of those for whom I represented the cliché of "monarcho-fascism." I would use advice from Silvio Berlusconi: not responding immediately to questions, but rather reading a prepared statement as an answer so as not lose my temper. The members of Parliament would often yell. I remember one harangue coming from the ranks of the right: "Leave, Mr. Saxe-Coburg, go away, you are harmful to the country!" Or even a member from the left: "You, sir, are no longer 'Your Majesty,' you are 'Your Uselessness'!" I wasn't expecting it; it was out of context, and, as we say in Bulgarian, "lightning struck me from a blue sky." But, let's be honest, I had to stop myself from laughing, because I thought the line was catchy, even while members from my party were loudly protesting. These are only samples. I sometimes spent three hours standing without showing any feeling so as not to let the cameras catch the slightest unfavorable shot to show in the papers the next day. Only once was I unable to contain myself, responding briefly to a representative who had changed parties three times and was lecturing me on the direction I should follow. I stood up to have the floor and exclaimed, "I am ready to be lectured by many people, but certainly not by someone who is on his third party in two years."

I still wonder where the resentment came from. Even after all the years, there was still hatred in some people. I was never aggressive to anyone or answered in a disrespectful way questions that were truly rude. Some of those around me would have preferred that I answer in the same tone, with the same lack of arguments, but I was always careful not to. I think this difference exasperates some. Insulting people doesn't come with me. I have never done it.

I err on the side of "possibility" and am only interested in the *possible*. I tried to apply pragmatic decisions, but ones that were not always politically profitable or popular. One question that I often asked myself, and that seems essential to me, was how a democracy could be created without democrats: too many people remain fundamentally intolerant, only rarely accepting the opinion of others. Everything should be based on proof of reciprocal respect.

The single most important question for me was how to best serve my country, unconditionally. I was obsessed by the idea of improving the conditions of life of my fellow countrymen and boosting the economy. Already in October, we began to increase the minimum salary, then doubling subsidies for families and launching an important program for fiscal reform. The latter was intended to lead to the exoneration from taxes for the lowest incomes and, above all, to encourage investment by exonerating firms that reinvested their profits domestically. I wanted to make Bulgaria a more attractive country for investors. We made tremendous efforts with my team. I called on my long-standing network of contacts to encourage large international groups that lack so sorely in our country. Foreign investors felt that the government was in competent hands, and all this allowed us to show Bulgaria in a better light. The world economic atmosphere was quite different from what it has become since. We were still in a remarkable phase of growth and investments of billions of euros came in. We were thus able to work with Italian, Spanish, French and German firms. Belgium was our primary investor for several years. I must also underline that I was careful to ensure that foreign ambassadors had more direct access to my office than they had had during the terms of my predecessors. I accepted invitations from the different embassies, again stressing my desire for openness. I was sometimes obsessed by the challenge, seeing the potential of my country and all that there was to catch up with after years of isolation. Our needs were great, and this was a godsend for entrepreneurs. My other major idea was to pursue our European policy, but I will come to this topic a bit later.

I remain persuaded that Bulgaria had great potential at its disposal, whether in terms of qualified workforce or of all the products of modern agriculture, in addition to forest and water resources, summer and winter tourism and its cultural aspects, including the archeology of which I am so fond. *Innovate or evaporate* was, during these years, a recurrent theme in the policies of my government.

My meetings with my ministers were often longer than the time normally scheduled for them, for I wanted to hear each person's findings and to discuss them afterward, much to the regret of the more impatient. We always began on time. My work hours at the ministry as well as my punctuality became a trademark—and contagious. My ministers and team members were quickly infected. I don't like waiting or making people wait.

For various reasons related to dealing with political issues, I was compelled to do some limited government reshuffling, and each time it was at great personal cost. It is never easy to ask someone to leave, but I didn't want to delegate this thankless task. It was part of my responsibilities. I discovered the mysteries of political life, with its highs and lows, and its violence. The media graciously accorded us one hundred days before starting to criticize our actions. The "yellow press," as we refer to tabloids in our country, was particularly ferocious. By the way, I remember when one of my ministers—the one in charge of public works—had had his reputation tarnished because of a rumor accusing him of taking bribes. Not long after, he became seriously ill and did not have enough money to pay for his medical treatment. We got together with several of his ex-colleagues to help him. This is what evil gossip can lead to, and it is not the only case of the same kind I could mention.

*

In the meantime, President Stoyanov's term of office came to an end. In the elections in the fall of 2001, he was beaten by the leftist candidate, Georgi Parvanov, former general secretary of the Socialist Party. People believed that this political "cohabitation" would be very challenging for me, but this was not the case—so much so that at the end of his second five-year term, Parvanov confided to me that I was the prime minister with whom he had worked the best. We made a habit of meeting to bring each other up to date on issues. I sounded with him on issues that I considered important. To go to meet him, I would take the underground public way that connects our two buildings. The president in turn came once or twice to see me in the Council of Ministers building, something unusual given state protocol.

According to the Constitution, the president has the last word on approving of ambassadors, but the government remains in charge of foreign policy. During a summit concerning our candidature to the European Union, we surprised our partners by showing up together. We had come to an agreement between us that we would show the face of a united Bulgaria abroad. After my term in office, my Movement was present in the Socialist coalition in the form of five ministers, including justice, defense, education, civil service and European affairs. This is when representatives of the media, along with members of the rightist opposition, accused me of suffering from Stockholm syndrome, since I was so "close" to ex-Communists.

At the end of our four-year[1] term, my Movement ran again in the parliamentary elections of 2005. The results were not in our favor, and we were beaten. The Socialists won, but without an outright majority. As we were in second position, we naturally agreed to form a coalition with them and with another partner, the Movement for Rights and Freedoms. Despite widespread criticism, I wanted to participate in this alliance—qualified by many as "against nature"—because I was convinced that with such a wide political unity, we would stand a better chance at joining Europe. Without bragging, I think I provided a stable

---

1. My first mandate was the second government to complete a full term since 1989.

point of reference, compared to the large number of political shooting stars that I have seen go by.

The majority in parliament was Socialist, so there was no way I would remain prime minister: I thus presented my resignation to the president. Still, as head of one of the three coalition parties, I remained involved in country affairs. I attended the meetings of the executive committee of our coalition where, along with the ministers, the general direction of the government was decided. Thus, from 2005 to 2009, I pursued my political life in another manner. My appointments calendar was always full: among others, I received numerous foreign visitors, encouraging them to come to Bulgaria and reassuring them about the nature of our coalition. My office was now at the headquarters of our Movement, and it was from there that I continued to direct the party machinery. I had little time to return to Spain to see my family, doing it only very occasionally, such as when my oldest son Kardam suffered a terrible car accident in 2008.

The defeat of our coalition in the parliamentary elections of 2009 was blamed on me personally. Some of our representatives declared that we should have left the coalition the day that we were admitted to the European Union, two years before in January 2007. But I would have found it disloyal to cause the government to fall merely as a political maneuver. I thus continued to support the Stanishev government that had followed mine, so that it would also make it to the end of its mandate, proving that Bulgaria had the stability it needed at a time when other European countries were looking us closely. Apparently, this was a strategic error, and one that we paid dearly for, since our party was swept out of government in the elections after eight years of power. But no other party had stayed as long! Since 1989, not a single prime minister has ever been reelected. The public quickly becomes bored with new faces. I am proud to have been instrumental in providing eight years of political stability and continuity to Bulgaria.

*

The only black spot—and it is a large one—concerns the attack made against me at the end of my term of office, which I found unforgivable. It relates to my family properties and is a subject that now must be explained.

This affair came at me like a bomb from nowhere. I certainly did not see it coming. Certain individuals, out of wickedness or pure spitefulness, sought to punish my success. The attack seems particularly unfair to me when one knows that some scandals on their end—too shameful to mention—were silenced. Obscene fortunes were made over a few years and never attracted the attention of parliament or of the courts.

Several properties without which I had lived for fifty-five years were at the heart of the attack. I had every right of inheriting from my father, like any ordinary citizen; this would have allowed me to feel at home after such a long absence. Above all, it would have been proof of a successful transition into democracy, where the rights of all are respected. Unlike others, I never threatened or blackmailed anyone, nor did I exercise the slightest pressure.

When I returned to Bulgaria in 1996, I deliberately avoided visiting all of the houses that we owned, among them a dwelling near Bania that my father built in 1929 on a hectare of land, and a beautiful property in Krichim, near Plovdiv, one that my parents particularly liked. As for the palace at Euxinograd—much beloved by Princess Clémentine—it had been bequeathed to the state in 1912.

After 1993, the question of restitution of confiscated property was raised. Any Bulgarian citizens who could prove ownership had the right to take their case to court. The principle of restitution had been applied by other former members of Comecon, including East Germany. Since private property was not recognized during the Communist period, hundreds of thousands of properties of all sizes had been nationalized or even confiscated. Since 1878, the laws in Bulgaria were such that the land was split among all the heirs, making it difficult to farm the tiny plots of land that resulted. After the war, the Communists took advantage of this situation to collectivize the land in order to make more rational use of it, even if this tactic ultimately did not work. Then, after 1989, disaster struck: in the chaos of privatizing these huge state-run farms, what little remained of our agriculture was wiped out. Herds of animals were stolen, machinery was sold off on the cheap, and former owners claimed their land back. The large plantations put together during the Communist period were also destroyed. In brief, the solution was politically impossible to manage.

In rural areas, abandoned buildings and land lying fallow can still be seen, almost a quarter of a century later. I find this sad and terribly wasteful, for our soil is rich. I am convinced that sustainable, integrated agriculture that is respectful of the environment is the gold of tomorrow. Already today we could be one of the important players in agribusiness of the European Union, especially in fruits, cereals and even livestock.

Today there are plots of land that still have no owners. The latter moved abroad, or disappeared in the camps of the Communist period, or, because the records of the land registry disappeared, are still discussing among themselves the boundaries of neighboring land allotments. In the 1990s, a system based on sworn statements from witnesses was put in place to settle such disputes. Most often these were elderly people who remembered how the fields were divided among neighbors before being confiscated. Human nature being what it is, this method led to abuses. The situation has still not been settled and is the subject of endless debate.

But despite this litigation, those who have been involved in the restitution process have generally won their cases thanks to the law.

When restitution began, I was still living in Madrid. Several times my advisors in Bulgaria urged me to put together a case. Each time, I answered that I had other priorities in mind. I maintained this position until 1998, when most of my fellow citizens had recovered their property—when the cases were clear-cut. It was not on my initiative, but on that of the public prosecutor of the time, Ivan Tatartchev, that the case concerning my property was referred to the government. The government handed the case on to the Constitutional Court, not without certain awkwardness. My sister and I let the matter follow its course, with no intervention on our side. I was certain that we were quite within our rights and couldn't imagine that we could be refused what had already been granted to so many of our fellow citizens. Finally, the court announced its decision in June 1998, ruling unanimously in favor of our family.

The legal base for the restitution of these properties was the list drafted in 1946, given to my mother by Kimon Giorgiev, then presiding over the first Communist government. The thought that one day we would need it surely did not occur to him.

The decision restored our property to us in its entirety. It made me feel at home again. I found childhood memories and, in turn, could welcome my own children to the family home. Each of them discovered Bulgaria with great joy. I had bored them thoroughly for so many years with stories of a country that remained an abstract idea for them. They could now come to Sofia without living in a hotel and stay in houses built by my grandfather and father with their own funds.

My wife and I began to restore Vrana shortly after its restitution, as it was in a very poor state. We first began work on a wing that is adjacent to the palace and in which I continue to live. I was also given access to our Tsarska property, and the one that was near Sarigöl, in the mountains. In these two spots with their many memories of childhood for me, I saw that many valuable objects had disappeared. And yet it never occurred to me to ask for the slightest compensation.

The restitution of these properties was later disputed only for political reasons. I no longer have free access to the estates that my grandfather bought with his own money; a sort of moratorium has been imposed on me, meaning that I can use them but without really being certain that I own them. I am forbidden to sell timber from the surrounding forests, which allowed me to pay for their upkeep. For a country under the rule of law, this procedure is shocking. When I compare my situation to the spoliations of state property organized in the course of the wildcat privatizations that followed the fall of Communism in 1989, it sickens me to see how I continue to be dragged through the mud and harassed about my family inheritance. One hardly surprising detail: the attacks made on me often come from less than innocent hands.

But let us come back to our house. My wife and I have spent much of our own money in its restoration. I would I have never been able to undertake such a task if the sixteen hundred hectares of forest surrounding the Tsarska property did not bring in enough for their maintenance, including paying for the necessary staff.[2] As the owners of forests, we were subject to a ten-year forest-management plan, and I adhered strictly

---

2. Bulgaria is a country that is rich in forests, with more than 40 percent of its surface covered in them. This is an important environmental bonus and one that I respect.

to it—respect for nature is in the family genes. I took a personal interest in the matter, taking long walks with the forester—a competent, experienced engineer, and as scrupulous as I was when selecting trees to cut.

Around 2007, in a fit of spite, a member of parliament who wanted to harm me launched a campaign to defame me. This effort was soon taken up by the Bulgarian media, and I found myself accused of illegally cutting thousands of cubic meters of wood and wanting to "empty" Bulgaria. They even went to the extent of publishing photos of hundreds of stumps piled by the side of the road—photos that, of course, had not been taken on our property, which was easy to prove.

After this fake news, the accusations followed, fanned by obscure political interests aimed at making "Simeon" everyone's target. All of this had to do with my role in the coalition, of course. In December 2009, this affair brought about an unprecedented decision by parliament: to vote a moratorium against me, preventing me from disposing of my property as I see fit, with the pretense that the legitimacy of my rights as an owner needed to be reexamined. In fact, not only is such a moratorium in violation of our Constitution—Parliament is not supposed to deal with individuals—but it also violates the principles of European justice. It was to fight this injustice that I went to Strasbourg and not, of course, to sue my country, as I have shamefully been accused of doing.

Let us remember that in 2000, when my sister and I donated the eighty-eight hectares of the park at Varna to the city of Sofia, in memory of the family and to thank Providence for having allowed us to return, no one had a thing to say! There was no question that we were the legitimate owners. The mayor thanked us enthusiastically, and the park was opened to the public. I wanted it to be called "King Ferdinand Park" since he was the one who designed it.

It is interesting to note that, aside from the political controversy, the misunderstanding comes from an error in interpretation of the term *estate management*. This was an institution in charge of managing the property belonging to the sovereign, including his own money and his salary. In no way was this public property, but none of my accusers ever tried to clarify any doubts, preferring ignorance and bad faith. Said institution was copied from the Kingdom of Belgium, for its sovereign was at the time a close cousin of King Ferdinand. Management of the property of the Belgian royal family has prevailed like this until today. It would be easy to establish a parallel: "estate management" for the king is done independently and not by an institution of the state. The opposition pretends not to understand this important detail, preferring to consider that our personal holdings were acquired with public monies. In fact, there is supplementary proof of their mistake. Since 1900, in no budget of the Bulgarian state has there ever been a single line devoted to the payment of salaries to civil servants in charge of "estate management," meaning that they were paid directly by the sovereign.

Finally, to close this painful subject, I would like to underline that, contrary to the practices in some countries at present and to the embezzlement of funds attributed to many leaders, my family did the opposite: we used owned funds brought from abroad as donations or investments in the country. A large part of the fortune of the Orléans and the Koháry families was invested in it. I believe that these examples, like many others, should not be forgotten. The personal fortunes of my ancestors, like that of Princess Clémentine, from the Orléans family, brought considerable wealth to Bulgaria at the time. The practices of the time were really quite different. The construction of the railways in Bulgaria that allowed us to be connected to the rest of Europe was possible only because of a loan guaranteed by Louis Philippe's youngest daughter. It surely is the height of ingratitude to hear, as I did, a nasty piece of gossip suggesting that her generosity had been a "good deal" for the princess. Not only does this perspective ignore the visionary dimension of such an investment, but it also, and above all else, disregards the financial risk that it involved—very great at the time in a country that was just emerging from Ottoman occupation.

To end, I will borrow a witty remark made by the renowned Bulgarian journalist Velislava Dareva on the matter: "Oh, tsar, do not give your palaces to the mob. They'll turn them into toilets."

CHAPTER FOURTEEN

The European

DURING MY TERM IN OFFICE, MY FOREIGN POLICY WAS BASED ON THE two headings that I considered essential: our entry into NATO in 2004, and the acceleration of our European dream, with our final accession to the European Union in 2007. These two objectives were but the implementation of specific goals that had motivated me for years.

Again, you must put yourself in the context of the years of exile at the end of the war. People of my generation dreamed then of building a Europe at peace. After the suffering endured by my people, and many other Eastern European countries, we found it hard to believe that one day this dream could come true. It seemed to me important to tie Bulgaria as closely as possible to the West, to avoid us falling into the mistakes of the past. I knew how much my country had suffered as a token in the games played by the Great Powers before the First World War and during the Second. This is how the idea of being a full member of these two successful organizations was quickly adopted as the main driver of our diplomacy.

NATO was an important step in our moving closer to the Western world. It represented a clear perimeter for our actions. Today, with the hindsight of a decade, we can see how very judicious the choice was, even if the path leading to it was cumbersome. At the beginning of the negotiations, I made it a condition that enough time should elapse to allow a smooth transition away from the pro-Russian past of Bulgaria. For me, this was also a way to avoid irritating the Russian government, which had already suffered other humiliations. Let us not forget that in one of his more pro-Soviet speeches in the 1970s, Zhivkov had envisaged our becoming part of the Soviet Union!

The conservative opposition spread the rumor that I was dragging my feet on NATO, accusing me of a lack of enthusiasm and of leaning eastward. This was, of course, complete nonsense. I thought that it was not very appropriate to enter the North Atlantic Treaty overnight. Until 1989, we had been one of the most active members of the Warsaw Pact, especially because of our shared borders with Turkey, Greece and even Yugoslavia, suspected by Moscow of double-dealing. Our armed forces up until then had depended on Soviet support and technology; our officers spoke Russian, most had been trained in Soviet military academies, and the war plans of military headquarters still followed the Warsaw doctrine. This meant that I also needed to be sensitive to the reaction of our officers, for whom such a change was far from obvious. For years, they had been taught that NATO was the enemy that had to be fought: a general in command of our anti-aircraft forces did in fact resign from his duties just before we joined. While I did not agree with his decision, I found his attitude worthy of respect.

The Eastern European countries little by little became candidates for NATO. Each at a different pace, as soon as it was possible taking into consideration the—oh so important—sensitivity of Russia. They had to examine their own strategic preferences with respect to their new needs and address issues related to armament (what should be done with missiles?), energy, and other economic issues with their former "Big Brother."

While these negotiations were going on, some countries were called upon to demonstrate their commitment to NATO. Among other things, we showed it by sending troops to Iraq. This is how Americans tested us, and the pressure was difficult to resist.

In return for membership, NATO required us to drastically reduce our troop numbers, going from 120,000 to 35,000 in just a few years. This was a real sacrifice for the officer corps but was endured with an abnegation that I wish to emphasize. As prime minister, I had to go to Mons, in Belgium, to the General Headquarters of NATO to undergo a thorough interrogation to verify our intentions and know how far we were willing to go in adopting technical-administrative measures in order to join. This was a wide-reaching reform. To manage all the stress that I had built up before the presentation, I thought about my oral exam for the *baccalauréat*. Seated at a wide round table where civilian and military representatives from each country met for their sessions, I answered the questions addressed to me in five languages. From all the years I had spent in board rooms, I knew that my ability with languages helped me understand the subtleties of different cultures, as well as the psychology of my counterparties. Working with an interpreter was already a handicap.

That day, I really became aware of the responsibility I bore: the decisions that would follow would have lasting consequences for my country. I was happy about this. From the American military side, I constantly felt a sort of friendliness toward me, surely because I was a graduate of one of their military academies. It just so happened that General Norman Schwarzkopf, the commander-in-chief of the first Iraq war, had studied at Valley Forge Academy. The meeting went very well; I felt the support of all the ambassadors present, which encouraged me. At the end of the meeting, the general secretary, Lord Robertson, who had already visited Bulgaria, said to me in his strong Scottish accent, "Prime Minister, I have never been present at such a multilingual performance as yours before!"

Prior to this time, I had met with the ambassadors of Russia and those NATO countries who were accredited in our country, each presenting his arguments to me. To be honest, on a few occasions I could tell that the Russian representative—with whom I had otherwise a good relationship—was very worried. We had let them know that we were unhappy about some logistical issues. The delivery of spare aviation parts, which were entirely Soviet, posed a particular problem. We should not forget that we were in a strategic position, possessing on our territory a series of S22 and S23 Scud-type missiles that we would necessarily have to dismantle and return to Russia.

We had dealt with a somewhat delicate matter when the United States requested access to the missile sites in order to learn more about similar weapons possessed by Saddam Hussein's Iraq. At the risk of attracting the wrath of the Pentagon, I resisted the request, for it seemed to me that if Bulgaria had signed an agreement with Russia, it should stick to it and not violate that agreement. The Americans would have been pleased to obtain the material, but they might also have said to themselves that we were acting only out of self-interest and thus thrown doubt on our long-term loyalty to the Atlantic alliance. I did not give in, and all the material was returned to Russia as agreed.

Despite this incident, our candidacy moved forward, and we were accepted into the alliance in April 2004. Eight countries joined at the same time. All were received at the White House by President George W. Bush. He congratulated us one by one. We had a short American-style briefing, so that we knew in what order we should present ourselves. I was already familiar with the famous Oval Office, since I had already attended an important working meeting there during a bilateral visit at the beginning of my term of office. What is more, I had been acquainted with the corridors of power since the 1960s, for I had visited Washington twice with American Bulgarians who had prepared a series of encounters with senators and congressmen to make them aware of issues concerning Bulgaria. At the time, we were in the middle of the Cold War, and they wanted me to take part in a sort of Bulgarian government-in-exile.

But the times had changed, and it was as prime minister now that I was presenting myself. President Bush, flanked by several advisors, received me in the Oval Office and showed me where he met with his department heads. I quickly counted the number of chairs, including his. There were sixteen, and there were already seventeen of us for little Bulgaria alone. President Bush was cheerful. Contrary to many rumors, he always impressed me as someone who was alert and dedicated and who paid attention to his guests. I had already met him in Prague, early in our candidacy, and then in Istanbul for a large NATO meeting with all the other heads of state.

In Prague, I had words with Donald Rumsfeld, secretary of state for defense, about an issue that was a reflection of the mindset at the time. Our customs services had made a mistake about some goods. A cargo of 180 gearboxes for farm tractors available in Bulgaria and supposedly destined for Sudan almost ended up in Iraq after suspicious handling. Like most Soviet-manufactured equipment, the gearboxes could also have been used for the tanks used by the Iraqi armed forces.

We were not responsible for the incident, but I very much wanted to defuse the issue, one that could have had disastrous consequences for our candidacy. Again, my attention to detail. I thus took the initiative and went to talk to Rumsfeld. The piercing look in his eyes through his thick glasses struck me: "Secretary, I am the prime minister of the Republic of Bulgaria, and I suppose that you are furious with us about the gearboxes." "I am not angry, but I worry about you guys." By that, he was clearly making a reference to the future of our candidacy. He was threatening us. Then we moved on to another subject, and I didn't wait around. I simply did not want us to be suspected of messing behind their backs. This example shows that there are no insignificant matters in politics. You have to keep an eye on everything. In the modern world, information circulates very quickly and the politician, like any other decision-maker, must above all be well informed. Information is the key to power. You can see it clearly enough in stories about spying that regularly make the headlines.

Bulgaria's membership of NATO changed our strategic vision. The presence of other countries from the late Warsaw Pact also modified the chessboard in Central and Eastern Europe in a significant way, one that is still visible today. The process of rebalancing power begun when the Wall fell is still not over. History with a capital "H" has come back with a vengeance, and we should not be surprised by it. You need the perspective of a historian to understand the period and beware of the loads of information swamping us from TV channels specializing in live reporting. The Russians were of course very annoyed with the three Baltic countries, Estonia, Latvia and Lithuania, becoming members. They were the first, in 1987, to rise up against Moscow. They had been very courageous.

In Bulgaria, public opinion was widely in favor of this, our first membership in an international organization.[1] It was clear from then on that we had turned the page from our recent past. We were perceived in the international arena as credible partners. During a military parade in Sofia to celebrate the event, I was surprised by the number of spectators who turned out: the streets were crammed with people who had come as families.

---

1. I want to add here that our membership in La Francophonie, in the early 1990s, was the first time that we had received international recognition since 1989 and a membership that was symbolically important for us.

In the early 1980s, while I was still living in Madrid, a huge polemic preceded Spain joining NATO. I remember the controversial arguments. A portion of the left was openly hostile to it and a march of political personalities had been organized in the city. On banners, the anti-Franco slogan could be read: *No pasarán!* Felipe González and Javier Solana, still Socialist militants at the time, were present. This did not prevent either of them from having brilliant careers afterward, the former becoming prime minister of his country in 1982, and defending its entry into the Atlantic Alliance, and the second, years later, becoming secretary general of that same NATO and subsequently head of European diplomacy between 2002 and 2007. The career of Javier Solana is full of break-throughs. A man of fine intelligence, he has now become one of my fellow members in the Order of the Golden Fleece. During a meeting with the Austrian chancellor Bruno Kreisky following the death of Franco, I indirectly contributed to his return (and that of his brother Luis) to Spain—from which they had been exiled for political reasons. This was a real paradox, since I was an exile from my own country. I can understand the path he followed when I look at my own. Control of our destiny largely escapes most of us—happily—and this situation can sometimes lead to situations full of irony if one is sensitive to the sense of History. For me, NATO was above all an agreement for joint defense among countries sharing the same values.

*

While I was satisfied with this first membership, I nevertheless had my sights firmly set on joining the European Union as well. Starting in 1998, the government of my predecessor, Ivan Kostov, had begun negotiations, and I took them up afterward with all of my team. We were all very enthusiastic about successfully completing our mission.

This phase seemed quite a serious one to me in terms of our future, being the "civilian" part of our joining Europe, which had already begun with NATO. I wanted to put the whole weight of my experience into it—that of my past life, my international contacts, my influential friends and those of my relatives. In Athens in 2004, when ten countries were accepted into the European Union, I thought to myself, "I hope Europe doesn't get indigestion." This, moreover, is what happened. I did not consider myself at the time prime minister only, but also the result of a strange, unexpected life, one that was made cosmopolitan by way of exile. Time has made me realize how fortunate I am to have this heritage.

In the spirit of the European Union, we had instituted safeguards that seemed essential to me for a democracy as frail as ours. Naturally, I put my all into it in terms of work and hours of discussion. I had to swallow many insults. Fortunately, we made an excellent team—motivated and competent—all pushing in the same direction. Without that, we would have never obtained the results we did.

I arrived in Brussels for the negotiations as a man who has known how to get around just about everywhere: in the private sector, where I was known in many large European companies, and in political circles as well. I believe this really made a difference. I had the opportunity to see my country benefit from the goodwill of my network and experience. It would not have been the same if I had remained on the throne of Bulgaria for all those years instead. I fundamentally believe that behind any setback, some hope or compensation is always hidden. I am the type of person who always wants to see the glass half full. I am a bit like Albert Camus, who defined himself as a "cautious optimist." I have never wanted to become embittered or bear grudges, despite the adversities that life can bring. I have always demonstrated it, from the time of the death of my father and the execution of a large number of those close to us.

I was fortunate to meet the Dalai Lama after a speech he made at the European Parliament in October 2001. He had come to Strasbourg to defend the idea of the Union: "I believe that the European Union constitutes an eloquent demonstration that peaceful, supportive coexistence between different nations and peoples is possible." His optimism pleased me greatly. We met one-on-one for forty minutes, and I was touched by his fascinating personality and wisdom. We were in agreement on one point: our exiles were also a source of our good fortune. It just so happens that we are the same age and that both of us can look back on our past and our misfortunes with pride.

I can say without hesitation that the European Union is an institution that I respect enormously even if it finds itself regularly questioned.

It protects and contributes to prosperity not only for Bulgarians but also for the rest of our dear old continent. I have no question on the subject despite the current wave of Euroskepticism, a trend that I find dangerous. Coming from a generation that witnessed the atrocities of war, I can assure the younger generations that the peace that we enjoy is an enormous asset.

From an economic point of view, the Union gives us the necessary weight to negotiate on equal grounds with the other large blocks of nations. From an American perspective, it is clear that Europeans have maintained their significance internationally thanks to the creation of the Union. We do not realize the economic power that we represent together: the number one zone of economic exchange if all of our GDPs are put together! And then we are still the continent whose way of life is envied by people from around the world, a society increasingly conscious and determined to blend economic development with respect for the environment. Let alone the richness of our cultural heritage, our museums, our castles, our cathedrals, and our landscapes, all of which stems from a rich history that is also part of our identity. We can be proud of it.

We must speak with one voice, and despite criticism, the creation of the euro gives a practical sense to the Union, just as there is a certain geographical unity and freedom of movement. I understand that the bureaucracy, which was created in Brussels, and keeps growing, worries people. An excess of detail and a growing number of civil servants—despite my respect for the work they do—have sometimes seemed to steer the Union away from the principles of its founding fathers. I am thinking of Robert Schuman, the first president of the European Parliament, and Konrad Adenauer, the former chancellor of Germany (West Germany), for example. But civil servants are not the decision-makers, and we must not let ourselves be biased by the rise of various kinds of populisms! Politicians must propose a new vision, and above all take the time to explain it to their citizens, far from the slogans and demagogy that bring nothing to the table.

In my youth, I met an odd person, one who was a visionary. Richard Nikolaus von Coudenhove-Kalergi was the son of an Austro-Hungarian diplomat and a Japanese lady. I read his political program for Europe and was very taken with it. In the period between the two world wars, in 1922, he was the first to design a modern plan for a united Europe, successfully convincing numerous intellectuals and politicians, including Aristide Briand, several times president of the European Council of Ministers. But the idea went no further, as we know, except for a "European Union" being proposed at the League of Nations. Defending such an idea at the time was nothing short of daring! This was also the case of Ernst Jünger, who in 1941 began to write a very beautiful essay titled "Peace: An Appeal to the Youth of Europe and to the Youth of the World," an interesting paradox considering that at the time he was wearing the uniform of the Wehrmacht in occupied Paris. Alas! It is often in the midst of dramatic events that great ideas are born. Afterward, with prosperity, they are seldom forgotten.

As I see it, though I could be wrong, relevant policies are those designed as a continuous process. It is only this that enables long-lasting results. We must avoid getting lost in the details and instead develop a new dimension of the European mindset by leveraging our heritage—a history of more than a thousand years—to meet the expectations of new generations.

I am not a dreamer: I know that we still have a long way to go. But I remain convinced that we have no alternative. We must continue to improve the tool that we have given ourselves stay united, even if only streamlining it. The generations to come will not forgive us if we stop or reverse in the middle of the journey. Where would we be after these years of economic and political crises if we did not have our European institutions?

I am open to other views, but I have yet to be convinced by a better option. Having a Europe of regions is a proposal I often hear about: the idea is entirely honorable as long as these regions remain within their respective countries, but it becomes a dangerous syllogism if taken literally. Most of our countries have been built over centuries, and I find unacceptable the idea that the construction of Europe should serve as an excuse for the dismantling of nations. This brings to mind the regional nationalism in Spain, one that exists elsewhere as well. The problem becomes a bit thornier with each political crisis. To my mind, the principle of a supranational union, often criticized, does not prevent national identities from continuing to exist, quite the contrary. Reciprocal stimulation means that we cultivate even more the things that differentiate us from our neighbors. I believe in the respect of our individual history as the cornerstone of a future in common. I am well placed to know about it: my family history is studded with drastic choices made by my ancestors. It is not by accident that I am such a staunch supporter of the European idea.

I feel at home just about everywhere in Europe. Wherever I look in my family tree, there is not a branch that has not taken root in one of its green valleys! I have yet to find a European country where there are no family traces. I am not bragging here, but rather trying to make a point as to how interrelated we Europeans are and to what extent I am convinced of the benefits of a united Europe. As an enthusiastic reader, I know my History: I know all too well the harm caused by our divisions and the damage done by leaders who are ignorant of the past.

During a conference in Vienna where I spoke as part of an official visit, Austrian chancellor Wolfgang Schüssel called me "Mister Europe" before those gathered. I took it as a great compliment. I could not help but think of my uncle, Otto von Habsburg, who spent all of his life fighting for a unified Europe. His life is exemplary: Son of the last emperor of Austria-Hungary—the Empire itself already being a multinational entity—and speaking many languages, his family was exiled in 1918, following the fall of the monarchy. He was subsequently chased out of Germany by the Nazis, leaving for the United States before returning to Europe after the war. We always met with great pleasure at conferences or family reunions. I listened to him carefully. He sat on the benches of the European Parliament for twenty years and was admired by all. One of the ideas that he liked promoting was the Europe of the Danube, taking the longest river in Europe as an axis for cultural, economic and even environmental exchange. I remember having heard him for the first time in public during a conference in Madrid in 1955, at a time when Spain was still isolated. In many ways, I consider him one of my political mentors, a role model I deeply admired. I believe that he was a unique link between the mindset of old Europe, of which he was a product, and contemporary Europe, which he embraced and is still a work in progress.

When the controversy about the Christian roots of Europe began, I was surprised. I would have never thought that this question could be sufficiently important to justify the constitution being rejected. I was present at the famous summit in Brussels where we discussed this, and it was the Greek minister of foreign affairs, George Papandreou, who had the final—witty—word: "In that case, Hellenic influence should also be mentioned, for it goes back much further than Christian." This remark, full of humor and also quite true, relaxed the atmosphere. I consider myself a deeply religious person, but, as I see it, religion is personal. The fact that Europe has a long history of Christianity is beyond question—it is a fact. However, I couldn't see how the formula could bring us together and make us progress. I felt the emotional weight of the question led to nothing positive and had each one defending his opinion.

I remain very fond of the beauty of our churches and our monasteries, especially in our country, where the Orthodox Church has preserved all of the pomp and rigor of ancient liturgy. The great abbeys of the West, too, participated in the safeguarding of knowledge at a crucial moment in the history of our continent, and then in the preservation of the values that provided a framework for our democracies, even to the very idea of human rights, in turn influenced by the Christian message in all its variants.

Often during our negotiations, I felt the sympathy and friendship of President Jacques Chirac toward our application. We enjoyed exchanging remarks in French. He was a lively and energetic person, the impression he gave me was one of a man convinced by the idea of Europe. The Italians and the Germans also provided us with relevant support for our candidacy.

Since the beginning, I had understood that it was in our best interest to propose a dual application with our neighbor Romania, as a team. Going off on our own, like some politicians in Bulgaria wanted to do, was to be avoided.

My contribution was to give a personal touch to the negotiations by going to see the persons in charge in Brussels directly to try to convince them one by one. You need to know how certain mechanisms work, and to give of yourself. Brussels is not an abstraction but a human entity. I followed the file closely. Little by little, we grew closer to meeting the criteria of Maastricht. I remember the joy of seeing one of the forty-three chapters concluded when the minister in charge of the matter, Meglena Kuneva, informed me of it by telephone.

One of the greatest satisfactions in my political career was to have been invited, on January 1, 2007, to the ceremony for the raising of the European flag in Sofia, not far from Alexander Nevsky church, even if I was no longer prime minister. The representative of the Union, the German minister of foreign affairs, Frank-Walter Steinmeier, hugged me when he saw how moved I was.

*

Joining Europe was not without headwinds. Here, I would like to give just one example of the obstacles that we had to overcome. Starting in 1976, Bulgaria equipped itself with six nuclear reactors in a single plant, at Kozloduy, located on the banks of the Danube. This type of energy is so important for our country that until now, even the Green Party was not necessarily anti-nuclear. When we began our discussions with Europe, around 1995, we were still in the post-Chernobyl period, and the subject of the safety of Soviet technology remained a sensitive one. As countries bordering on the Soviet Union, the Czech Republic and Slovakia had the same problem. We were told by the commissioner in charge of enlargement, "Either you close the two oldest reactors in the power plant, 1 and 2, or your candidacy will be suspended." This was very difficult for public opinion to accept and above all was contrary to our own interests as far as our energy supply independence was concerned. Indeed, this power plant produced all by itself 41 percent of our electricity, while also allowing us to export to neighboring countries. Greece, Austria and the Netherlands were the most active opponents to our power plants. We were forced to close the first two reactors before turning off 3 and 4 as well. Blocks 5 and 6—of a generation well after that of Chernobyl—continued to generate. The energy chapter was challenging to negotiate, and our team found itself in an impossibly tight squeeze: on the one hand, we were accused by Bulgarian public opinion of betraying our national interests; on the other, our access to the Union absolutely depended on it.

The decision to build a new power plant was also particularly complicated. In the 1980s, Zhivkov's government had already decided to build a second one, but after 1989, work had been interrupted by lack of funds, even though Bulgaria had already invested nearly a billion dollars in the project. In 2002, I wanted to see what state it was in with my own eyes. It was located facing the island of Belene, which was home to the worst of the gulags during the dictatorship. I was so astonished to see how advanced the construction was, and its high quality—its upkeep carefully maintained by its engineers—that I wanted to reactivate the project to avoid such a terrible waste. I thus requested specialists to examine. Would it be possible to resume construction after fifteen years? One of the reactors had been delivered by Czechoslovakia: it had been paid for, was in perfect shape and ready to be installed. Seeing that our engineers were competent, and that it was possible to carry on, we finally decided to relaunch the work site. The European Union had not forbidden us to continue exploiting this energy source, and we needed to innovate.

Problems began, though, when the new reactor was supplied. My idea was to replicate the Finnish way, establishing a consortium of suppliers so that sourcing could be diversified and more than one country made happy. My thought was to keep the Soviet material already delivered, while asking the French group, Areva, and the German, Siemens, to supply what was missing, and to reach out to the American firm Westinghouse to guarantee the safety of the whole. The Canadians offered us the tenth and last reactor in series before beginning a new generation facility. Our engineers and experts advised us to wait before embarking on the new series, so we decided to turn down this proposal. My term in office came to an end in the meantime. The next government continued along the same lines, and it was only later that the file got bogged down in endless discussions between our energy agency and the Russians, unhappy to have been passed over for the second project, with each side accusing the other of not respecting deadlines and agreements. There were suspicions, in fact, that bribes had been paid, the hidden intention being to reject all that I had done previously and cancel the project. One excuse given was seismic risk, despite all the studies having ruled that out, and the potential flooding of the Danube having been taken into consideration. Alas, everything became heavily politicized, and that is where things stand today, as the seventh block is under construction in the existing power plant.

I prefer not to think of the huge sums that were invested for no use. Today, a good number of years later, neither of the two sites has been finished. Without being a technician, in my somewhat simplistic view, I've always thought that the development of a country leads to increased energy needs over the long term. Moreover, the European Union requested that we increase production of renewable energies while decreasing polluting fossil fuels like coal and diesel. And yet we could build no more dams, under pressure from Greece and Turkey, because of international treaties regulating the use of upstream water. And we did not have enough investment funds to develop wind and solar power, whose price per kilowatt was too high at the time.

Eventually, we did not have much choice. I give the Soviets credit for having allowed us to become a member of the club of nuclear-energy-producing countries. The Russians supply us with the necessary fuel and take the waste back. I don't know how we would manage otherwise.

Often, and unintentionally, Brussels technocrats put us in annoying situations, underestimating our technology even though it had already overwhelmingly proved itself. Coming from a relatively small country, I confess that I am particularly sensitive to dictates. It was difficult to juggle between the sensitiveness of our public opinion and the conditions imposed to obtain membership.

This situation saddens me, for we are wasting precious time and large amounts of money to secure our independence in energy. With hindsight, this dilemma, which cost me so many sleepless nights, needs to be explained by Europe in a more consensual fashion: I sometimes had the impression that the tone of certain instructions from Brussels were close to blackmail.

If I can agree with the concept of European directives, a common set of rules for its member countries. But I question the way in which some bureaucrats behave, with a lack of sensitivity and even communication that made things unnecessarily difficult. Having been for four years in a front row seat for many international decisions, I know that many facts are not conveyed in an objective manner. I am convinced that many thorny issues could have been avoided by a little more flexibility. Perhaps the lack of accountability of those sitting on the other side of the negotiating table or the asymmetry in the relevance of the matters discussed are to blame as well for a certain bitter taste left in my mouth.

I have noticed that, when it comes to technical blockages, widening the perspective to include the long term has a tendency to destabilize a purely technocratic vision. "What will be irrelevant in five years can't be relevant today," I liked to say. My only ambition in the negotiations with Europe was to defend the interests of my country. As I wasn't necessarily seeking reelection, I had little to lose and could do as my conscience dictated.

I do not like clichés and always try to fight unconscious—let alone conscious!—bias. One can find a set of clichés for every country in Europe, but I find the one that sees Bulgaria in terms of the drama of its Romany or gypsy population being forced to leave particularly irritating. Obviously, I know that every country must have its laws, public safety and property respected, for these are essential values in a democracy. Whoever goes to a foreign country must respect the traditions and hospitality of that country.

But it seems to me delicate to stigmatize an entire people and thus to discriminate against a whole part of our population: all Romany are certainly not bad citizens. An effort must be made to understand their culture and mindset, linked to nomadism. I have always refused to make ethnic or religious distinctions between my fellow citizens. Nor do I like the term *minority*, which is often used.

In 2003, I was committed to participating in a large international conference in Budapest (sponsored by the World Bank and George Soros's foundation), the Open Society Institute, whose goal was to bring together the nine countries with the largest Romany populations. The opening session took place in the magnificent neo-Gothic parliament of the Habsburgs. The rostrum was full of ministers and delegates.

My friend James Wolfensohn, president of the World Bank, stood up and spoke: "Times have changed. In these imperial surroundings where in the old days only aristocracy sat, we see here today Romany representatives from all over Europe, including the chairman of this session. Here, we have a king who became the prime minister of a republic, a poor Hungarian refugee who became a world personality, George Soros, and you have before you a little Jewish boy from Australia who became president of the World Bank." I was struck by the summary of this encounter linking History and Culture. Who could have ever imagined such a meeting taking place one day? A reminder that we should never look down on anyone today, as he or she may become a decision-maker tomorrow.

I would also like to point out that one of my great-uncles, Archduke Joseph of Habsburg-Lorraine, showed great interested in gypsy culture at the end of the nineteenth century. In 1888, he published a grammar of the language as well as an ethnographic study of their habits. Nicknamed the "Gypsy Archduke," he even authorized entire families to settle in the lands of his estate, Alcsuth, in Hungary.

The other recurrent cliché about Bulgaria is the issue of its "Mafia," as if we had an exclusivity on it in Europe. This is unfair, for organized crime is internationally widespread. Its ramifications reach the so-called most advanced countries. Having gangsters is not our privilege alone, and there are people who would do well to sweep in front of their own front doors before lecturing others.

It is certainly in our interest to fight the underworld. From both totalitarianism and unbridled capitalism, we have inherited—I agree—a lack of personal ethics that has enabled the boom of ruthless and speedy fortunes, but we must keep a sense of proportion. The more we are integrated in the European Union, the more our judicial system will be able to free itself from political influence and dirty money. This is a priority. Cooperation between member countries in the Union to reform our justice is important, as is the cooperation of Europol, OLAF (the European Anti-Fraud Office),[2] and the American services of the DEA (Drug Enforcement Agency) that help us fight the scourges of drug trade, human trafficking and other illegal activities.

Bulgaria is capable of playing an important role in the stability of southeastern Europe. Our country lies between Turkey and Europe, and its 300-kilometer seacoast forms an entry to the European Union. It is

---

2. The European Anti-Fraud Office investigates affairs of corruption and serious crimes committed within European institutions.

also for this reason that Bulgaria is sought after and that ill-intentioned people see it as a hub for their activities.

The presence of our much larger Turkish neighbor allows me to open a short chapter, as it is a subject to which I am attached. The country has always interested me. Every day, hundreds of Turkish trucks cross our country, on the way to Central Europe, Germany and France. We have a duty to maintain good relations with our large neighbor. I see Turkey as a strong economic power that can be very useful for us. It represents an enormous market for our products and also invests in our country. We must not forget that we share membership in NATO. Turkey has always been a key partner in it, equipped with a mighty army, whose hundreds of kilometers of border shared with the Soviet Union played an important role during the Cold War. The West has never had to complain about its loyalty. At the time, no one asked whether the country was Eastern or European, but when it became a question of joining the European Union, the "Asian" argument was brought out like a bogeyman.

Of course, I know that NATO and the European Union are not the same in nature. Many Turks already live west of the Bosphorus, in Istanbul, in eastern Thrace or Edirne. Also, many of my fellow citizens live in there. Those who were driven out in 1984 continue to voice their attachment to Bulgaria by voting, for example, in the parliamentary elections of May 2013 in the eighty-six voting stations set up for them. Turkey has been part of our history for several centuries, and I take that as an opportunity rather than an inconvenience. For me, the country is already in a certain way in Europe, and there is no point in denying it. Whether it should integrate entirely in the European judicial system is a question that deserves an objective analysis. Let us stick to reality and not make of Turkey an argument about internal politics that we throw at each other.

The Turkish population, with its grand history, is difficult not to respect. And perhaps its history has the same difficulties as ours of being known and understood? Furthermore, an often degrading view of Islam needs to be fought. I believe that European influence can be of help in reinforcing a spirit of secularism. I am not among those who fear this religion—far from it, since I have been used to living in contact with Muslim cultures since my childhood in Egypt.

Also, the Black Sea allows Bulgaria to belong to the Organization of the Black Sea Economic Cooperation (BSEC), founded in 1992 along with other member states: Turkey, Romania, Ukraine, Russia and Greece. This hardly known association is for me a successful example of what could be done on a Mediterranean scale. The Black Sea allows countries with different cultures to meet together to put in place economic projects of common interest, like the sharing of natural resources. Its headquarters are in Istanbul, while the Black Sea Bank is based in Salonica, already a promising symbol.

Speaking of this point, I would also like to say how delighted I am with our excellent relations with Greece, despite the fact that for years we turned our backs to each other. A country whose past I admire—not just for its archeology, of which I am a great fan—and whose businesses invest in our country. This also makes me think of another neighbor, Macedonia, for which Bulgaria feels great friendship and which I visited as prime minister. I was able to verify the reciprocity of these feelings.

Continuing along our borders, there is Serbia, which is rapidly advancing toward membership in the European Union to my great satisfaction. As to Romania, whose population is three times that of Bulgaria, our affinities allowed us to complete the path to Brussels together. It is basically the spirit of the Union that pushes Bulgaria and the countries that border it, to cooperate and be good neighbors.

*

If Bulgaria has close historical ties with Turkey, another country whose influence is important for us is Russia, with which we share something of a common heritage. I cannot forget that it was Russian troops that helped us end Ottoman rule in the nineteenth century. Today, Russia has returned to the center of the world stage and should be neither underestimated nor, even worse, ignored. For the Russians, we are a Slav country, and thus close to them, sharing many values and traditions. I have a weak spot for these two nations, Turkey and Russia, which are almost continents by themselves, and I encourage Bulgaria to find a balance between these neighbors and its membership in the European Union. This is not easy.

Russia is relevant in part because of its resources: gas pipelines, oil, coal and nuclear fuel. Considerable Russian capital is invested in Bulgaria: thousands of people have purchased apartments in our ski resorts and our beautiful coastal areas. They feel comfortable in our country again; the wounds of the recent past have healed with time. After my election, I quickly organized a visit to Brussels, and then to Moscow to carefully underline the importance that I attributed to Russia. During a bilateral meeting at the Kremlin, I met President Vladimir Putin. An hour before, our ambassador announced to me that it would not be my homologue, Mikhail Kasyanov, who would preside over the Russian delegation, but in fact President Putin, catching me unawares. The points on our agenda were dealt with in less than an hour, since Putin tends to be energetic and expeditious. As we were putting away our respective documents, he leaned back in his chair and looked me straight in the eye: "Prime Minister, I have learned some not very good things about you." I immediately felt the tension grow in my entourage; our chief of staff seemed about to faint. For a moment, I thought we were going to be subjected to a wave of complaints. The seconds passing seemed like an eternity. Then Putin grinned: "I heard them from King Juan Carlos himself, who came to see me a few days ago," he said. I began to breathe again. "President," I answered, "in that case, you should ignore them, as the king and I are too close friends for anything bad to have been said." And that was it. I was still curious to know what he was planning on saying, but now, with hindsight, I think he was demonstrating his sense of humor—and perhaps even testing me. I had the opportunity of seeing him again twice, including once in Bulgaria.

This international overview would not be complete without reporting the sad episode of the Bulgarian nurses held prisoner in Libya, which haunted us all during my term of office. They had been arrested at the Al-Fateh Children's Hospital in Benghazi in 1999, accused of having spread "an epidemic by injecting HIV contaminated products to 393 children," of whom twenty-three were already dead. Strangely, the Libyan doctors in charge of the hospital had not been bothered. This was never explained.

Our relationship with Libya went back to the period of the Cold War: Communist Bulgaria supplied engineers, doctors and technicians to several countries in the Maghreb, since technical cooperation was a means for Zhivkov's Bulgaria to make itself known on the international scene. From the very beginning of this dreadful story, we felt that the whole thing was an excuse for internal propaganda: through it, Gaddafi appeared as the guardian of his people against foreigners who wanted to harm them. In addition, the nurses worked in Benghazi, the territory of Cyrenaica tribes who, by their very nature, were opposed to the government in Tripoli. How shameful to have made up an accusation that had no truth to it!

In the course of a long trial, the Pasteur Institute helped us with the analysis of samples and Professor Luc Montagnier, one of the discoverers of the AIDS virus, testified several times in our favor, excluding the possibility of deliberate contamination, given the fact that some of the children had already been infected before the nurses had begun practicing in the hospital. I contacted the oldest son of Colonel Gaddafi, Saif al-Islam, and several other people who had go-betweens in Libya, in an attempt to convince them of the nurses' innocence and our good faith, but to no avail.

Twice the nurses were sentenced to death, and twice their execution was postponed. I leave it to the reader to imagine how these women were traumatized by this hell on earth that lasted eight long years. One can easily imagine the psychological harm to these unfortunate women.

From the very beginning of the scandal, public opinion was outraged that a story that reeked of lies and manipulation should be believed. The Bulgarian media adopted this sad story as their war horse against me, blaming poor bad management of the issue, among other things. Wrongly: the entire administration of the state was deeply involved and committed to solving the crisis, including the president of the Republic, the parliament, the rest of government and civil society, and even the Red Cross of Bulgaria and that of other countries.

We were victims of international blackmail. In fact, Libya owed a great deal of money to Bulgarian companies that had drilled for oil on its territory and did not want to pay its debts or even to return the material that had been taken there. And now Gaddafi was demanding a ransom instead!

We had come to an impasse, until that morning in July 2007 when our ambassador in Tripoli let us know that the hostages were going to be freed. An airplane was provided by French president Nicolas Sarkozy—elected a few weeks earlier—and was ready to bring them back to Sofia. But we were not yet at the end of our pain: in the middle of the night there was an umpteenth attempt to demand a ransom. When learning that Cécilia Sarkozy was onboard the plane, the Libyan authorities must have realized that it wasn't possible to prevaricate yet again. I must admit that the drive of President Sarkozy was the determining factor in the final unlocking of this saga.

A documentary film by the journalist Velislava Dareva analyzes this tragedy in detail—one that disgusted public opinion.

EPILOGUE

A Life Lived in Full

We live in a period
Where clichés are accepted
As verdicts.
—TOLSTOY.

IN 2009, AFTER EIGHT YEARS OF INVOLVEMENT IN GOVERNMENT, IT WAS time for me to resign from my duties, assuming the responsibility for the voting defeat of our party. I had not been prime minister since 2005, but my Movement had continued to support and participate in the government that succeeded me. In the end, I was relieved, though sad not to have completed all our reforms. I thus left the party's offices in the center of town, close to the Alexander Nevsky church, for a new office in Vrana, the house that is so dear to me despite some painful memories from childhood. I work at a desk facing the garden, organizing my trips, answering interviews, and, most of all, welcoming visitors—fellow countrymen, diplomats and politicians. Since the end of my term, I have been regularly invited to participate in conferences abroad, to attend international meetings where my experience is of interest. Recently, I lectured about it and about the future of the European Union in front of a crowd of students in Cambridge. I was proud to see several young Bulgarian students among them. In Turin, I spoke on the topic of good governance before a group of decision-makers. In Moscow, on Palm Sunday at the invitation of Patriarch Kyril, I attended a sumptuous celebration in the Cathedral of Christ the Savior.[1] The patriarch was the epitome of a religious leader, oozing gravitas and with the profound sense of faith that Russians sometimes have. In the course of my life, I have had the pleasure of meeting prelates, heads of the Church, and simple monks, and I have visited countless monasteries, from Mount Athos in Greece to Saint Catherine's in Egypt, as well as sites in Germany, Austria, France and Spain. Among other things, these experiences have taught me that we need ecumenicalism and tolerance. In the face of atheism—which is winning over more and more people—I believe that the faithful need to be united, not to debate about which chapel you sing in.

I took advantage of this trip to see friends in Moscow, including Igor Ivanov, former Russian minister of foreign affairs, and my godson "Micha" Orloff, grandson of King Farouk. In Berlin, I recently attended the enthronement of our new metropolitan for Western Europe, a man of thirty-five, something rather unusual for the Church. As for gatherings of royal families, the sixtieth coronation anniversary of Queen Elizabeth II was the peak of the monarchial ideal such as I see it. Thanks to her wisdom and the exemplary manner of doing her job, the queen incarnates the quintessential constitutional monarch, all of what a crown may bring a country. My admiration only continues to grow for this extraordinary sovereign. The celebrations for her jubilee, in London in May 2012, which I attended with my wife, demonstrated her power as a symbol and her popularity. With very few exceptions, all the monarchies of the world were represented. Since I was proclaimed king in 1943, my seniority granted me the privilege of being placed next to her for the photograph immortalizing this historic day.

In late April 2014, my wife and I attended the mass celebrating the canonization of their Holinesses John XXIII and John Paul II in Rome. I was received at the Vatican three times in the early 1960s in connection with our marriage. John XXIII had been close to my parents when he was posted as representative of the Vatican to Sofia, between 1925 and 1934.

---

1. Razed by Stalin in 1931, it had been built in memory of the defeat of Napoleon's Grande Armée and was recently reconstructed to its original state.

My mother had even been invited to his coronation in 1958, for before leaving Sofia she had predicted that one day he would become pope. "Still and all, these women are quite amusing with their imaginings," he had written in his journal. As for Pope John Paul II, I had received him during his visit to Sofia in May 2002 on his way back from Azerbaijan. He looked very tired but wanted to go to the monastery of Rila to pray on the tomb of my father. After his prayer, he took me aside and spoke to me about what Cardinal Stefan Wyszyński had done against the Communists and the low blows that Moscow had dealt Poland in response. He wanted me to know, to be informed. I admired the worn-out old man who took the time to share this important and sometimes ignored chapter of his life with me. I could read in his eyes a hint of satisfaction: "We succeeded! We got 'em!" He also mentioned the fact that the Jews in Bulgaria had not been deported. His visit was a landmark for Bulgaria, for it was the first time ever that a pope had come to our country. And as he was very popular, the inhabitants of Sofia came out in crowds to welcome him. By declaring that he had never believed in the "Bulgarian trail" in his assassination attempt in 1981—so often inferred by the press at the time—he cleansed our country of all suspicion.

*

My life has always been very full. I enjoy a fascinating correspondence with my former homologues, friends of long date. I receive foreign ambassadors, who always ask to see me even if I no longer play an official role in the Republic. Perhaps it is curiosity that motivates them, and yet I know as well that they receive instructions to do so, particularly when they come from a country that has a monarchy. I am curious to learn what they have to say about their country and take the opportunity to talk to them about Bulgaria, suggesting personalities who might be of interest them—writers, researchers, historians. I note that this type of dialogue, outside the usual official channel, is useful, for they get a broader view than that found in the usual networks.

The quality of the diplomats sent to Sofia is of a high level; perhaps this is due to our very interesting geopolitical position, or our relationships with the Middle East via the Black Sea, or our role at the heart of the so-called Balkan countries, of which we were the first to be accepted into the European Union. Numerous Bulgarian diplomats come to see me before taking up their posts, especially those who are named to countries that I am supposed to know well. They also come to sound the ex-prime minister who is reputed for his high-level contacts.

After a discussion or lunch, I sometimes like to take the time to show my visitors the hidden parts of Vrana Palace, those that are being restored. Since the moratorium imposed on our properties, we have been directly responsible for paying for the project; this is a large expense that I assume willingly, for I think of the future of my country and hope that one day its citizens will be proud of such restoration. I am trying to refurnish it with historic and family objects that have either been brought back from Madrid or come from Coburg, as well as recovered in Bulgaria. My objective is to create a museum dedicated to the "Third Kingdom," something that does not exist in our country yet. This period was systematically erased from history books or, at best, denigrated. My sister, my wife, and I are devoted to this project, as is a young historian, Ivaylo Schalafoff, who spends long hours working on it with a praisewor-thy sense of duty and of historical precision. Basically, the house where I lived until I was nine years old (and which would be much too large to be a home) is ideal for housing such a museum. The part where I live with my wife is a smaller addition to it. The original was the first residence that King Ferdinand had built on the spot where the Turkish governor-pasha who occupied these lands before our arrival had his dwelling.

To carry this project forward, I created the "King Boris and Queen Giovanna" private fund in 2011, whose goal is to preserve the royal her-itage of Bulgaria with the means at our disposal. After years of indiffer-ence, lies, and propaganda, I thought it was too bad to let such a legacy, its archives and its paintings, fall into oblivion. I believe it is important for the public to be able to benefit from it. We would also like to create an institute dedicated to our dynasty, with its own specific library. I have brought together archives consisting, on the one hand, of documents I have stored during my sixty years of activity and, on the other hand, of the personal files of Ferdinand I that were in Coburg. I had repatriated the latter in 2006 from Stanford University in California.[2] They include agreements and treaties between Bulgaria and other countries, letters from my grandfather with sovereigns of the period, photographs, and even his bills, allowing us to re-create everyday life in Sofia during this long-ago period. They take up eighty-eight boxes filled to overflowing. I gave them to the university in the 1970s, with, however, a provision—which turned out to be premonitory—that if the country returned to democracy, they could be returned to me. I still have today several large photo albums that illustrate palace life and that of Sofia under the reigns of my grandfather and my father.[3] All these documents could be useful in recovering a heritage that was dispersed by the ups and downs of History.

It is with great joy that I keep an eye on the work as it advances, the rooms opening up one by one, the display cases filling with personal objects brought from all over the world—uniforms, decorations, dinner menus, royal flags, collections of porcelain and family paintings. Alas, a large part of our furniture was "lost" during the years of the Communist regime, and some of it can now be found in private collections.

My windows give onto superb trees planted by my grandfather in the park at the beginning of the twentieth century: a type of giant plane tree, pines that are forty meters high, Douglas firs, a Wellingtonia, beech trees and lindens. I smoke my cigarillos while contemplating them. I watch the passing of the seasons, the same natural beauty that delights me every day. In Bulgaria, the seasons are quite distinct, for we have a continental climate. I remember how the absence of such transitions in Alexandria bothered me.

For a little while now, I've had the pleasure of feeding a few couples of jays and woodpeckers that knock on the windowpanes at the first light of day. My passion for nature is a sort of link with my ancestors. My grandfather was a bird lover, an ornithologist recognized by his peers and the founder of a reputed museum of natural history in Sofia. I also learned a great deal from my father concerning plants, even their names

---

2. The choice of this university was twofold. The first was that it had very important archives on Eastern Bloc countries, the Hoover Institution on War, Revolution and Peace, and the second was that California is a zone far from the Soviet Union.
3. The selection of photos for this book was taken in part from these archives.

in Latin (which I still remember). Protecting nature is an obsession with me. I am very sad when I come across city children who don't know the difference between a pine and a walnut tree. Working with the minister of the environment, I tried to get a series of laws passed to safeguard our forests, one of the riches of Bulgaria. A law thus was written forbidding exports of whole cut trees, requiring them to be sawed into large planks of cut lumber in order to limit the amount of wood smuggled out the country; another, inspired by a Portuguese law, requires that when a wooded parcel of land burns, a minimum of ten years must pass before anything can be built on it, which has clearly reduced cases of arson.

In one part of the park, we have restored two greenhouses dating from the time of my grandfather. One of them is full of exotic plants, some of them coming from Africa: cacti, a ficus, and the famous Victoria regia—giant waterlilies large enough to support the weight of a small child! When I returned, I was amazed to see that some of these plants had survived since the years of my grandfather's reign. But despite the beauty of the park that surrounds me, I have less time to enjoy it compared to my father.

I continue to go back to Spain for visits that are all too brief, to be near my children, but the place that touches me the most is in Bulgaria: our Tsarska house, in the mountains, high up in the Borovets, is where I really feel that I have come home. The proximity of the city makes it an ideal spot for weekends, and I like to drive there myself. This former hunting lodge was built in the middle of a vast forest full of game, deer and wild boar. Unlike Vrana, I found it exactly as we had left it in 1946; we had only to rearrange the rugs and the paintings and to update the utilities. Suddenly, I found myself living my childhood memories, transported to the past by the heads of the big wood grouse hanging on the walls, hunting trophies of my grandfather that greatly impressed me as a small child.

*

As time goes by, I have the impression that people are becoming conscious that my government gave the country a period of development and stability such as it has not known since. I attempted to apply a policy of reassurance and tolerance, even if this was misunderstood at the time due in no small part to the adverse media coverage. There are people who are never forgiven, and this was my case. I suffer from it, for I find it unfair, especially for those within my team who willingly devoted all of their time and energy. It takes time for people to realize what they no longer have. Numerous politicians now tell me that.

Despite the difficulties, leaving Bulgaria has never occurred to me. I will remember the day of my return forever. But I admit with sorrow that I sometimes feel exiled inside. I am tired of constantly having to remind people of my family's role and place in our history, as well as having to justify the tiniest of my actions. I am weary of seeing people trying to erase the fact that I am king. I didn't invent it: it's a fact of history. I don't ask citizens of the Republic to change their opinions, but I don't see the harm in leveraging the continuity that I represent. I served the Bulgarian Republic as Prime Minister Saxe-Coburg Gotha: I am proud of it, and it in no way changes my original identity. God knows that I have acquired a great deal of political experience, and that my international relations are numerous and reputed, and yet this irrational resentment toward "the king" remains constant. I do not believe that one betrays the republican ideal by respecting one's past. Many officials are quite considerate to me when I meet with them individually, and I am pleased that they are, but then in public their behavior changes. I am not angry with them, for at this stage in my life, I know that is how human nature is. I merely note it.

The fifty years that I lived without a hope of seeing my country again seemed like an eternity. I believed that the Soviet system would remain in place forever. History played quite a trick on us, and, like many people of my generation, I adapted to a new perspective. I do not regret at all the work I accomplished during the years of silence and loneliness, for they allowed me to grow as a person and have an international, multicultural perspective. If I had remained on the throne all that time, I would have never had such a full life. I think now of my children and of the spiritual legacy that I leave them, of peace reestablished with the history of their family and with Bulgaria. I know that they think about it, even if we don't talk about it often, and that their attachment to this past will prevail. I will leave the major part of Vrana open to the public so that visitors who are curious about it may see for themselves what life was like before Communism. In my mind, this museum is dedicated not just to my forefathers but also to a lifestyle that was, for ideological reasons, thrown away by Bulgarians. The thought of all those people who worked with us and whose memories were also erased is still with me. Bulgaria was then a country gladly facing in the direction of a Europe that was synonymous with prosperity.

I remain convinced that a better knowledge of the past cannot but help the younger generations to better face the future while being proud of their roots. You can only know where you are going if you know where you come from, the saying goes. For years, this idea has been key to my approach, whereas political fights are only ephemeral.

Today, I reflect on the process that we followed in 1989 to put an end to a regime. While I am proud of the fact that there were no deaths, I wonder whether it would have been better to have a more clear-cut transition, one triggering the general catharsis that the country needed to turn the page in a healthier way. Perhaps I was wrong to preach recon-ciliation at all costs? A radical change would have enabled a society with better-defined foundations, free from the politico-economic legacy that still causes us so much harm. I am somewhat regretful that I was not more categorical with the Communists and that, in a certain way, I legitimized the acquittal of some. This was an error, and I admit it willingly. My faith has me reject acting out of revenge. I was compelled to understand the position of others, even if I considered them adversaries. I have always avoided biases, and despite the pain of exile and the fate of my fellow citizens inside the country, I resisted stigmatizing only a portion of them. I realize that this attitude was not understood. Perhaps I mishandled it? My liberal convictions had me appeal for national reconciliation, relying on the judicial system then to do its work correctly; this was not the case.

I was coming from another background, and events demonstrated that I had underestimated the power of money—you never know "which God is served," as we say in Bulgarian. It is always easy to justify oneself afterward, but it seems to me that if we had followed Germany's example, with the famous Stasi files available for consultation only by the person involved, it would have been helpful. However, in our country, the same kind of files were soon made accessible to the public, and many people took advantage to blackmail others or to exonerate themselves by making compromising evidence disappear. Such lowballs poisoned our society, and, despite the efforts made to fight this state of mind, I was not able to leave my mark. Twelve years after the fall of the regime, it was too late: everyone had had time to organize their dirty little schemes.

*

Reading is my salvation. It is a form of meditation for me, one that allows to see the world through the eyes of personalities. I began to read when I was relatively young, after a health problem that called for rest.[4] I thus did not have to take gymnastics at the *Lycée Français* and consequently returned home early every day. After my homework, I spent long hours in the company of my mother and her lady-in-waiting, reading hundreds of pages. As prime minister, journalists used to ask me regularly what book I would like to read again. "If only I could read them for the first time!" I thought to myself, since I spent my time with my nose stuck in paperwork.

Certain periods in life are more prone to reading. Others less. It is only now that I have gotten back to reading, very late in the evening when I am suffering from insomnia, or when traveling by plane. My first choice is historical accounts and biographies of famous personalities. But I also read Saint-Simon with relish, as well as thinkers from the Renaissance, from the time of the Reformation—for example, the Swiss Zwingli, known for having countered some of Luther's doctrines. Each time I go to Zurich, I like to stop at the chapel where he taught. I am also redis-covering the philosophers I studied with curiosity in times past—Ortega y Gasset, Albert Camus. I still remember the phrase written during the war in one of his *Letters to a German Friend*: "I love my country too much to be a nationalist." There is also my fellow citizen, Tzvetan Todorov, and

---

4. My mother worried about my growth: while she recited novenas, I went to see doctors who insisted that I needed to rest.

Ismail Kadare, who describes our eighteenth century so well, and, further back, Descartes, Montaigne and Erasmus, all of whom marked me.

This period in the history of ideas lacked in Bulgaria, as it did in other countries under Ottoman occupation: it's as if we were isolated from thought for several centuries. I was always intrigued by Erasmus in particular. I discovered his work when I was still young; I believe it was while rummaging in the shelves of bookstores in London, Paris or Geneva, perhaps forty years ago, that I found my first volumes. I was attracted by his life and his precepts—his humanist side suits me. He is an author whose wisdom I often called on when making decisions. I keep one of his maxims close to hand: "If in some way I haven't succeeded, this is a mistake, but not a fault; I deserve to be corrected, I do not deserve to be attacked. For if there is one thing I recognize above all, it is that I know nothing. Let others make all the grand declarations that they want to: weak as I am, I will declare nothing, but show what I can do, and I will readily admit my error if, like any man may, I have erred; I will be my own censor if I catch myself in the wrong."[5]

I also enjoy Bulgarian literature, particularly Ivan Vazov, a reputable writer who brilliantly described the end of the Ottoman period. *Under the Yoke* was published around 1894. He then became minister of education under my grandfather.

I know little about more recent literature, for which I hope I will be forgiven. This gap exists in part because I have given priority to history. But I know that it is rich: there are magnificent books by Yordan Dimitrov Radichkov, who has been compared to Gabriel García Márquez and put up by our academy for the Nobel Prize for Literature, and Anton Donchev, a contemporary author of several books whose *Time of Parting* is a masterpiece.

Of course, on the Spanish side, the writings of Camilo José Cela—he invited us to Galicia to eat giant eels—touch me deeply, as do those of my friend Jorge Semprún or Mario Vargas Llosa.

Bulgaria is a country that reads; there is a great deal of translation of foreign books. Often, I have noticed that there is a tendency to put all

---

5. Preface of the *Novum Testamentum* (1516).

Slav peoples in the same basket, but this is a mistake. We Bulgarians have a wry, finely tuned sense of humor. In fact, we are shy and fearful above all of ridicule, and we have a habit of brooding. I think this is deep in our national character. When I read Ivan Hadjiiski, a Bulgarian freethinker from the 1930s who became the most well-known sociologist of his time, I feel like I recognize myself in the description he gives of the people he met then. It seems to me that little has changed since.

There is one place that I have not spoken of very much and that is essential for me: the monastery at Rila, which is two hours by road from Sofia, nestled in the heart of an imposing mountain range. This place was founded in the tenth century by Saint John of Rila, a hermit who settled in the gorges situated above the river of the same name. From that period, there remains a large tower and many precious objects displayed in a rich museum that has been recently set up. In the eighteenth and nineteenth centuries, the complex was rebuilt after parts of it had been torn down. This type of construction was mainly made of stone, wood and mortise. The church itself is impressive: its frescos and its iconostasis make it a masterpiece of the art of the Balkans. The monastery has never been occupied, even in the time of the Ottomans. It is for us a symbol of resistance and of the continuity of the Bulgarian Orthodox Church, present in the hearts of all. When the Marxists drove out the monks, many Bulgarians took it as the sign of the end of the country, for in the centuries before, this had never happened. Abbot Kalistrate, the father-abbot, whom I had known as a child before leaving Bulgaria, was shot. My mother was very fond of him. A good man, cultivated and a former military officer. The monastery was closed around 1956, then transformed into a museum, and finally reopened as a place of worship in the 1970s under popular pressure. An abbot was put into place who had been a novice in my time—Father John. He had studied law at the University of Leipzig and was there when I returned. In 2002, he blessed the marriage of my daughter Kalina in the small chapel at Borovets.

We built a memorial chapel at Tsarska where visitors can go to light a candle. Father John explained to us that the Russians seized over eleven thousand objects of art before Rila Monastery was closed, giving restoration as an excuse. Most of them were never returned. Many other relics were hidden by the monks in coal storage areas, including part of the ribbons from the wreaths sent by foreign governments for my father's funeral. They are now once again displayed in one of the rooms of the monastery.

In May 1996, when our car arrived close enough for us to see the walls of the monastery, Margarita—who was, of course, visiting Bulgaria for the first time—was convinced that she had already seen it, since I had talked about it so much. Ever since childhood, I had never forgotten this idyllic, spiritual place, one that I had come to several times with my father and my Uncle Kyril, and then later with my mother. We would go there by car, with one of our two chauffeurs, Lazarus or Sava. There used to be a little cog railway, like the one that went up to the Mer de Glace at Chamonix, to reach the monastery. Alas, it hasn't been restored because the previous father-abbot was afraid that tourists would come in masse and destroy the peacefulness of the spot. But the place is so unusual that I wouldn't think so.

The monastery remains the ultimate in "Bulgarian-ness" for me, a place where I feel well and where I can recharge my batteries. Nothing has changed, as if monastic seasons were not subject to the same calendar as ours, with the ancient stones gracefully acquiring their patina over the centuries. When I returned to Bulgaria, I saw the same landscape and crossed the same villages and the same forests, hundreds of years old; the main road at the time was still a country road of paving stones.

I know that my mother loved it as much as I have just described; she spoke about it at length when she returned from her own visit. It is odd how my memories of my early years came back to me: in 1996, the monks received us in great pomp; there were many people, and in entering into the huge courtyard, I remembered very well the set of antlers under the entrance that had so impressed me when I was a child. On this spring day, I saw it from a distance, as if it wanted to salute the little king that I was then. We were given the royal suite intended for us, consisting of a pretty corner sitting room and two bedrooms. Fifty years later, the decoration hadn't changed—the same kilims, the same furniture, the same ornaments. The service had been followed by a very large breakfast that reminded me of long ago.

After the death of my father, we had established a ritual: on the 28th of each month, we left for Rila for a requiem mass in his memory. My mother was very insistent that we go there together, while my uncle stayed in Sofia. This was to decrease the risk of being attacked, since the presence of partisans from April 1944 had become a real threat.

On those days, my mother wore a black veil and no makeup. We recited the service for the dead. I still remember it—I could say it in its entirety. Then we were given a little boiled wheat, mixed with chopped walnuts and sugar, with the wheat symbolizing the resurrection. I was allowed the little silvered sugar cross on top of the cake. We often stayed with the father-abbot for a light meal, or sometimes for a night, before returning to Sofia. This period was hard for all of us.

We kept up this habit until April 1946, when the Communist authorities—worried about the constant pilgrimage to Rila—judged it a good idea to move my father's remains. We then buried him in the park at Vrana during the night from Thursday to Good Friday. I remember this horrible moment very well. Later, we learned that the abbot at the monastery had refused to collaborate and that the monks had had to be confined to their cells. During this transfer, the marble tombstone covering the grave of my father was broken up with sledgehammers. The queen, who had only been informed of this decision by telephone the night before, had just had the time to have a hole dug in the spot she had chosen, in a clearing where my father liked to walk. Our teeth chattered from emotion and from shivering, since it was still night and cold. Imagine the children that we were then! The palace staff that had not yet been shot was there beside us; then the coffin was let down into the grave in front of us. One of the putschists, General Marholev, who had been forced on me as head of the house, then said, "Open it!" My sister and I were extremely shocked: through a small window, we made out the embalmed face of my father as we had seen it on his deathbed several years before. Surprised at its state of preservation and caught in his own trap, the general drew back and couldn't help but utter, "The king!"

The next day the construction of a small chapel began; we saw its roof completed on September 16, the day of our final departure from Vrana. I still remember the smell of that fresh cement. Alas, there is not a single photo. We held the first and only requiem mass there and then never knew what became of it.

The story doesn't end here because in the months that followed, the head of Communist Bulgaria, Georgi Dimitrov, had the chapel used as a shed to store garden tools. This man was undoubtedly motivated by a spirit of revenge, one that did not, however, prevent him from blithely taking advantage of the comfort of our family home. Then, in the 1950s, the government destroyed it and removed the body of King Boris without our knowledge.

I still think of my father when I wake in the middle of the night with murky thoughts.

No witnesses betrayed the secret, nor can any trace of it be found in the archives of the state, since the orders were probably given orally so as not to leave any proof. In 1991, my sister tried to contact four soldiers who supposedly took part in the second exhumation to know more. Despite the fact that the statute of limitations applied to such an event, none of them dared own up; their minds were still consumed by fear. Apparently, they were sworn to silence.

I am grieved that there still has been no official initiative to shed light on the issue—one that concerns our collective history—while countries like Russia have done the research on, and thus mourned, the assassination of the imperial family. As prime minister, I did not have an investigation undertaken because I did not want people to think that I was taking advantage of my position to satisfy personal vendetta. The great mystery of this second removal is, at the heart of it, a second death, a sacrilege. On reflection, I imagine that this outrage was carried out at night and that King Boris was incinerated in the ovens of the nearby steel plant at Kremikovtsi. A popular legend even says that his body was transported in secret to the monastery at Rila.

Nevertheless, we learned in 1991 that his heart had been found in a jar on the shelves at the Medical Institute of the Ministry of the Interior. It had been secretly preserved in a formalin solution. When my father died, there had been no autopsy, at the request of my mother, who was still in shock at it all. But my Uncle Kyril had made the decision to have his blood analyzed to see whether he had been poisoned. His heart must

have been extracted during the embalming and most probably was preserved then. When my mother returned to Rila in 1993, it was in fact to
put the urn containing his heart back in its original tomb.

Today, people who come on weekends to walk in the park at Vrana,
open to the public, can see in the clearing the outline of the chapel that
the faithful have traced on the ground in memory of this painful story. I
go there often, alone, to meditate a bit after a day's work.

In late August 2013, I visited Rila again to close a chapter, or even a whole
section of my life. I attended a religious ceremony to commemorate the
seventieth anniversary of King Boris's passing. My sister made the trip
from the United States. We had not been together at Rila since 1946. We
were very moved by this day of reunion organized around the memory
of our father, in a way reviving our childhood and shared ordeals. I had
a very warm feeling, an impression of being reconciled with a period of
history that had been fragmented, as if in the end we had won. During
the ceremony, the songs of the choir from Alexander Nevsky, who had
come especially for the occasion from Sofia, carried us so high that I felt
like I was floating in the air.

August 28, 2013, marked something of a round number for me,
since I acceded to the throne in 1943: seventy years! This anniversary
went unnoticed since we were there for the memory of my father. But
during the requiem mass, in the presence of the patriarch neophyte and
the president of the Republic, Rosen Asenov Plevneliev, it occurred
to me that this was an important date for me. All those decades spent
serving my country, as I always thought it right to do! I shared this
thought with no one. For me, the idea of posterity means little, and I do
not think in terms of it. I want to leave behind a fair image, one of a life
determined—almost predestined—by my obligations and the historic
role I inherited, which I have tried all my life to honor the best I could.

After seven decades of good and loyal service to my country, I suddenly felt the weight of time on my shoulders, a great tiredness, and I
understood that this anniversary was also that of my own epilogue.

Postscriptum (Winter 2020)

In reading these pages again, four years later, I realize that God has blessed me with a long-lasting life. I was looking for a well-deserved retirement upon finishing these memoirs, which were meant to be a firsthand recollection of my life for my children. I thought that I would be able to retire gently from public life—a public life that began during the Second World War, at age six, and which has granted me so much other than headwinds. The journey has been a bridge between two very different political systems. I think of Marxism, an ideology that seemed like it would last forever, and of such a fast transition to a market economy, hoping to become one day like the rest of European democracies. I believe that today's technology—and the speed of change it allows—is at the heart of the difficulty in adapting to the new world. The society in which I was born belongs to History, and ever since I entered politics my obsession was to help my country's fate up to that of the European Union. Despite the progress made, I am still concerned with issues such as migration, energy, and its environmental impact. And with finding an economic model capable of providing a stable, long-term growth with enough job opportunities for all Bulgarians who have emigrated in recent times. The brain drain has become a worldwide issue since the 1990s. It is up to governments to come up with effective wealth distribution policies to reverse this exile trend. Those lucky enough to have received an education abroad should not forget about their home country, their roots and language, and should share their experience back home. I am renewing this message of hope, one that I specifically conveyed to our youngsters at the time of the signing of Bulgaria's accession to the European Union on April 25, 2005.

In this respect, as a staunch pro-European, I believe Brexit to be a mistake: it brings an uncertain economic future, a troubling precedent for member countries and a blow to the symbol of the Union. We should not forget that the Brexit campaign was based on a series of lies and inaccurate data, and it took for granted very relevant achievements such as a single market of goods and services for 450 million people, one legal system or the absence of military conflicts. The Euroskeptics, so in fashion nowadays, ignore the fact that any of the twenty-eight member countries would be irrelevant on its own in this globalized world.

It was impossible for me to retire in the way Emperor Charles V did in the Spanish monastery of Yuste. Bulgaria is not a monarchy, and therefore I could not abdicate as some of my cousins have done in recent times. As king, I have to continue with the lifetime duty of serving my country. I have tried to balance the various roles in my life in a rational way, sparing no effort. I have no regrets for having done so. I continue to meet many people at home in Sofia, first and foremost Bulgarians from all walks of life. Diplomats, both foreign and Bulgarian, as well as corporate executives and entrepreneurs, welcome my political experience, both domestic and international. I enjoy each and every one of those meetings, which allow me to be up to date in world affairs and always open minded. I also meet with journalists and historians; I participate in charity activities and spend considerable time dealing with all the correspondence. When abroad, I enjoy attending conferences and family reunions as well, considering COVID restrictions.

Some of these trips even have an official angle, as was the case in the recent visits to Saudi Arabia or China. I was asked to join the Bulgarian delegation to Riyadh in November 2017, and my presence made the audience with King Salman possible. In China, I attended the World Tourism Organization's congress (UNWTO) in Chengdu in my capacity as "special ambassador." Having witnessed Spain's economic boom in the 1960s and 1970s, which was in part due to an explosion in tourism, I am convinced that Bulgaria could experience a similar growth thanks to its exceptional nature—forests, lakes, coastline—its winter sports or its reputed archeological sites.

I have also been invited to religious commemorations in Moscow together with the patriarch of the Bulgarian Orthodox Church, as well as to the Orthodox Synod summoned by His Holiness the Ecumenical Patriarch of Constantinople Bartholomew in Istanbul in 2015. Besides my religious convictions, I am one of the two Orthodox monarchs left, along with my cousin Constantine of Greece. The anointing I was given at birth grants me a special stature within the Bulgarian Orthodox Church. In fact, in 2015 the tradition of naming the tsar in their prayers was restored during a synod to commemorate the 1,150 years since the conversion of Bulgaria. In so doing, our church showed fewer complexes than our civil authorities.

*

Having said this, I would like to highlight two issues that hurt me and that can help the reader understand me. They related to the very essence of justice. The first is private property, which is recognized by the Universal Declaration of Human Rights as a fundamental right in article 17. I have already explained earlier in the book the issue of the properties acquired by my grandfather King Ferdinand and my father King Boris; their ownership has been questioned in Bulgaria in a smear campaign against me. One of the most upsetting—and humiliating—lies is that I returned to Bulgaria exclusively to recover my family's assets. I see with great sorrow that, far from trying to find a solution, the government continues to harass me with litigations. To this day, and after ten lawsuits, the "moratorium" that prevents me from enjoying these properties freely, and which was voted by Parliament in 2009, has not been lifted. Needless to say, this moratorium is illegal, as only a judge can impose such a measure. This is why I have been compelled to seek arbitration by the European Court of Human Rights in Strasbourg. This litigation has conveyed a poor image of our judiciary and political system at home and abroad, and it is the only legal way I have to defend myself as a European Union citizen from such blatant injustice. My political opponents blamed me for suing my country, which is absolutely not the case.

These trials are the result of a political vendetta, and so far nobody has had the guts to find a solution to this impasse, despite all sorts assurances to the contrary in private. I will not give in, out of respect for the memory of my ancestors, as well as their integrity and commitment to the development of the country since 1886. I am also keen for my children and grandchildren to perpetuate our ties to Bulgaria. These are places where I spent my first nine years, with all my childhood memories. Despite returning to them after fifty years in exile, I feel like I was never gone. My children and grandchildren have every right to enjoy them too, as I have the right to pass these properties on to them. It is a matter of principle for me.

The second issue is of ideological nature. I place statesmanship and respect for unaltered history at the top of my values. My parents taught me strictly to differentiate between what belongs to the state—i.e., the public domain—and what is private property. This distinction is not as obvious and straightforward nowadays. These are properties that have belonged to us for three generations, not acquired after just a few years in power. We serve, whereas others take advantage—rather generously, I would add. I am clearly the scapegoat of murky political demeanors. Contrary to what people may think, I am first and foremost free, which seems to upset some. I do not depend on anyone. Unlike others, I have never fiddled, and yet my opponents try to taint my reputation with outright slander. "The bigger the lie, the more people will believe it" (Lenin dixit).

In my country, there is a persistent ambiguity with respect to its recent past, and hence its identity and what I represent. Under Communism, my family was systematically vilified and denied its founding role in modern Bulgaria. I am shocked by the fact that mean cleavages keep on without anyone stepping in to provide an unbiased view. I thought these methods belong to the Communist past. In fact, today's politicians seem unwilling to turn the page, both left wingers who do not admit the failure of their theories and conservatives who have never forgiven me for winning the 2001 elections on a liberal ticket. The left blames me for being what I am—the son of a king—and the conservative monarchists blame me for not trying to restore the monarchy after my triumphant return in 1996. I fail to understand how, thirty years after the fall of Communism, the country is still struggling to get around this problem. I want to point at those responsible for preventing citizens from moving on, for perpetuating this collective amnesia. They are not just former Communists, but rather a large part of the political establishment that, in the early 1990s, refused to embark on the radical change that was needed. Even I, as prime minister, avoided revenge and sought social peace, perhaps contributing to this misunderstanding that has lasted all too long. I had to face the statesman's dilemma of preserving truth while preventing violence at all costs. I have noticed a similar pattern of behavior in other countries, whereby historical revisionism and manipulation are on the agenda.

I am concerned that this example may part of a general trend primarily fueled by personal interests, where everyone is primarily interested in securing his or her own place in the "new" democratic society. I am particularly disgusted when my legitimacy is questioned despite having been head of state and later elected prime minister—especially in a country such as Bulgaria, where everyone knows each other and oligarchs are easily legitimated! I have served Bulgaria and my fellow countrymen all my life. I have done so with all my heart, even at a time when my country's reputation abroad was poor, leveraging precisely my legitimacy, which is both historic and democratic.

I have been living in Sofia for the past twenty years, and I still lack a clear stature. I can see this when the authorities consider inviting me to an official event. It is funny to see them confused, as though I had shown up accidentally. The Republic does not know how to place me, literally, its protocol team often not knowing what to do, to the point of ridicule. Placing me is often shocking and done wrongly, for I combine two distinctions, that of former head of state and that of former prime minister. The first is deliberately ignored, and yet it is a historical fact. This was the case again on the occasion of the opening of the Bulgarian presidency of the European Council of Ministers in January 2018 in Sofia. At this ceremony, attended by twenty-eight European commissioners, including the then president of the European Commission, Jean-Claude Juncker, and the president of the Council of Europe, Donald Tusk, I was seated in an upper gallery far from them. This faux pas was noticed by the foreign delegations, who were surprised not to find me at a place in accordance with my status and the active role I played in Bulgaria's accession to the European Union.

With hindsight, perhaps one of my mistakes was to have always behaved as a constitutional monarch, and thus with a duty to stay above political parties. I realize that since I entered politics in the early 2000s, I should have turned into a politician and fought in the political arena using the same weapons as my opponents. Despite the insistence of my advisors, I was handcuffed by my principles and integrity, at the cost of reelection in 2005. Today I regret it, for we could have accomplished most of our goals needed to modernize the country and open its economy. Twenty years later, I see that we were right in our priorities and that there is an increasing number of Bulgarians supporting them. Political commentators used to laugh at the words I used to describe Bulgaria's situation, but today they are widely accepted. I am amazed how current politicians boast any small achievement, and more so in comparison with what my government did back then and how little credit we got.

Personally, I keep on trying to help my country. It is not easy. I stay up late at night, and that is when I had the idea of turning our Vrana home—formerly a royal residence—into a museum dedicated to the history of the Third Kingdom. Vrana was empty and run down when I returned; I have been filling it with furniture from my home in Madrid, with souvenirs of my mother from her house in Estoril and from my sister Princess Maria Luisa, as well as priceless family objects from the Coburg, where my grandfather died in 1948. Since 2015, the display cabinets also include antiques donated by Bulgarian collectors who share our sense of philanthropy. This museum brings to mind the fact that Bulgaria has not had a Renaissance. The Ottoman domination, which lasted five centuries, left us without this period of unprecedented cultural development, one that has allowed other European nations to enjoy today's Western civilization. As I always insist, we must understand, and not judge. We haven't enjoyed an Age of Enlightenment, and this has unconsciously had an impact in our reactions and complexes. Nonetheless, as I look into the future, which I shall not live to see, my hope remains that of a united people within a European Bulgaria. Our national motto is "Unity makes strength," and rightly so. Thus our homeland shall be the preferred place for all those who at some point had to leave it!

Vrana, December 2020

CHRONOLOGY

April 1876: First revolt of Bulgarians against Ottoman presence.

1877–1878: The Treaty of San Stefano, ending the Russo-Turkish War, provides for the establishment of an autonomous Principality of Bulgaria.

1879: Prince Alexander of Battenberg becomes prince of Bulgaria, until 1886.

August 2, 1887: Ferdinand of Saxe-Coburg becomes prince of Bulgaria. He comes from Vienna.

1896: The young Prince Boris is baptized an Orthodox; Russia then recognizes Prince Ferdinand on February 2.

1908: Proclamation of the independence of the "Kingdom of Bulgaria" by Ferdinand I.

1918: King Ferdinand abdicates after World War I. His oldest son becomes King Boris III.

October 25, 1930: Marriage of King Boris and Princess Giovanna of Italy in Assisi, Italy.

June 16, 1937: Birth of Simeon in Sofia.

August 28, 1943: Death of Boris III at 4:20 p.m.; Simeon becomes King of the Bulgarians.

January 1944: Beginning of Allied bombardments over Sofia.

February 1, 1945: Prince-regent Kyril is executed in Sofia after a coup d'état supported by the Soviet Union.

September 16, 1946: Departure of the royal family to Istanbul and Egypt.

1951: Arrival in Spain; family settlement in Madrid.

January 21, 1962: Marriage with Margarita Gómez-Acebo y Cejuela in Switzerland.

November 1989: Beginning of political changes as a result of the fall of the Iron Curtain.

1991: Princess Maria Luisa becomes the first member of the royal family to return to Bulgaria.

1993: Queen Giovanna of Bulgaria returns to Bulgaria on the occasion of the fiftieth anniversary of the death of Boris III.

May 25, 1996: Return of Simeon II to Bulgaria.

2001: The Simeon II National Movement wins the parliamentary elections. Simeon of Bulgaria becomes prime minister until 2005.

2004: Bulgaria becomes a member of NATO.

2007: Bulgaria enters the European Union.

August 28, 2013: Commemoration of the seventy-fifth anniversary of the death of King Boris at Rila Monastery.

Bibliography

Bourboulon, Comte de. *Ephémérides de Bulgarie, 1887–1913*. Typed document.

Braudel, Fernand. *La Méditerranée et le monde méditerranéen à l'époque de Philippe II*. 3 vols. Paris: Livres de Poche, 1993. (*The Mediterranean and the Mediterranean World in the Age of Philip II*. 2 vols., 2nd rev. ed. Translated by Sian Reynolds, 1972 and 1973.)

Bulgaria, Giovanna di. *Memorie*. Milan: Rizzoli, 1964.

Defrance, Olivier. *La Médicis des Cobourg, Clémentine d'Orléans*. Brussels: Éditions Racine, 2007.

Delorme, Philippe. *Les dynasties perdues*. Paris: Éditions Express Roularta, 2011.

d'Espagne, Eulalie. *Mémoires de S.A.R. l'infante Eulalie, 1868–1931*. Paris: Plon, 1935. (*Memoirs of a Spanish Princess, the Infanta Eulalia*. London: Hutchinson, 1936; reprinted New York: Norton, 1937.)

Dontchev, Anton. *Les cent frères de Manol*. Arles, France: Actes Sud, 1995.

———. *L'épopée du livre sacré*. Arles, France: Actes Sud, 1999.

Grèce, Michel de. *Mémoires insolites*. Paris: Pocket, 2006.

Groueff, Stephane. *Crown of Thorns: The Reign of King Boris III of Bulgaria, 1918–1943*. Lanham, MD: Madison Books, 1987.

Hassan II. *La mémoire d'un Roi*. Paris: Entretiens avec Éric Laurent, Plon, 1993.

Hugo, Victor. *Actes et paroles depuis l'exil, 1876–1880*. Œuvres complètes, Vol. 3. Paris: Hetzel, 1880.

Jélev, Jéliou. *Le fascisme*. Sofia: Izdatelstvo na BZNS, 1982. (Traduction française, 1997.)

Kantorowicz, Ernst. *L'Empereur Frédéric II*. Paris: Gallimard, 1987.

Lacarrière, Jacques. *Men Possessed by God: The Story of the Desert Monks of Ancient Christendom*. New York: Doubleday, 1964.

Maradji, Mohamed. *50 ans de photographies au Maroc: Témoin de époque*. Morocco: La croisée des chemins, 2009.

Ortega y Gasset, José. *L'histoire comme système*. 1935–1941.

———. *La révolte des masses* (1929). Translated by L. Parrot. Paris: Éd. Les Belles Lettres, 2010.

Pérez-Maura, Ramón. *Simeón de Bulgaria, el rey posible*. Madrid: Belacqua, 2002.

Raditchkov, Yordan. *Les cours obscures*. Paris: Gallimard, 1966.

Schaufelberger, Constant. *La destinée d'un roi: La vie et le règne de Boris III, roi des Bulgarians (1894–1918–1943)*. Uppsala: Boktryckeri Aktiebolag, 1952.

Sergheraert, Gérard. *Syméon le Grand (893–927)*. Paris: Éditions Maisonneuve, 1960.
Simsir, Bilal. *The Turks of Bulgaria (1878–1985)*. London: K. Rustem and Brother, 1988.
Todorov, Tzvetan. *Mémoire du mal, tentation du bien*. Paris, Robert Laffont, 2000.
———. *Au nom du peuple: Témoignages sur les camps Communistes*. La Tour-d'Aigues: Editions de l'Aube, Regards croisés, 1998.

ACKNOWLEDGMENTS

My sister Princess Maria Luisa
My daughter Kalina
Prince Michael of Greece
Alexandra Chrobok, Princess Koháry
My dear wife, Margarita, once again

Mia Morero
Paulina Mihaylova
Professor Ivaylo Schalafoff
As well as my other assistants . . .

King Boris and Queen Giovanna Foundation
www.dvoretz-vrana.bg
Contact: info@dvoretz-vrana.bg